YET I LOVED JACOB

YET I LOVED JACOB

Reclaiming the Biblical Concept of Election

JOEL S. KAMINSKY

Abingdon Press
Nashville

YET I LOVED JACOB
RECLAIMING THE BIBLICAL CONCEPT OF ELECTION

This book is printed on acid-free paper.

Library of Congress Cataloging-in-Publication Data

Kaminsky, Joel S., 1960-
Yet I loved Jacob : reclaiming the biblical concept of election / Joel S. Kaminsky.
p. cm.
Includes bibliographical references and indexes.
ISBN 978-0-687-02534-3 (binding: pbk. : alk. paper)
1. Bible. O.T.—Criticism, interpretation, etc. 2. Election (Theology)--Biblical teaching. I. Title.

BS1199.E63K36 2007
234--dc22

2007008448

07 08 09 10 11 12 13 14 15 16--10 9 8 7 6 5 4 3 2 1
MANUFACTURED IN THE UNITED STATES OF AMERICA

CONTENTS

ACKNOWLEDGMENTS

This book began to take serious shape during my stay at the Center of Theological Inquiry in Princeton, New Jersey, during the fall of 2001. I owe a debt of gratitude to the other fellows in residence with me, most especially Jacqueline Lapsley and Mark Reasoner, as well as Robert Jenson, then the Center's director. While in residence in Princeton I had much helpful feedback from scholars at Princeton Seminary, most particularly from Dennis Olson and Patrick Miller, as well as from Leora Batnitzky at Princeton University. Jon Levenson from Harvard University has read many parts of this book and provided invaluable assistance along the way. His previous work in this area has been deeply inspirational. Some of the most valuable help and criticism has come from my students at Smith, most especially my former research assistant, Anne Stewart. She has spent hours chasing bibliography and reading various drafts of this material.

Since that time I have had the ongoing support of the Department of Religion and Biblical Literature at Smith College as well as of the administration, who granted me a Mellon course release in spring 2004 to continue working on this project. I also owe thanks to Annette Reed and Dana Hollander, who invited me to present my work at a conference titled "A Covenant to the People, a Light to the Nations: Universalism, Exceptionalism, and the Problem of Chosenness in Jewish Thought," held at McMaster University in May of 2005. This conference was followed by two additional panels at the Society of Biblical Literature in Philadelphia in November 2005 on election in the Hebrew Bible, New Testament, and rabbinic Judaism.

I was able to bring the project to completion during my stay at Durham University in Durham, England, in the spring of 2006. A number of colleagues and students at Durham have given me invaluable feedback, most particularly Walter Moberly and his advanced graduate student Joel Lohr, who both read and carefully annotated an earlier draft of this book. I also wish to thank Robert Hayward for inviting me and the Departmental Chair, John Barclay, for hosting me as a visiting Jewish Studies Fellow in the Department of Theology and Religion while at Durham.

All of the above have substantially enhanced the book in innumerable ways, but I have not always heeded the advice others have offered. I am certain errors remain and many additional improvements and expansions could (and perhaps should) have been made. However, my publisher has a deadline as well as a wish to keep the book to a reasonable word count, thus putting some helpful limitations on the scope of the project. Nevertheless, I remain in debt to so many for so much help along the way.

In addition, I wish to acknowledge a number of publications and their editorial staffs who published earlier forms of parts of this manuscript over the past several years. By doing so they not only helped bring the material into better shape, they also permitted my ideas to reach a wider audience, who in turn could give me much-needed feedback. These include the following:

"Chosen." In *New Interpreter's Dictionary of the Bible*. Vol. 1. Nashville: Abingdon Press, 2006. This is a six-thousand-word entry on chosenness in the Bible.

"Attempting the Impossible: Eliminating Election from the Jewish Liturgy." *Midstream* (January–February 2005): 23–27. Aspects of the introduction and "Concluding Reflections" first appeared here.

"Reclaiming a Theology of Election: Favoritism and the Joseph Story." *Perspectives in Religious Studies* 31.2 (Summer 2004): 135–52. This contains much of chapter 4.

"Did Election Imply the Mistreatment of Non-Israelites?" *Harvard Theological Review* 96.4 (October 2003): 397–425. This contains much of chapters 7–8.

"The Concept of Election and Second Isaiah: Recent Literature." *Biblical Theology Bulletin* 31.4 (Winter 2001): 135–44. This is a very early form of part of chapter 9.

I also owe thanks to current and former members of Abingdon Press and some of their contract employees. These include Greg Glover, who before leaving Abingdon oversaw the initial proposal for this book and strongly encouraged me to publish it. Since then I have benefited greatly from the assistance and encouragement provided by Kathy Armistead and John Kutsko. I would also like to thank the copyediting staff, who helped me turn the copy text into a more refined form, and my indexer, John Muether.

Of course books cannot be written without a supportive group of family and friends. My brothers and their significant others (Jeff and Ann, Jordan and Michele), parents (Charlotte and Elliott), in-laws (Reva, Amos, Marsha, Phil, Tammie, Joe, and Sue), my cousin Steve (and his wife, Rhona), and my many friends (Greg Spinner, Nus Deutsch, Morris Rosenthal, and others)—all have been tremendously supportive of me and my rather obscure interests over the years.

My largest debt of gratitude goes to my wife, Jody Rosenbloom. She has put up with my disappearing for two extended sabbatical retreats as well as with endless hours of my working on aspects of this book and other related projects it has spawned. My initial interest in this topic arose from her questions concerning the meaning of chosenness. In particular, she wanted to know what exactly this notion implied about those chosen and those not chosen, and could it still hold meaning today? Jody's love and support have helped me through difficulties in life as well as with this book. But more important, Jody's deep and abiding love for the Jewish people has given me an intuition into the meaning of Israel's election. Jody, like the wise woman from Abel Beth-maacah, is certainly among the שלמי אמוני ישראל, those who seek the welfare of the faithful in Israel (2 Sam 20:19a NJPS). This book is lovingly dedicated to Jody with thankfulness for all that she has brought to my life.

Brief Note on Stylistic and Other Considerations

I have generally relied on the NRSV translation for biblical quotations and note when I have departed from it. I have devocalized the Tetragrammaton in all quotations and references. I have employed vowels in the Hebrew text only when they were necessary to make a specific argument. To reduce the notes somewhat, I have listed only those scholarly sources I directly engage with in Section 1. The secondary literature on Genesis is vast, and a fuller bibliography is easily obtainable from the many fine commentaries published on it. Inasmuch as the notes are indexed, I have opted to forgo including a bibliography to reduce the size and thus the cost of the book. I will post a link to the full bibliography on my website at www.smith.edu/~jkaminsk.

ABBREVIATIONS

AB	Anchor Bible
AJSR	*Association for Jewish Studies Review*
AnBib	Analecta biblica
BA	*Biblical Archaeologist*
BASOR	*Bulletin of the American Schools of Oriental Research*
BJS	Brown Judaic Studies
BTB	*Biblical Theology Bulletin*
BZAW	Beihefte zur Zeitschrift für die alttestamentliche Wissenschaft
CBQ	*Catholic Biblical Quarterly*
CBQMS	Catholic Biblical Quarterly Monograph Series
ConBNT	Coniectanea Biblica: New Testament Series
DSD	*Dead Sea Discoveries*
FS	*Festschrift*
HAR	*Hebrew Annual Review*
HSM	Harvard Semitic Monographs
HTR	*Harvard Theological Review*
HUCA	*Hebrew Union College Annual*
Int	*Interpretation*
JAOS	*Journal of the American Oriental Society*
JBL	*Journal of Biblical Literature*
JES	*Journal of Ecumenical Studies*
JETS	*Journal of the Evangelical Theological Society*
JGRChJ	*Journal of Greco-Roman Christianity and Judaism*
JJS	*Journal of Jewish Studies*
JPOS	*Journal of the Palestine Oriental Society*
JQR	*Jewish Quarterly Review*
JR	*Journal of Religion*
JSNTSup	Journal for the Study of the New Testament: Supplement Series

JSOT	*Journal for the Study of Old Testament*
JSOTSup	Journal for the Study of the Old Testament: Supplement Series
JSPSup	Journal for the Study of the Pseudepigrapha: Supplement Series
JTS	*Journal of Theological Studies*
NCB	New Century Bible
NJPS	The New Jewish Publication Society Translation of the Tanakh
OBT	Overtures to Biblical Theology
OTL	Old Testament Library
OTS	Old Testament Studies
OtSt	*Oudtestamentische Studiën, Leiden*
RBL	*Review of Biblical Literature*
SBL	Society of Biblical Literature
SBLDS	Society of Biblical Literature Dissertation Series
SJLA	Studies in Judaism in Late Antiquity
SJT	*Scottish Journal of Theology*
TDOT	*Theological Dictionary of the Old Testament*
TST	Toronto Studies in Theology
VT	*Vetus Testamentum*
VTSup	Supplements to Vetus Testamentum
WBC	Word Biblical Commentary
WUNT	Wissenschaftliche Untersuchungen zum Neuen Testament
ZAW	*Zeitschrift für die alttestamentliche Wissenschaft*

Abbreviations for Jewish Postbiblical Sources

'Avod. Zar.	*'Avodah Zarah*
b.	*Babylonian Talmud*
Gen. Rab.	*Genesis Rabbah*
ER	*Eliyyahu Rabbah*
Exod. Rab.	*Exodus Rabbah*
PRE	*Pirke de Rabbi Eliezer*
Sanh.	*Sanhedrin*
Shabb.	*Shabbat*
t.	*Tosefta*

Introduction to the Topic

> In modern Biblical studies the doctrine of election has received little attention. Yet it would seem to be fundamental to the thought of the Bible in both the Old and New Testaments. To the writers of the Old Testament Israel is the chosen people of God; to the writers of the New Testament the Church is the heir of divine election. In both Testaments individuals are presented as chosen of God for their particular work. Whether we like it or not, the doctrine of election is a Biblical doctrine, and whatever our view of its validity, it demands some attention from the student of the Bible.[1]

So began H. H. Rowley's now classic study of election theology in the Bible. Rowley's lament concerning the lack of attention this central subject received in his day continues to be true today among biblical scholars and Jewish and Christian theologians. This is so for a number of complex reasons that deserve discussion. The most obvious is that the idea that God favors certain individuals or groups over others is theologically and morally troublesome to modern Western thinkers, as succinctly summed up by Will Herberg.

> A truly rational and universal God, it is maintained, could not do anything so arbitrary as to "choose" one particular group out of mankind as a whole. . . . God is the God of all alike, and, therefore, cannot make distinctions between nations and peoples. To this is added the moral argument that the doctrine of "chosenness" is little better than crude ethnocentrism, in which a particular group regards itself as the center of the universe and develops doctrines that will flatter its pride and minister to its glory.[2]

Criticisms such as these have led some recent Jewish and Christian thinkers to argue that the biblical idea of election has outlived its theological usefulness, while many others either empty the notion of its theological content or simply avoid directly addressing this central biblical concern. Before exploring more recent Jewish and Christian thinking on the idea of election, it is important to trace the deeper roots of the modern critique of chosenness, which reach back to Spinoza and Kant. The ways in which these major Enlightenment figures treated the idea of chosenness continue to reverberate today, a point less surprising once one notes that Spinoza was not only a philosopher who critiqued religion, but was also, in the view of many, the first modern biblical critic.

Spinoza argued that while the Jews had been once chosen by God, a close reading of the Hebrew Bible demonstrated "that God chose the Hebrews neither absolutely nor forever."[3] He arrived at this conclusion by arguing that chosenness applies only to a group's socio-political organization, not to individuals of a group.

> We conclude, therefore (inasmuch as God is to all men equally gracious, and the Hebrews were only chosen by Him in respect to their social organization and government), that the individual Jew, taken apart from his social organization and government, possessed no gift of God above other men. . . .[4]

Since the Jews lacked an independent state in Spinoza's time, they were currently not chosen, although they could be chosen once again in the future. However, this would not elevate them over any other well-organized and prosperous nation. Spinoza's philosophical approach to election preserves the shell of the biblical idea while excising its theological content. Now in fairness to Spinoza, he was writing in the wake of a series of religious wars, and his criticisms of the Bible were aimed at creating more stable political conditions. While interreligious warfare is indeed a great concern, this past century has taught us that the ability to commit atrocities is not contingent on subscribing to a traditional religious viewpoint. Rather, any human institution or ideology has the potential to be distorted and then used for nefarious purposes. More important, while emptying religions of their particularity may at times lessen intolerance, it does so at a very steep price by creating a climate of total indifference for all things religious.

The Enlightenment critique of election was extended in a new direction by Immanuel Kant, who argued that Christianity "from the beginning bore within it the germ and principle of the objective unity of the true and universal faith" and that Judaism, while it provided "the physical occasion for the founding of this church," stands in absolutely no essential connection to the Christian faith.[5] Kant supported this rather tenuous idea by reducing Christianity to a purely ethical system of moral truths that are universally knowable through reason alone. Both Spinoza and Kant attempted to prove their points through combining reason with a very selective reading of the Bible, obscuring the centrality and pervasiveness of the idea of election within the Hebrew Bible and the New Testament. Equally important, these Enlightenment figures were able to marginalize election by arguing that it was in fundamental contradiction to certain universalistic ideas, particularly monotheism.

Many Jews and Christians have sensed that such Enlightenment thinking misrepresented and misunderstood the biblical text. However, few thinkers have been willing to defend the Bible's highly particularistic ideas of divine election. More usually, the attempt has been made to try to fit the Bible's truth into certain Enlightenment notions, and generally speaking, the biblical ideas have been distorted in the process. Thus, the Bible's core truths are equated with Enlightenment universalism. On the other hand, the Bible's more particularistic claims are seen as an accident of history that can be discarded as chaff once the valuable universal truth within has been recovered. Furthermore, even those who have sought to defend the biblical notion of election have had difficulty freeing themselves of certain deeply ingrained Enlightenment biases such as the tendency to favor the universal over the particular, or the notion that Israel's understanding of God's universal nature ultimately conflicted with her election theology, necessitating a rejection of the particularistic dimensions of that theology.

Election in Recent Scholarship

Even a thinker like Rowley, perhaps the modern commentator who most articulately defends the biblical idea of election, has unwittingly absorbed problematic elements of the Enlightenment worldview that stand in deep tension with the Bible's theological claims. While Rowley resisted certain aspects of the Enlightenment critique of religion, he (along with many scholars since his time) tends to meld a deep-seated Christian supersessionism with an Enlightenment preference for a universal religion.

Thus, Rowley's understanding of the nature and function of election in the Hebrew Bible is tainted by his tendency to read the Hebrew Bible through the New Testament and subsequent Christian history, as demonstrated by his assessment of Judaism. He argues that Judaism failed to carry out its election responsibilities in two major ways. To begin with, the vast majority of Jews rejected God's self-revelation in Christ.

> That Judaism has cared so little for One who, on lowest count, is the greatest of her sons, and the One who has most powerfully influenced the world, is a singular fact. . . . If, then, the first element of the service of the elect was to receive and cherish the revelation of God given to Israel, then the church performed it more fully than did Judaism.[6]

Second, Rowley sees election as involving Israel's duty "to mediate to all men the law of her God, and to spread the heritage of her faith through all the world."[7] And here, too, Rowley argues that Israel has forfeited her status by abandoning her responsibilities.

Whereas initially Rowley's views seem attributable solely to his Christian supersessionism, on further inspection they are a rather complex mix of Christianity and various Enlightenment ideas. This is not surprising once one places Rowley in his context and notices that he was writing during the height of the Biblical Theology movement, a movement that often mixed biblical and Enlightenment ideas in a troubling fashion. Rowley's move to make the idea of an active mission to convert the world to biblical religion central to the Hebrew Bible's message is based on a Christian reading of the Hebrew Bible with little support in the text itself (as discussed in chapter 9). Here Christianity's deep commitment to mission, which Rowley wholeheartedly embraces, may be driven at least partially by the sense that either one is elect or one is lost to God. By this I mean that Christians of Rowley's mind-set would want to save as many souls as possible from damnation. However, while not usually noticed, much of the Hebrew Bible offers three categories of election, which include the elect, the non-elect, and the anti-elect (categories discussed at length in chapters 7–8). The anti-elect, like the Canaanites, are generally seen as beyond the pale of divine mercy and doomed for destruction; the non-elect have a place within the divine economy even while they retain a different status than Israel, the elect of God. Within the Hebrew Bible's three-tiered scheme there is little, if any, need for Israel to missionize the Gentile nations of the world.

On the Enlightenment side, Rowley assumes that Christianity is superior to Judaism because Christianity is a more universalistic religion, that is, it is inclusive and tolerant as evidenced by its pervasiveness in the world today and its openness to converts. Rowley represents the view that Judaism became an exclusivistic and intolerant religion, thereby forfeiting its elect status to Christianity, which brought God's message of salvation to the Gentiles. Yet in much of the Hebrew Bible (as well as in much of rabbinic thought), being non-elect is in no way equivalent to being damned. Thus, a Jewish exclusivism that allows the non-elect to serve God in their own way might be more tolerant than a Christian inclusivism that recognizes only a single path to salvation. Furthermore, while there is a widespread tendency for contemporary Christians to see Christianity as a universal religion, historically it would be quite inaccurate to think of New Testament Christians as all-embracing universalists. When Rowley and other more recent scholars who follow in his path presume that the truest or best parts of the Bible are those that correlate most closely with a certain idea of universalism, this universalism is an Enlightenment ideal that is more indebted to Kant than to anything in either the Hebrew Bible or the New Testament. As Joseph Blenkinsopp notes, theological reflection on the Bible has been distorted by the unconscious way in which biblical critics absorbed these Enlightenment patterns of thought.

> The term "universalism," with its antonym "particularism," is one of those slippery words the precise meaning of which is rarely defined. In biblical theology it tends to recur in discussions of opposite trends in early Judaism, and especially where Judaism is contrasted unfavorably with early Christianity. The categories themselves are a relic of the Enlightenment with its postulate that true religion must be in conformity with the universally valid laws of reason and a universally accessible moral law derived from them. . . . It was in this prejudicial form that the terms came into use in the new discipline of Biblical Theology, which was itself a product of the Enlightenment.[8]

While most contemporary scholars of the Hebrew Bible have managed to avoid Rowley's explicit supersessionism,[9] many actually end up embracing various forms of Enlightenment universalism even more fully than Rowley did and by doing so endorse an implicit supersessionism. Most interesting is that even those who appear to be making radically different arguments often flatten the theological landscape of the text and not infrequently reach similar conclusions. Rather than attempt to provide an extensive survey of the field, I will briefly explore two quite common contemporary approaches for dealing with the problem of election and try to uncover their underlying logic.

One strategy, represented by Rolf Knierim's theological program, recognizes the anti-Judaic bias in much of biblical theology but sees the root of the problem in biblical particularism itself. Knierim argues that other parts of the biblical canon authorize one to dissolve the Bible's particularistic concept of election, because of his belief that there is a "claim, found in both the Old and the New Testaments, that all humanity is elected into the blessing of God's universal justice and salvation."[10] Knierim must be complimented for not simply replacing Jewish exclusivist claims with Christian supersessionist ones that are equally exclusivist, as Rowley ends up doing. Rather, he wishes to eliminate all such exclusivist claims. In this, Knierim is simply carrying the Enlightenment embrace of universalism to its natural conclusion, and by doing so he overcomes a serious flaw in Rowley's work. However, he can only accomplish this feat by giving no voice to the Bible's deep and pervasive particularism. Although his goal is to be sensitive to issues of cultural diversity and pluralism, his solution ends up requiring Jews and Christians to give up one of their most cherished and central theological beliefs.[11]

On the other end of the spectrum, an essay by Jorge Pixley advocates a newfound appreciation for biblical particularism. He sees God's election of the Jewish people as a biblical endorsement of the modern ethic "that the survival of peoples with their own particularities is a human value" and that we must build "societies in which 'all can find a place.'"[12] Such a view celebrates the notion of cultural particularity over against some generic universalism; however, it does not do justice to the Bible's particularistic theology of Israel's election. As Jon Levenson notes, Pixley is only able to use the biblical idea of chosenness as a support for the continued maintenance of other ethnicities and cultures today by ignoring one of its most distinctive dimensions: "In short, though the Hebrew Bible conceives of Israel as an ethnic group, its very existence is a standing reproach to ethnicity and, for understandable reasons, arouses the hostility of the unchosen."[13] Levenson is pointing out that although the Hebrew Bible emphasizes the value of Israel's uniqueness, the elect people of Israel stand over against the Gentile nations as a whole. The preservation of the particularism of each individual non-elect nation receives scant attention within the Bible. Unlike Pixley's approach, the New Testament redefines who Israel is, but it still sees the early church as God's people standing over against the rest of the world, rather than viewing all ethnic groups as equally chosen.[14] Pixley is to be commended for his sensitivity to issues of cultural diversity, but his attempt to utilize the Bible's election theology as a resource to support the contemporary drive to preserve threatened minority cultures indicates that he has not reckoned with the specific particularism of the biblical text. Rather, Pixley has reconfigured the Bible's highly particularistic idea of Israel's election into a distributive universalism that views every human culture as elect. While Pixley and Knierim start off from opposite directions, one stressing the importance of particularisms and the other speaking of God's universal justice trumping any notion of particularism, both end up dissolving the Bible's particularistic election theology by extending election to everyone.

The fact that Pixley and Knierim end up in similar places is not surprising once one realizes that much of the current discussion of this issue is animated by the tendency to read the biblical text through certain contemporary events and ideas (much as in Spinoza's time). In particular, the vivid memory of recent occurrences of ethnic cleansing and attempted genocide in combination with current views of race, ethnicity, and multiculturalism that have grown out of and affected our understanding of these terrible events has shaped contemporary scholarship on the concept of election in ways that cannot be ignored. While it is inevitable and even appropriate that this should occur, one must recognize that the biblical text might not be compatible with the now pervasive liberal, democratic, multicultural ethic. More important, one must provide a corrective to the tendency to read the Bible through the lens of current popular notions of race, ethnicity, and democratic pluralism when such readings lead to serious distortions of the biblical text, especially those parts that deal with the idea of election.

Election in Modern Judaism

As one can see, Christian discussions of election theology have been strongly affected by secular currents reaching from the Enlightenment to contemporary issues of race and ethnicity, as well as by theological currents, most especially by supersessionism and the tendency to read the Hebrew Bible through a New Testament lens. However, a broader audience may be unaware that election theology has remained equally problematic and misunderstood within modern Jewish thinking. In recent decades, there has been a growing discomfort with the notion of chosenness—the idea that the Jewish people were specially elected by God—among some

Jews from all three of the more liberal Jewish movements (Reform, Reconstructionist, and Conservative).[15] The intellectual roots of this uneasiness were articulated as far back as the Reform prayer book adopted by the Berlin Reform Congregation in 1844, a prayer book produced during the period when European Enlightenment ideas began to penetrate German-Jewish culture:

> [T]he concept of holiness and of a special vocation arising from this has become entirely foreign to us, as has the idea of an intimate covenant between God and Israel which is to remain significant for all eternity. Human character and dignity, and God's image within us—these alone are signs of chosenness.[16]

This discomfort with the notion of Jewish election was further exacerbated within the pluralistic democratic environment of the United States, resulting in various attempts to redefine the meaning of election or find an alternative central purpose for the existence of the Jewish people.[17] In fact, Arnold Eisen has argued that the problems posed by the notion of election have driven much of the explicit theological discourse in American non-Orthodox Jewry over the past century. The most serious Jewish critic of election theology was Mordecai Kaplan, the founder of Reconstructionist Judaism.[18] Kaplan felt that the traditional idea of Jewish election was no longer defensible and that modern Jews "must be prepared not only to foster their nationhood but to see in nationhood as such, whether it be their own or that of any other people, the call of the spirit. *By this they will achieve a revaluation of the doctrine of election.*"[19] In other words, Kaplan, like Knierim and Pixley, sees all nations as elect, thereby dissolving the Bible's highly particularistic idea of chosenness. The Reconstructionist movement continues to be committed to eliminating the idea of election from the Jewish theological landscape. More recently, other prominent Jewish voices, such as the feminist thinker Judith Plaskow, have called for the rejection of the notion of election and suggested replacing it with the rather weak notion of Jewish distinctness.[20] Clearly, Judaism, no less than Christianity, has been deeply affected by Enlightenment universalism as well as by contemporary discussions of ethnicity, multiculturalism, and gender, and this has led to a call within some Jewish circles to eliminate the notion of Jewish election. However, as Eisen notes, while the concept of chosenness remains troubling to American Jews, very few have embraced the call to eliminate its presence from Judaism.[21]

Reclaiming Election Theology Today

The above survey indicates that many Jews and Christians are unwilling to part with the classical notion of election theology despite centuries of modernist critique aimed at dislodging it from the Jewish and Christian theological universe and regardless of the fact that it is in deep tension with certain widely held pluralistic sensibilities.

Interestingly enough, significant changes are taking place on the contemporary cultural front that make this an ideal time to take a new look at the notion of election. The power of Enlightenment universalism is beginning to wane in the face of the realization that this universalism is itself a particularistic ideology, albeit one that won large acceptance throughout the Western intellectual world. The problematic nature of the Enlightenment project is most clearly revealed in the ways in which its claims of universalism were used to further various imperialistic aims. The ebbing of Enlightenment universalism has led to newfound respect for particularistic religious and cultural ideas suggesting it is time to reconceive the way in which interreligious dialogue should be conducted. During the period in which Enlightenment ideals held sway, there was a tendency for each religion to explain how it was best suited to fit into such an Enlightenment world. Both Jews and Christians tended to emphasize the universalistic aspects of their respective traditions while downplaying their radically particularistic claims. Thus, each tradition's theological claims were tailored to fit into the Enlightenment philosophical project in ways that distorted their unique theological identities, which in turn obscured the deep theological differences between the two traditions. Now a growing list of thinkers is arguing that religious dialogue only works when traditions engage one another in all of their particularity.[22] To do anything less is to make a mockery of interreligious and intercultural dialogue.

The waning of the Enlightenment worldview coupled with the growing tolerance for deep assertions of religious particularity (albeit sometimes sincerely and sometimes more as a bow to a weak multiculturalism) suggests that the time is right for a reappraisal of this most particularistic biblical concept, that of election, an idea that remains central to classical Jewish and Christian theological claims. In fact, certain Jewish and Christian theologians have articulated compelling visions of how election theology might speak to contemporary Jews and Christians.[23] This book explores how these broader theological insights might be supported or refined by careful attention to the Hebrew Bible and the ways in which it was appropriated by early Christianity and rabbinic Judaism.[24]

This book is driven by the awareness that the notion of chosenness first articulated within the Hebrew Bible is central to the Bible's theological worldview, as well as to the worldviews of both Judaism and Christianity that grew out of and continue to sustain themselves from the Bible's theological wellsprings. Inasmuch as this is the case, I do not think that either tradition can sidestep, marginalize, or jettison election theology without severing its connections to its biblical roots, a move that would greatly impoverish or perhaps even destroy both of these venerable faith traditions. While one must squarely address the difficulties posed by election theology to anyone living in the modern world, too often the cultured despisers of the notion of chosenness have portrayed it in inaccurate and simplistic terms. In addition, as noted on occasion within the body of the book below, a number of secular critics have recently argued that Israel's monotheism is the root cause of violence against the outsider in Western culture.[25] These critics rightly note the deep biblical connections between Israel's elective claims and her understanding of God's nature, even while they draw negative—and in my mind wrongheaded—conclusions from this linkage. In any case, these critics clarify that the Enlightenment's attempt to marginalize the Bible's particularistic claims while seeking to preserve the so-called universalism of biblical monotheism is intellectually incoherent. Thus, recovering a richer and more sympathetic portrait of the biblical concept of election is a necessity for anyone wishing to affirm the Bible's fundamental theological claims. The hope is that the following chapters will reveal that the idea of God's special love for his people Israel can indeed speak to us once again today and in doing so that these chapters might lay the groundwork for articulating a post-Enlightenment understanding of the Bible's core ideas.

Outline of This Book

This particular treatment of election will proceed in a somewhat unusual fashion. First of all, unlike some previous forays into this area, I will not focus on a set of close word studies. Such studies can be of value, yet they tend to overlook the many ways in which election theology suffuses the larger biblical corpus. On the other hand, neither will this study seek to give a comprehensive catalog of every biblical text that has some linkage to chosenness. Other works have pursued this path, and while valuable, such works are inevitably longer and less accessible to the more general reading public.[26] The attempt here is to explore the Bible's election theology by carefully analyzing certain biblical texts, discussing major motifs or themes, and engaging contemporary concerns.

Quite often treatments of election theology in the Hebrew Bible begin by treating a book like Deuteronomy in which one finds highly developed abstract theological language describing Israel's divine election. However, this book begins with an extended literary theological analysis of the four stories of sibling rivalry within Genesis. Although certain scholars would deny that these stories contain any election theology inasmuch as they lack the more developed vocabulary of election found in books such as Deuteronomy, as will be seen, the narratives of brotherly struggle in Genesis are a major locus of election theology. Thus, chapters 1–4, after a brief introduction, are dedicated to exploring four stories of family rivalry: Cain and Abel, Isaac and Ishmael (as well as Hagar and Sarah), Jacob and Esau (as well as Isaac and Rebekah along with Leah and Rachel), and Joseph and his brothers. Other narratives in the Hebrew Bible probe elective issues (e.g., God's choice and then rejection of Eli and Saul in 1 Sam 3–4 and 8–15 as well as the story of David's rise to power in 1 Sam 16–2 Sam 5); however, the Genesis narratives are particularly well-suited as an introduction to biblical election theology. This is so because they raise a number of central issues concerning election theology that recur in the more abstract theological reflections on election that helped shape the Pentateuch, and they had a strong influence on the Former and Latter Prophets, thereby providing links between Section 1 and Section 2 of this book.

In order to avoid digressing too far from the narratives in Genesis, I opted to treat some of the major abstract theological ideas broached already in Genesis in a separate chapter at the beginning of Section 2. Thus, chapter 5 explores the relationship between election and the themes of promise and covenant. Chapter 6 briefly compares and contrasts the election theology within Priestly texts to that found in Deuteronomy by focusing most especially on each collection's ideas of holiness.

The next two chapters explore issues surrounding the ways in which Israel's election theology affected the treatment of "the other" in ancient Israel. There has been a strong propensity to assume that Israel's election theology is ethnocentrism at its worst and that genocide flows naturally from it. The problem in my view has been the assumption that ancient Israel's treatment of the Canaanites was paradigmatic for her treatment of other outsiders. Chapter 7 examines the theological problems raised by texts that deal with the category I prefer to call "the anti-elect," consisting of groups such as the Canaanites who are destined for destruction. Chapter 8 examines "the non-elect," those many other peoples, often portrayed positively, in relation to whom Israel works out her destiny.

Chapter 9 examines election theology within the prophetic corpus with particular attention to the question of how ancient Israelite thinkers imagined the eschatological relationship between Israel and the Gentile nations of the world. Christian commentators have tended to see many of these eschatological texts as authorizing the ideas of mission and conversion. However, a careful analysis of these materials will demonstrate that, while a few rare passages might have something akin to the notion of the conversion of the nations, it is God, not Israel, who brings about such changes. More important, Israel's unique status is upheld in the vast bulk of eschatological oracles within the Hebrew Bible. Chapter 10 explores election theology in relation to the third section of the Jewish canon, the Ketuvim, or Writings. After briefly surveying elective themes in Psalms, a book pervaded by such notions, I turn to the difficult question of what, if anything, wisdom texts have to say about election theology. Here I point out that while at first glance such texts seem to have little connection to election theology, certain elective themes occur even in older wisdom texts. Furthermore, I argue that later wisdom texts found in the Apocrypha have no trouble at all melding wisdom and elective ideas in highly creative ways. Finally, chapter 11 attempts to survey the unique but related ways in which the New Testament and early rabbinic Judaism each appropriated the Hebrew Bible's views of divine election as well as showing how a clear understanding of each religion's election theology illuminates and enriches contemporary Jewish-Christian dialogue. We will then finish with a summary and a set of concluding reflections.

This book is not intended to be the final all-encompassing study of the Hebrew Bible's election theology. Rather, its purpose is to provide a new and relatively accessible discussion of some of the most interesting aspects of this topic with the hope that others will be drawn into this theologically central but much-neglected area of study.

Section 1

INTRODUCTION TO CHAPTERS 1–4

ELECTION AND THE RIVALRY STORIES OF GENESIS

This first section of this book is a study of the four sibling rivalry stories in Genesis: Cain and Abel, Isaac and Ishmael, Jacob and Esau, and Joseph and his brothers. While the most explicit and developed statements concerning God's election of Israel are found in Deuteronomy and 2nd Isaiah, there are a number of compelling reasons to begin this study of the Bible's election theology with the Genesis stories of brotherly struggle. My suspicion is that the most elaborate statements on Israel's election, found in books like Deuteronomy, are in fact later texts that are drawing out the deeper implications from Israel's core narratives such as the sibling stories in Genesis, stories that gave rise to Israel's earliest sense of herself. These four narratives of sibling rivalry have much to say about Israel's understanding of her chosenness. Moreover, as the reader will soon see, these individual stories are linked to one another, and taken together they contain a sustained and profound exposition of the biblical concept of election.

In analyzing the sibling episodes in Genesis, my approach, while fully cognizant of historical criticism, will be focused mainly on literary and theological concerns. This approach might best be called holistic or canonical, and its goal is to produce a narrative reading that elucidates Israel's election theology. Although various historical critical issues will be discussed in the notes, they will be introduced into the main text only when they bear directly on a literary and/or theological point being made. Each story will be analyzed independently, but the overarching set of literary and theological tropes that connects all of these stories will be highlighted during the course of the argument. It is hoped that this procedure will allow the reader to see why, individually and collectively, these four stories deserve this attention in an examination of the biblical concept of election.

The larger framework that binds these stories together consists of recurring themes, motifs, word patterns, and wordplays. The use of shared literary patterns among the stories of brotherly struggle in Genesis and between these stories and certain other narratives elsewhere in the Hebrew Bible raises an issue that will come up periodically in this book: when should one limit oneself to the immediate narrative frame of a given passage and when should one utilize pieces from elsewhere in the Hebrew Bible to clarify textual and/or exegetical issues under discussion? Clearly, one must strike the right balance between recognizing that each of the stories of brotherly struggle is unique while they are also connected to one another as part of a canonical whole. Although drawing out the connections between the various sibling stories is useful, one must avoid flattening out the unique contours of each story, or dissolving them all into one another in order to derive a single theological point.

Before we turn to the analysis of the first sibling story, that of Cain and Abel, it may be helpful for the reader to have a sense of the larger argument of chapters 1–4. In broad terms, I hope to demonstrate that the four rivalry stories in Genesis are an extended meditation on the concept of election, which seeks to give a full articulation and defense of this powerful idea, even while it highlights many of the problems flowing from it.

This examination poses a challenge to a number of recent treatments of the same literature that regard the idea of divine favoritism (and its reflection in the favoritism exhibited by certain patriarchs and matriarchs toward one special child) as unfair and therefore morally and theologically retrograde. For example, Regina Schwartz, taking a political and ideological view toward the various sibling rivalry stories in Genesis, argues that the Hebrew Bible's propensity for favoring one sibling, family, or nation over another is rooted in a worldview dominated by scarcity, which inherently engenders violence against "the other."[1] Other recent writers such as Burton Visotzky and Norman Cohen offer a psychologizing and moralizing approach by claiming that the text of Genesis critiques the notion of favoritism by portraying the family strife such favoritism brings in its wake.[2] Scholars like Mark Brett pursue a historical-ideological approach, seeing this material as a thinly veiled way for certain exilic groups to critique exclusivistic notions of election that he believes were in vogue among the ruling elite in the Persian period.[3] While each of these scholars makes astute and insightful comments on certain aspects of the sibling rivalry stories, all of these approaches inevitably miss many of the theological nuances within the text because they read a modern predisposition against ethnicity, exclusivism, and particularism back into the biblical text. Thus, although Schwartz thinks these sibling stories endorse the violence that arises when differing groups and/or individuals compete for favored status and Visotzky and Brett see the text as critiquing these same ideas, all appear to agree that the root of the problem is the notion of human and divine favoritism and the exclusivism and particularism accompanying it.

Yiu-Wing Fung's recently published monograph on the Joseph narrative clarifies the limitations of the above-mentioned approaches to the question of favoritism in the Genesis sibling stories. His analysis is dedicated to unmasking what he views as the problematic nature of any theology that promotes the favoritism of some over others who are required to submit to and accept such favoritism.[4] In the final chapter, Fung points out that while some modern commentators condemn the human favoritism of characters like Jacob because it is harsh and unfair, almost all commentators accept the same unfairness when it comes from the divine realm. Few commentators have bothered to articulate why such unfair favoritism should be unacceptable when humans engage in it, while the same unwarranted partiality is acceptable when it comes from God. This leads Fung to reject both human and divine favoritism, a sensible idea if one finds chosenness repugnant.

Following in the footsteps of Michael Wyschogrod, I argue that such favoritism, though highly unpalatable to most people living in a modern democratic world, is at the very center of the Bible's theology and points toward a profound intuition about God's relationship to the human community.[5] Like many recent commentators, I too think the Bible is offering a critique of certain human behaviors. But the evidence presented below will show that the critique is not a rejection of the notion of the mysterious favoritism finding its fullest articulation in the concept of God's special election of Israel, an idea that inevitably brings in its wake some level of exclusivism and particularism. Rather, as will be demonstrated in the following analysis of the stories of sibling rivalry, Genesis offers a critique of the human rebellion that occurs when others malign the elect, as well as when the elect misuse or fail to accept their special status and the responsibilities it entails.

Chapter One

Cain and Abel

Genesis's sustained meditation on the idea of chosenness begins with the story of Cain and Abel in Gen 4. Several aspects of this disturbing and enigmatic episode directly or indirectly touch on the issue of election. As most readers know, the story is set immediately after the first couple's expulsion from Eden due to their failure to obey God's command. In a mere two verses Eve gives birth to two children, Cain the elder, who becomes a farmer, and Abel the younger, who becomes a shepherd. Each brings an offering: Cain, produce from the ground, and Abel, some firstborn of his flock. When God accepts Abel's offering but not Cain's, Cain is troubled. God and Cain have a rather cryptic conversation in which Cain appears to be advised not to let his rejection lead him to any rash acts. But in the very next verse Cain kills Abel. The story ends with God's indictment and punishment of Cain, which are slightly tempered by God's promise to protect Cain from anyone seeking to kill him.

The story line appears rather straightforward, but its terseness raises a number of issues, many of which will not receive attention here because they are not of direct relevance for this investigation into the biblical concept of election. Thus, one might wonder how the brothers know that God had accepted one offering and not the other when all the text says is that God "had regard for" or, more literally, "looked upon" Abel and his offering but did not look upon Cain and his offering. Did fire come from heaven as in Lev 9:24 or 1 Kgs 18:38? Did the glory of God appear as it did in Lev 9:23 or Exod 40:34? Do Abel's cattle prosper and Cain's crops not? How quickly is this known?[1] These types of questions, while interesting, are secondary to the focus of this book.

However, four questions are highly pertinent to any attempt to understand what this narrative might contribute to our view of the idea of election. (1) Were Cain and Abel not only siblings but actually twins inasmuch as Abel's birth is prefaced with the words "next she bore his brother Abel," rather than the expected fuller formula "Adam again knew his wife and she conceived"? (2) Was God's acceptance of Abel's sacrifice and rejection of Cain's due to the fact that Cain brought an inferior offering and, thus, Cain had no one but himself to blame? Several interpretive possibilities attribute YHWH's rejection of Cain's offering to some deficiency in its type or quality. The strongest of these is the notion that while Abel brought from "the firstlings of his flock, their fat portions," Cain just brought "fruit of the ground," not the most select vegetables or the firstfruits. But another possible explanation is that Cain's vegetable offering was doomed to fail either because God preferred meat offerings over vegetable ones or because vegetables were tainted by God's earlier curse upon the ground (Gen 3:17-19). (3) Is it possible to grasp the meaning of the conversation between God and Cain in verses 6-7, especially since verse 7 contains a number of unsolved grammatical and textual problems? This conversation may help illuminate what, if anything, Cain did wrong before he killed his brother, and what his relationship to God was in the short period after his sacrifice was rejected and before Abel's murder. (4) What is the nature of Cain's punishment, and what does it reveal about Cain's status at the close of the narrative? Is Cain utterly cut off from God, or is he still within the pale of God's mercy?

Are Cain and Abel Twins?

The first question about whether Cain and Abel are twins is relevant to the discussion of election in that if Cain and Abel are twins, the issue of who is the firstborn and who is the younger child turns on a few short minutes. This would heighten the rivalry between the siblings by stressing their near equality. Furthermore, it might lead one to see this narrative and the Jacob and Esau account as a pair of narratives that should be read over against each other. Unfortunately, whether Cain and Abel are twins or just brothers is not a question that can receive a definitive answer from the language of the verses themselves. The possibility that these brothers are twins is raised by the fact that there is only one verb indicating Adam had sexual intercourse with Eve (ידע in Gen 4:1) as well as only one verb describing a single conception (ותהר in Gen 4:1), but each birth is described separately (4:1 using ותלד and 4:2 using ללדת). The ambiguity is that the second use of the birthing verb may have been just a shorthand way of summarizing Abel's conception and birth.

While many commentators assume that Cain and Abel are siblings rather than twins, some favor the idea that they are twins based not just on the ambiguous language of verse 2, but because they recognize that this story shares a host of similarities to the Jacob and Esau episode. That story also contains two siblings born from the same mother in very close temporal proximity who each take on different vocations, with one receiving God's favor and the other not. And there the elder almost kills the younger, but the younger is the one driven into exile, albeit not for a whole lifetime. The close relationship between these two narratives may be a textual signal that one should assume that Cain and Abel were indeed twins like Jacob and Esau. My suspicion is that Cain and Abel are not twins, but that the author(s) of the text may have been purposefully ambiguous in order to have the first story of brotherly struggle serve as a paradigm for all the subsequent ones—those about twins like Jacob and Esau and those about regular siblings as in the Joseph story. Thus, while the Cain and Abel story will surely be helpful in illuminating various aspects of the later sibling stories, particularly the Jacob and Esau narrative, the argument for using evidence from this latter narrative to solve a textual ambiguity in Gen 4 is less compelling.

Why Might God Not Have Accepted Cain's Sacrifice?

The second question mentioned above, about whether Cain's offering was defective in some way, is perhaps the most pivotal issue in connection to the concept of election raised by this passage. This is because it directly relates to the Bible's view of how people are chosen. Is election primarily a divine decision with little or no human input, or one that is strongly influenced by a variety of human factors (i.e., can God's choice be rationalized)? Some scholars argue for the latter position by claiming that Abel's sacrifice earned God's favor and/or that Cain's displeased God. As indicated above, numerous theories propose exactly what Cain might have done wrong or what Abel did correctly. Two weaker hypotheses center on the fact that Cain brought a vegetable offering, either arguing that such an offering was inherently inferior to a meat sacrifice,[2] or claiming that while a vegetable offering became acceptable later in the biblical period, at this point the ground is still under the curse it received in Gen 3:17-19.[3] Such theories draw additional support from the widespread acknowledgment that this narrative's oldest kernel is likely an etiological tale explaining the eventual cultural triumph of shepherds over farmers. But while an older etiological tale about shepherds and farmers may have formed the earliest kernel of the now extant narrative, it is no longer the dominant point of the story. There is less support for the even more far-fetched Girardian reading that Abel's meat sacrifice was "an appropriate outlet to control violence," but Cain "does not have the violence outlet of animal sacrifice at his disposal."[4] Any hypothesis that seeks to fault Cain for failing to bring a meat sacrifice must reckon with the fact that there is no explicit evidence in Gen 4 that God was upset with Cain because he failed to bring a meat sacrifice. Such theories draw their evidence from elsewhere in the Bible but can muster little or no basis for importing such notions into Gen 4.

A much more viable possibility is that Abel's sacrifice was accepted because he offered "the firstlings of his flock, their fat portions" (Gen 4:4), while Cain brought "fruit of the ground," not the most select vegetables. This line of interpretation, which is found not only in modern scholarship[5] but also in ancient Jewish and Christian sources,[6] certainly has merit to it; nevertheless, there are problems with it as well. After all, Cain could bring only what he produced, and to be fair, one cannot bring fat portions or firstborn pieces of grain in a way that one can bring firstlings from the flock and the most delicious parts of an animal. Although it is conceivable that Cain is being condemned for failing to bring firstfruits (Deut 26:1-11), a number of factors speak against this possibility. To begin with, if one wishes to pin so much on a word or two in the text, one could easily come up with a reading that turns Cain into a pious person and Abel into a mere imitator. As Jon Levenson notes, "Whereas Cain brought his sacrifice 'to the Lord' Abel, on this sort of microscopic over-reading, did not."[7] Additionally, while the first conversation between God and Cain in verses 6-7 is admittedly cryptic and difficult to interpret, God does not tell him, "Well, next time all you have to do to please me is to bring better produce."

Perhaps the greatest piece of evidence against the view that Abel influenced God's decision to favor him is that it is quite difficult to find much support from other biblical texts for the idea that God's initial decision to bestow favor on some individual or group is primarily dictated by human behavior rather than by mysterious divine fiat. Internal biblical evidence suggests that one should read this as the first of many stories about brotherly struggles set off by God's mysterious choice to elevate one brother to preeminence, sometimes in consonance with a parental choice to favor the same child.

> It is a misunderstanding of the real meaning to look for the reason for the inequality of God's regard. . . . The reason why God regards Abel's sacrifice and not Cain's must remain without explanation. And the narrator wants to make clear that this is one of the decisive motifs for conflict wherever there are brothers.[8]

The point of introducing this motif of divine favoring is not to argue that such favoring is deserved by those who receive it, but that it is inevitable even in egalitarian circumstances. No matter how fairly things are divided up, soon enough one person will outshine another and human jealousy will be unleashed.

Most mysterious is the fact that the elder brother, Cain, whom one would expect to be favored by the rule of primogeniture,[9] is overshadowed by the second-born Abel. This unusual occurrence is repeated in the cases of Ishmael and Isaac, Jacob and Esau, and Joseph and his ten older brothers. Toward the end of Section 1, I will offer some explanations for the prominence of this motif in these sibling stories and elsewhere within the Hebrew Bible. The point to be noticed here is that God's recurring mysterious elevation of the younger sibling over the older one strongly indicates that God's attention to Abel's sacrifice is not driven by either Abel's proper or Cain's improper behavior.

The Theological Implications of the Cain and Abel Story

If the Cain and Abel story is not one about the human ability to influence God's mysterious choice, then what is this story about? Unfortunately, this story will continue to remain somewhat enigmatic because, as indicated above, the conversation between Cain and God in verses 6-7 is quite cryptic and likely textually corrupt. Many scholars consider verse 7 to be one of the greatest cruxes in the Pentateuch. The most obvious problem is that the word חטאת (sin) is feminine, and the participle following it, רבץ (crouching), is masculine. Additionally, the use of the word נשׂא (from the root meaning "to lift up") can carry a number of possible meanings. It can be short for lifting up an offering, as in Ps 96:8; for forgiving one's sin, as in Gen 18:24, 26 (an interpretation favored by those who think Cain did something wrong with his sacrifice); or for lifting up one's head (Gen 40:13) or face (Job 11:15 or Deut 28:50), perhaps as an act of deference. Alternatively, it could be (and I believe likely is) intended as a contrast to Cain's fallen face mentioned in Gen 4:5-6, implying that if he overcomes his jealousy, his anger/depression will also abate. There is also a cryptic allusion to Gen 3:16 in that the identical words for "rule over" and "desire" are used in both places in strikingly similar phrases (ואל־אישך תשוקתך והוא ימשל־בך and ואליך תשוקתו ואתה תמשל־בו in Gen 3:16 and 4:7, respectively). The NJPS translation is better than most in that it allows one to glimpse the cryptic nature of the Hebrew verse: "Surely, if you do right, there is uplift. But if you do not do right sin crouches at the door; its urge is towards you, yet you can be its master." But no translation is likely to receive wide approval absent a newly discovered ancient manuscript that is less corrupt.

However, there are two reasons one need not solve all the textual difficulties in this verse for the purposes of the present discussion. First, it is clear that the general thrust of verses 6-7 is a warning to Cain to control his jealous reaction.[10] Furthermore, regardless of what exactly God said to Cain, the fact that God engages in a conversation with Cain after God's rejection of his sacrifice is itself quite significant. That Cain and God are having an intimate conversation suggests that the non-acceptance of Cain's offering does not mean that Cain is utterly alienated from God or somehow cursed, but only that he is not specially blessed. At this point in the narrative, Cain appears to occupy a type of middle ground best described by the term "non-elect." While this idea will be filled out in great detail in later chapters, for now it is enough to say that Gen 4 already indicates that those who are not divinely favored must learn to accept that God's blessing flows through the world in mysterious ways that, while merciful, are not, strictly speaking, equitable. God's "unfairness" in choosing some over others is not simply a benefit for the chosen or a detriment to the non-chosen. It is difficult to substantiate this claim only on the basis of Gen 4 in that Cain's murder of Abel truncates this narrative, but when one looks at the larger theology articulated by the full range of sibling stories, one discovers that often the non-elect also receive some form of blessing. Furthermore, the blessing of the non-elect is frequently brought about by their relationship to the elect.

Cain's failure is not in relation to the offering he brought, but in his reaction to God's mysterious favoritism of Abel. He allows his jealousy to get out of control, even after God has warned him of this danger. Rather than accept God's choice of Abel, he tries to overcome Abel's election by killing him. Interestingly enough, Cain's elimination of God's elect does not leave him occupying that role. Instead it results in Cain's becoming alienated from God and from the soil from which he earned his livelihood (vv. 11-12). At least initially, Cain moves down a rung from the middle ground of the non-elect and joins those who are beyond God's communion (v. 14). However, when Cain pleads with God that his sin/guilt or punishment[11] is too much to bear and that he can be killed by anyone seeking Abel's vengeance, God offers him a measure of divine protection. Whereas some maintain that the mark set on Cain may be from an earlier etiological tale that attempted to explain a tribal marking, within the current text it indicates that Cain is not destined for destruction like others who rebel against God's plan. Rather, he still receives a measure of God's mercy, even while he remains alienated from God (v. 16).

Another interesting facet of this story occurs several verses later in Gen 4:25, a narrative fragment that may have been more closely linked with Gen 4:16 at an earlier redactional point. This verse tells us that not only does Cain's murder of Abel, God's elect, fail to gain him the elect's position, which he jealously wished to assume, but the status of the elect instead passes to the latest born son Seth, who, as the text reports, is Abel's replacement. Thus, God's mysterious tendency to favor certain people remains unabated, offering evidence that the point of these stories is not to critique God for having elevated one brother over the other, but to critique the all too human propensity to become hateful and hurtful toward those whom God favors. Some of the later stories examined below do contain a critique of the elect who misunderstand the purpose of their election and thereby act wrongly, but it is difficult to apply such a reading to this passage where Abel is eliminated almost immediately. It is clear that this narrative is not focused on Abel, a character who does not even receive a full naming from his mother, whose name itself means "mist" or "vapor" and symbolizes the notion of the ephemeral, who is barely present, and who functions only as Cain's foil. Cain dominates this story by controlling much of its action and engaging in two extended dialogues with the Deity. The fact that the first narrative to struggle with the issue of election is so lopsidedly preoccupied with the non-elect strongly indicates that the concept of election was never assumed to be only for the benefit of the elect, but it was always about God's plan for the whole world, the elect and the non-elect alike.

One might ask whether the reading of this narrative proposed above, highlighting the manner in which God's mysterious favoritism affects the relationship between the chosen and the non-chosen brother, finds support in the Jewish and Christian interpretive traditions. As indicated above, some later Jewish and Christian sources bristled against the idea that God acted arbitrarily by attributing Cain's downfall to his human free will and Abel's election to his superior offering. Alternatively, other sources enhance the arbitrariness of God's actions. Thus, there is a line of interpretation found in both Jewish and Christian sources that sees Cain as evil from birth in that he was the offspring of the evil one who had led Adam and Eve astray.[12] In a sense, this ancient reading shares certain commonalities with the interpretations discussed above, which attribute Cain's rejection to the fact that God prefers animal offerings to vegetable ones either for mysteriously arbitrary reasons or for known arbitrary causes, such as Cain's hapless decision to become a farmer after God had cursed the ground in Gen 3:17-19. In all of these interpretations Cain is doomed to failure for simply being who he is. How both Judaism and Christianity deal with the concept of election, particularly with its more arbitrary aspects, is something that will be explored in greater depth toward the end of this book. For now, the reader needs to know that each tradition is complex, and both contain some interpretations that ameliorate the idea that God acts arbitrarily as well as others that heighten God's apparent arbitrariness all the more.

Before proceeding with a more detailed discussion of the other sibling stories, it is worth reflecting on the ways in which the Cain and Abel narrative is unique and what general attributes it shares with these later episodes. Unlike the other three stories of sibling rivalry discussed below, the Cain and Abel story does not contain all the elements of a full-blown theology of election. Certainly, God singles out Abel as the favored sibling, and this favoritism implies that Abel received some type of divine blessing that Cain did not. But the idea that God's special covenant will pass through only one brother's progeny, as occurs in the Isaac and Ishmael and Jacob and Esau episodes, is not present here. Without the presence of such a covenantal theology, it may be more accurate to speak of divine favoring rather than divine election here.[13] Of course, this narrative necessarily lacks a fully articulated theology of election because Cain's action truncates the possibility for God's plan to be wholly revealed at this time.

Nevertheless, one should not lose sight of the many ways this narrative is indeed linked to the three yet to be discussed sibling stories and thus gives voice to several of the central elements of the biblical concept of election. These include the mysterious divine elevation of the younger sibling over the elder, the fact that such divine favoritism does not signal that the non-chosen is alienated from God, the jealous reaction on the part of the elder sibling(s), the grave danger that such jealousy entails for the one chosen by God, and the fact that violence against the elect gains nothing for the non-elect because it does not eliminate God's propensity to continue to favor some over others. That many of these election tropes are adumbrated here but filled out in the next two episodes and heightened further in the Joseph story indicates that this is an intentional literary strategy to enrich the theme by continually returning to it and deepening it over time. If this is the case, the authors of Genesis then purposely linked the cryptic Cain and Abel tale to these other more developed ones. Having begun the process of unpacking Genesis's extended meditation on election, we now turn to the second story involving two siblings, the much more elaborate set of narratives about Isaac and Ishmael.

CHAPTER TWO

ISHMAEL AND ISAAC (AND HAGAR AND SARAH)

Before launching into an analysis of the Ishmael and Isaac stories, it is important to note that the trope of God's mysterious election occurs in shortened form numerous times between the Cain and Abel story and Gen 16 where the Ishmael and Isaac stories begin. There is the brief notice about God's special relationship with Enoch in Gen 5:24, as well as the rather mysterious favoritism Noah receives in the J account (Gen 6:8). Immediately after the flood, there is yet another tale of three brothers in which the descendants of one brother, those connected to Ham through Canaan, are demoted to the status of being landless, in this case through slavery. This follows Ham's sin against his father, just as Cain's landlessness is a punishment for murdering his brother. Another son, Shem, gives birth to the chosen line, and the third, Japheth, occupies the middle ground (Gen 9:18-27), adumbrating the existence of the medial category of the non-elect discussed at length in chapter 8.

This pattern of having three siblings in which one is elevated, one is of medial status, and one is eliminated is also found in the story of Abram[1] and his two siblings, Nahor and Haran, which begins in Gen 11:27. In this instance, Nahor occupies the medial position in that his family provides women to the Israelite patriarchs, and Abram is exalted while Haran's line is dis-elected.[2] Although this is the way things end up, there is initially a bit of ambiguity over which line will be chosen; Abram's brother Haran dies early, but unlike Abram, he has a male heir, Lot. The existence of this male heir and the notice that Abram's wife, Sarai, was barren leave the reader wondering whether Haran's or Abram's line will be elevated. Then suddenly, in an utterly arbitrary fashion, the mystery is slowly both clarified and complicated by an explicit set of promises God makes to Abram that include progeny, land, and special blessing (Gen 12:1-9).[3]

The promises seem to confirm Abram as the chosen one, but things remain cloudy in that immediately after they are delivered, Abram is exiled and in mortal danger in Egypt, having surrendered his wife to Pharaoh, king of Egypt (Gen 12:10-20). The episode ends with Abram receiving Sarai back and taking some of Egypt's wealth with him. But this occurs only after the Egyptians are afflicted with divine plagues on Abram's account, rather than receiving a blessing from Abram's presence. This short episode makes two points rather clearly. First, the nature of the interaction between the elect party and those not chosen affects whether the non-chosen reap a blessing or a curse.[4] Here a possibly unintentional offence against Abram brings down God's wrath on Egypt. Second, it seems that the promises God made to Abram will reach fulfillment in a very circuitous fashion.[5]

The suspense over how Abram, who is now seventy-five years old (Gen 12:4) and childless, will come to see the fruition of these promises is further heightened and somewhat clarified by Gen 13, a chapter focused on Abram's relationship with Lot. While Abram is the recipient of the promises in chapter 12, Lot may be the most likely figure to inherit these promises because Abram has no other viable heir. But chapter 13 makes clear that this eventuality will not come to pass, and by the end of the chapter Abram has title to what would eventually prove to be the more fertile portion of the Holy Land. However, the very action that leaves Abram as uncontested heir to God's promise concerning the land of Israel leaves God's other promises concerning Abram's becoming a great nation and a blessing to other nations further endangered. For now Lot, the only blood heir, is eliminated from the divine plan. Furthermore, his exit is due to strife engendered by the multiplication of Abram's and Lot's flocks, which may be attributed to God's blessing of Abram's household (Gen 13:2-7). Once again, Abram's election brings strife rather than blessing to others.

One might well have anticipated Lot's dis-election on the basis of Gen 12, but in an interesting twist Lot appears to bring this very reality to fruition through his free choice. This is not to say that Lot caused God's favor to turn against him, because God had already elevated Abram's line over Haran's and Nahor's. Rather, the Hebrew Bible often operates with a double causality in which events occur through a mysterious interweaving of divine providence and human actions. Thus Lot, further confirming God's promise to Abram from chapter 12, removes himself as a possible heir to these promises by choosing to settle in the (at that time) more verdant area of Sodom (Gen 13:8-13). And after this, God reconfirms his promise that Abram and his offspring, now predicted to become as numerous as the dust of the earth, will inherit all of the land of Canaan (Gen 13:14-17).

In some sense the relationship between Lot and Abram foreshadows the coming battles between opposing siblings, opposing wives, and opposing spouses that occupy much of the rest of Genesis from chapter 16 forward. These other narratives that are filled with intrigue about which heir will be the vessel of God's covenantal pledge cannot commence until Lot is completely excluded as a possible candidate for divine election, something that becomes clear once he chooses to settle in the vicinity of Sodom (Gen 13:14-18).[6] Thus immediately after the narratives dealing with Lot and his choice of Sodom as a home (Gen 13–14), God formalizes the promises he has made to Abram through a solemn covenant ceremony (Gen 15).[7] God is motivated to formalize his relationship with Abram by Abram's complaint that he lacks an heir (Gen 15:3), a fact that is all the more painfully clear in the wake of Abram's separation from his last remaining kinsman, Lot. The divine promise issued in Gen 12 and the covenantal pact found in Gen 15 (as well as its Priestly textual counterpart found in Gen 17) indicate that, unlike God's preference for Abel and his sacrifice, God's relationship to Abram and his descendants is more than simply a case of divine favoritism. In this instance it is certainly proper to speak of God's relationship to Abram and his future descendants as one involving election.

Quite interesting is that the covenant between the parts (Gen 15) exacerbates rather than lessens Abram's anxiety about his lack of children. In the wake of this covenant, Abram at Sarai's suggestion takes Hagar, Sarai's maid, as a concubine in hopes of producing a child to begin to fulfill the covenantal promises. This narrative twist once more introduces the question of how large a role human initiative plays in the working out of God's elective plan. While I argued that there is little textual evidence to support the idea that Abel earned God's favoritism and Cain lost it through certain behaviors, the question raised here is slightly different. Might election, once initiated by God, require human action to bring it to fulfillment? This question is very difficult to answer in a definitive fashion in this instance and in future biblical stories of chosenness.

Hagar and God's Plan

In the case of Gen 16, some perceive Sarai's initial attempt to produce offspring by suggesting that Abram sleep with her maidservant Hagar (Gen 16:2) as a failed attempt to force God's hand, proving that God, not humans, ultimately brings God's plans to fulfillment.

> Was it not inevitable that Abraham and Sarah should fall into temptation? There was no greater sorrow for an Israelite or Oriental woman than childlessness. . . . From the legal and moral standpoint, therefore, Sarah's proposal was completely according to custom. And yet, the narrator probably sees a great delinquency precisely in this.[8]

Joel Rosenberg bolsters this line of interpretation by noting the linguistic similarities between Gen 16:2-3, in which we are told Abram listened to his wife, who took Hagar and gave her to Abram, and Gen 3:6, in which Eve takes some of the fruit and gives it to her husband, who indeed is punished because he listened to his wife's voice (Gen 3:17).[9]

Other interpreters counter this argument by pointing out that later in this narrative, as well as regularly throughout the Pentateuch, the opposite message is communicated in that humans often bring God's plans to fruition or occasionally initiate actions that God then approves.[10]

> In defense of Abram and Sarai against the charge of faithlessness, however, it must be noted not only that the matriarch of the promised progeny has never been indicated, but also that the Hebrew Bible does not generally support an equation of faith and passivity. . . . If we view the decision in Gen 16:2-3 in this light, then the couple must be seen as willingly playing their role in the divine-human synergy through which the astonishing providential design will be realized.[11]

There are a host of instances in which humans suggest or begin actions that later receive divine approval. Subsequently in this very narrative, Sarah first suggests driving Hagar and Ishmael out of Abraham's house, an idea that upsets Abraham until God assures him that he should obey

Sarah because the promise will indeed pass through Isaac's line, not Ishmael's (Gen 21:10-12).[12] Further on in Genesis, both Rachel and Leah, on their own initiative, introduce the use of surrogates to produce children who become part of God's elect people.[13] Thus while linguistic echoes may exist between this cycle of stories and the Eden narrative, such echoes need to be evaluated on a case-by-case basis. It is possible that such similar language signals a common appraisal of the two husbands, but it is equally possible that the second narrative is using a wordplay to contrast the two stories and teach the reader that one needs to discern when one should or should not listen to one's spouse.

Rival Wives and Their Children

At this point in the narrative another element found in many texts dealing with chosen children occurs: the importance of the elect child coming from a chosen wife. Such a mother is often in rivalry with another woman who gives birth to children with much greater ease than the mother who will eventually bear the chosen one. Hagar and Sarai are pitted against each other as rival wives in a pattern repeated with Rachel and Leah as well as with Hannah and Peninnah in 1 Samuel. In this instance in particular one senses that the story might be better described as a rivalry between Sarai and Hagar rather than between their two children. As discussed below, there is some slight evidence of a possible strain between the two sons, yet the major tensions in the story are between the two women and the husband they share. This story might be better labeled as one of family rivalry or family strife.

Of course, the tension between Hagar and Sarai is ultimately tied to the question concerning which woman will bear the chosen son, an issue that is heightened by the many ambiguities within this narrative. As already noted, while Abram is promised progeny, before the announcement of Isaac's birth in chapter 17, God had not yet specified the matriarch of the elect line. And even when Sarah is named as the bearer of the promised child, the reader continues to have reason to wonder whether Hagar and Ishmael are dis-elected for a variety of reasons. In terms of Hagar's position in relation to Abraham and Sarah, a number of things raise the expectation that she, rather than Sarah, is the mother of a chosen child. While some of these markers, such as the fact that she is the first person to receive a specific oracle announcing the birth of a special child and the only person to name the Deity, occur before Isaac's birth, others occur after Isaac's arrival.[14] Furthermore, Hagar and Abraham share a common destiny, as do Isaac and Ishmael.[15] Just as Hagar is forced to watch the death of Ishmael, her only son, which is averted right at the last moment by a child's cry to heaven, Abraham is forced to bring about the death of his beloved son Isaac, an act that is stopped by a last-minute cry from heaven. That Hagar is a slave who is persecuted and then has her child endangered by those who have enslaved her calls to mind the story of another specially chosen one, Moses.

Turning to Ishmael, one discovers that his status is strikingly ambiguous in that for a non-elect child, Ishmael has more markings of election than perhaps any other non-elect person in the whole Hebrew Bible. Even when it becomes crystal clear that Ishmael is not the chosen child, he is blessed by God to father many progeny (Gen 17:20; 21:13; 25:12-17), and he is even given the sign of the elect, circumcision (Gen 17:25). Even more striking, Ishmael, like Isaac, has a death-nearly-averted experience, and as Jon Levenson has demonstrated, there is a very close relationship between being chosen and suffering a death or nearly averting one.[16] And as Larry Lyke has convincingly argued, chapters 21 and 22 in Genesis are artfully drawn together by a tight web of linguistic echoes, allusions, and curious grammatical constructions that blur the distinction between the two sons of Abraham in the mind of the reader.[17] Finally, at the very end of the narrative the reader learns that, oddly enough, Ishmael, like Jacob would later on, gives birth to twelve tribes (Gen 25:12-16). All of these facts indicate that while Ishmael is ultimately excluded from God's covenant and thereby is non-elect, his case is the least clear-cut instance of dis-election in the Hebrew Bible, and even after his non-elect status is confirmed, he still inherits those portions of the promise made to Abraham that deal with progeny, nationhood, prosperity (Gen 17:20), and divine presence (Gen 21:20).

What is clear from this narrative is that the understanding of election within Genesis is quite complex and filled with ambiguities. To anticipate my later argument, the Hebrew Bible did not endorse the notion that election meant that the non-elect were either damned or out of the purview of God's blessings, nor does it claim that the elect escaped all hardship. The concept of election is more nuanced, and these nuances need fuller attention than they frequently receive. Not only must one bear in mind that *an element* of election as articulated in the first of the promises God made to Abram concerns the blessing for the non-elect nations of the world (Gen 12:3), but furthermore, the Isaac and Ishmael cycle indicates that at least some of the non-elect are closer to the elect than others. Thus, there are degrees among the non-elect, and in any case, one should not confuse the status of being non-elect with that of being an enemy of God or what I prefer to call the anti-elect. Most important, some of the non-elect actually receive promises of special divine blessing, as is the case with Ishmael.

Those who view election as simply an assertion of ethnic superiority not only overlook the Bible's rather subtle portrayals of those not chosen, but also fail to reckon with unusual facts that tend to surround the chosen children and their mothers. Why is the elect child frequently born to a woman who has trouble bearing children, and why is the elect child (as well as the non-elect one, at times) subject to suffering and grave danger resulting in death or a death nearly averted? Also, what is one to make of the pervasive conflicts between rival siblings, rival wives, and/or husbands and wives? The failure to take theological stock of these facts has resulted in the tendency by some to misunderstand exactly what election entails. Inasmuch as the narratives surrounding Isaac and Ishmael are pervaded by these themes, a closer look at their function here and elsewhere within the Bible is warranted.

The motif of the child born to a barren woman is one marker used to indicate that the child who is eventually born to such a mother both comes from and belongs to God.[18] This idea is explicitly stated in the birth stories of Samuel (1 Sam 1) and Samson (Judg 13:2-5), and it seems operative in the narratives surrounding Isaac, Jacob, and Joseph. Frequently, the barrenness is ended by a direct prayer to God, as in the cases of Rebekah (Gen 25:21), Hannah (1 Sam 1:10-18), and Sarah in Gen 21:1-2, where Isaac's birth follows directly after Abraham's intercessory prayer for the women in Abimelech's household (who had been temporarily barren) (Gen 20:17-18). At other times the barrenness ends by means of a direct announcement from God or an angelic being, as in the case of Samson (Judg 13:3), the P and J accounts announcing Isaac's birth (Gen 17:15-19 and 18:9-15), and the birth narratives surrounding John the Baptist and Jesus (Luke 1). Whether the narrative approves or disapproves of Abram's attempt at Sarai's urging to produce an heir for Abram through Hagar, the narrative certainly suggests that Isaac, who is born to very aged parents who are well beyond the natural limit of childbearing age, is in some sense a supernatural miracle baby (Gen 17:17; 18:11-12; 21:7).

The sense that the child comes from and thus belongs to God is further heightened by the child's death nearly averted. In each instance in which one finds this motif, the child is saved by direct intervention of the Deity, as in the Isaac and Ishmael stories, or by a series of providential events that surely reveal the hand of God, as in the Joseph and Moses narratives. The near-death experience erases any claim by the human parents, who in each case surrendered the child to his death, thus allowing for God to claim the surviving person for himself in an uncontested fashion.[19] Not only is the child produced by God, but he now belongs to God as well. Of course, in this set of narratives both Isaac and Ishmael are saved through a last-minute divine reprieve. However, Isaac's supernatural status is marked by his highly unusual birth, which itself is linked to God's specific announcements that the covenant will flow through Isaac rather than Ishmael (Gen 17:18-21).

The rivalry between the fertile Hagar and the infertile Sarai (a pattern repeated later with Rachel and Leah in Genesis as well as Hannah and Peninnah in Samuel) serves as a bridge between the trope of the barren woman and that of the endangered child. Thus while it gives the reader a contrast between a natural child who is born normally and a supernatural one who comes into the world by means of divine intervention, it also raises the possibility that the promise may not reach fruition in that the rival wife's more easily born child or children may claim preeminence or may harm the chosen one.

Of course, the enmity between the co-wives frequently extends to a rivalry between their children. This sibling rivalry is surely an extension of the one between the adults in a particular generation about whose favored child will end up as the elect heir and the carrier of the divine promises. But it also links to the motif of the endangered child in that the rival sibling(s) frequently presents a grave physical threat to the chosen child. This clearly occurs in the cases of Cain and Abel, Jacob and Esau, Joseph and his ten older brothers, and may be hinted at in the rather cryptic Gen 21:9, in which some have argued that Ishmael was toying with or perhaps even persecuting Isaac.[20]

Many times the parents themselves contribute to the endangerment brought about through sibling rivalry, and sometimes they appear to endanger their children independently. Here one thinks of characters like Abraham, who endangers Ishmael and Isaac in Gen 21 and 22 respectively (albeit both times following God's command); Rebekah, whose plot to steal Esau's blessing endangers Jacob's life, which is only spared through an extended exile from the Holy Land and his immediate family (Gen 27:41-45); or the father Jacob, who openly dotes on Joseph and then sends him all alone to check on his brothers who hate him (Gen 37:1-14). A similar trope is found later in the Hebrew Bible when David initially accedes to Amnon's request to have Tamar prepare a meal for him, which leads to Amnon's sexually assaulting her (2 Sam 13:1-19). After this he (foolishly) lets Absalom convince him to permit all David's children to attend a sheepshearing party at which Absalom orchestrates Amnon's murder (2 Sam 13:23-29).

When one looks closely at the strained relations between family members, one notices that not only do the consequences and various counterreactions swirl around within a particular generation, but they also carry over to later generations. For example, Sarah is the force behind driving Hagar and Ishmael out, nearly leading to Ishmael's death. In the next chapter Abraham is forced to reenact the same movement with his and Sarah's beloved son, Isaac. But the deed of driving Ishmael out, an action initiated by Sarah and executed by Abraham, but approved of by God (Gen 21:8-14), comes back to haunt Joseph who, according to one source, is taken down to Egypt (Hagar's country of origin as indicated in Gen 16:1) and sold into slavery by Ishmaelites (Gen 39:1; cf. 37:36). The oppression that Israel would experience in Egypt, something hinted at in Abram's visit there in Gen 12 and mentioned explicitly in 15:13, can be linked to Abram's and Sarai's treatment of Hagar the Egyptian in Gen 16. In turn, the oppression of Hagar the Egyptian in Gen 16 ominously adumbrates the future oppression that the Israelites receive in Egypt. Particularly striking is the way in which just as Abram and Sarai attempt to raise an Egyptian's child as an Israelite, later Pharaoh's daughter attempts to raise the Israelite baby Moses as an Egyptian. These narrative connections are brilliantly brought into focus by Rosenberg.

> This ravaging of Hagar's own kinship is pointedly analogous to the narrowly averted exploitation of Abraham's family by Pharaoh in chapter 12. . . . Implicit punishment is visited on Abraham's descendants (a punishment "to the fourth generation" as stated in principle in Ex 20:5 and 34:8) for the callousness toward Hagar and her offspring manifested in complicity by Abraham and Sarah, albeit with apparent divine validation (16:9 and 21:12). If God is later to harden Pharaoh's heart (Ex 10:1), he has first hardened the hearts of Abraham and Sarah—who, as servant masters in their own right try to borrow the baby of an Egyptian subordinate. This complicated web of moral compromise and reciprocal

> political vicissitude makes clear the relation of Genesis 16 both to the Egyptian episode in chapter 12 and to the Egyptian sojourn oracle in chapter 15.[21]

Here Rosenberg has detected an intense mirroring effect in which Pharaoh's behavior toward Abram and Sarai in Gen 12 gives rise to their mistreatment of Hagar, but this deed itself carries in its wake negative consequences for Joseph as well as for the Israelites of the exodus generation, especially Moses.

There are a number of possible explanations for this thick web of interconnected motifs and stories. One is that the biblical writers were consummate storytellers, and they enjoyed weaving tales together. From the standpoint of narrative theology it appears to indicate that even when human actions are ultimately seen as part of God's providential plan, sometimes so much so that they are described as being authorized by God, this does not mean that those actions occur in a vacuum and entail no consequences. This is important to note because many readers today assume that if particular actions lead to undesired consequences, then by definition they could not have been part of God's plan and certainly not authorized by God.

God's Promises to Abraham

Before leaving the Isaac and Ishmael account, it might be useful to consider the nature of the promises that Abram receives within these narratives (Gen 12; 15; 17). As discussed at length in chapter 5 below, God promises Abram progeny, blessing, and land. Are these promises simply announcements of the assured future, or do they require some type of human response and participation to bring them to fulfillment? A Pauline reading that understands these promises as stemming from a mysterious divine grace that is in no sense contingent on any human action (Rom 9:6-18) has some grounding in the texts of Gen 12 and 15. But this reading is more difficult to sustain when one reckons with the Abraham cycle as a whole. While some have argued that the repetition of the Abrahamic promises in the immediate aftermath of the *Akedah* story is a later addition to the text (Gen 22:15-19), the existence of these promises at this point gives a much greater place to the human actor than he has in Paul's reading. This sentiment is further reinforced by Gen 26:2-5. It is possible that the fuller body of Jewish midrashic lore that attributes God's choice of Abram back in chapter 12 to Abram's merits as the first practicing monotheist stems from the humble beginnings of these two short passages in Genesis.[22] What these two Genesis texts and the rabbinic lore have in common is that they suggest that God's choice of Abram in Gen 12 might not be solely attributable to God's mysterious grace. Ultimately, it is warranted because Abraham proves himself worthy through his response to God. Thus even while it is fair to maintain that the Bible generally views God's choosing as mysterious, attempts to rationalize and explain such choices already occur in the biblical text itself, not so much by explaining the initial choice, which continues to remain shrouded in mystery, but by creating a sense that God's choice opens up a space in which the chosen party can fulfill his destiny, which thereby reinforces the divine choice and brings it to fuller fruition.

An additional text supporting the idea that the promises are at least partially conditioned by human response is Gen 18:16-33, the passage in which Abraham argues with God over the fate of Sodom. The passage begins with a strange internal debate in which God wonders whether he can hide what he is about to do to Sodom from Abraham. In Gen 18:18 God invokes language from Gen 12:3 about the nations of the world being blessed by or blessing themselves by Abraham and then links this language to something not explicitly stated in chapter 12, that is, Abraham's and his descendants' duty to do righteousness and justice. In fact, Gen 18:19 implies that the promises are contingent on performing such righteous deeds. And once Abraham hears of God's plans to destroy Sodom, he launches into a plea to save the city.[23] One wonders if calling God to account in an attempt to protect potentially innocent civilians is one way in which Abraham, and later Israel, becomes a blessing for the nations.[24] In any case, human deeds seem to be involved in actualizing a promise that once appeared to be based solely on God's unconditioned and seemingly unwarranted gracious action. Thus Claus Westermann, commenting on Gen 18:19, notes that "Abraham then is the father of צדקה and משפט 'righteousness and justice,' and is not seen here as the father of faith (as in Gen 15:6)."[25]

Toward the end of the Abraham story, one finds yet another narrative that supports the growing attention to human actions in the elective process, the episode of the wooing of Rebekah in Gen 24. Rebekah becomes the chosen bride who will bear the next generation's chosen child by her supererogatory actions at the well (Gen 24:18-20).

Interestingly enough, as Rebekah sets out to go to Canaan, she receives a blessing that contains aspects of some of the patriarchal blessings. The fact that she is the person who sets out on a journey to God's land and that she, rather than Isaac, receives the blessing that her descendants will inherit the gates of those who hate them (cf. Gen 24:60 to Gen 22:17) appears to indicate her chosen status.[26] And yet she appears to have come by this chosenness, at least in part, through her acts of kindness. I say in part, because in the Bible's view Rebekah is also sent in answer to the prayer of Abraham's servant (Gen 24:12-19, 42-46, 50).

Summary and Conclusions

Inasmuch as the Ishmael and Isaac passages just examined were much lengthier and more complex than the single story of Cain and Abel, a brief summary is in order before proceeding with the analysis of the third relevant narrative. The following ideas related to election were introduced or were taken up again and deepened in the Isaac and Ishmael sequence.

1. Perhaps the most important new idea introduced in these texts is that the concepts of promise and covenant are explicitly integrated into the narrative. Rather than just being a story of divine favoring like Cain and Abel, now one can use the theological term "divine election" when referring to this rivalry story and the subsequent ones. This is true in spite of the tendency among many scholars to deny that Genesis has any theology of election because it never uses the term בחר (to choose) in a theological manner as do Deuteronomy or 2nd Isaiah. Clearly, the use of an explicit term in an abstract theological fashion may suggest a further refinement of the theology of election, but its absence from Genesis does not mean that Genesis knows nothing of election theology. The absence of this term from Genesis may be attributable to the narrative genre of these materials inasmuch as many would argue that Genesis received its latest redaction after Deuteronomy was composed.

2. While much of the story turns on the question of which child is the chosen one, in this narrative the greater emphasis is on the rivalry between Hagar and Sarah. This demonstrates that at times such stories are better labeled family rivalry, rather than sibling rivalry, stories. The markings of chosenness that help distinguish the designated child can reach back to the chosen mother in the form of a barrenness that is resolved by a miraculous conception and birth.

3. These narratives further bolster a point I argued in reference to the Cain and Abel episode: the non-chosen sibling is not necessarily excluded from all divine favor. Ishmael, while not the chosen child and thus excluded from the covenant, does receive some of the elements of the original Abrahamic promise delivered in Gen 12: being blessed, being fruitful, and becoming a great nation.

4. As in the Cain and Abel story, one can see that God's choice of the elect remains shrouded in mystery and is not dependent on human action. But unlike the Cain and Abel story, the Abraham sequence makes clear that being chosen demands a human response and that chosenness is brought to fruition by human action, creating a synergy between divine initiative and human response. However, while humans must participate in bringing God's purposes to fulfillment, their actions can also complicate and at times even impede God's plans. Nevertheless, this is not a call for human passivity but a recognition that God works with imperfect humans to accomplish his greater purposes. Sometimes human actions are perfectly in sync with God's will, and at other times humans have the best of intentions but remain unclear on what God wants, thereby creating complications that God must now work into God's plan. Finally, as seen in the Cain and Abel story and as will be seen again below, sometimes humans try to block God's plan. While such efforts may delay, they never truly prevent the unfolding of God's purposes.

5. Being chosen often implies that such a child will be exposed to danger by God or other relatives, as well as posing a danger to those not chosen. Thus, Isaac's chosen status leads to his near sacrifice by Abraham as well as to Ishmael's exile and near death. In some sense this idea was already present in Gen 4 when Abel's favored status provokes Cain to kill him, resulting in Cain's exile. However, in the current story there is a glimmer of hope that this divine favoring need not always produce such negative results in that both Ishmael and Isaac show up to bury Abraham their father (Gen 25:9). As will be seen shortly, these themes of endangerment, family strife, and reconciliation will be further deepened in the next set of sibling stories, those concerning Jacob and Esau.

CHAPTER THREE

JACOB AND ESAU

The Jacob cycle, running from Gen 25:19 to 35:29, raises a host of thorny questions that pertain to this examination of the biblical concept of election. Some issues that will be raised here have been touched upon earlier; others are unique to this set of stories. This analysis will proceed in narrative order, even while recognizing that at times a question will cut across several stories within this cycle.

The narrative begins by reminding the reader about Abraham's successful quest to find Isaac a wife from Mesopotamia, thus linking the Jacob cycle to the Abrahamic one (Gen 25:19-20). Immediately after this, one finds another more ominous connection to the Abraham stories in a notice concerning Rebekah's barrenness (Gen 25:21), for it was precisely this issue that so troubled Abraham's household. Thus, one might be anticipating the sudden appearance of a rival wife who would bear a rival child on analogy to Hagar and Ishmael. However, in somewhat usual biblical fashion, a motif is invoked to call to mind a previous narrative only to have things turn out somewhat differently this time. In this instance Rebekah's barrenness is resolved quickly for the reader (although according to the narrative framework in Gen 25:20, 26, it actually took twenty years), when in the very same verse Rebekah conceives after Isaac prays to the Lord on her behalf. For a brief moment it seems that Isaac's family will lack the chaos of a family rivalry. But then the narrative swiftly turns again, and one learns that Rebekah is pregnant with twins who will surely be rival siblings in that they are already fighting in the womb (Gen 25:22). Suddenly, it is not the story of Isaac and Ishmael in which Hagar and Sarah battle for Abraham's and God's favor that is called to mind, but the even more tragic one of Eve, who gave birth to two sons in quick succession who indeed were mortal rivals for God's affections. Distressed at the pain that she was experiencing, Rebekah seeks an oracle from God—how we are not told—and is informed that "two nations are in your womb, and two peoples born of you shall be divided; the one shall be stronger than the other, the elder shall serve the younger" (Gen 25:23).

Before discussing the larger import of this oracle for understanding the Jacob cycle as a whole, one must reckon with R. E. Friedman's argument that the oracle is more ambiguous than commonly assumed. Friedman notes that the grammar of Gen 25:23b can support the reading "the elder, the younger will serve," just as easily as it can the usual translation "the elder will serve the younger."[1] While Friedman's suggestion is provocative and points to a potential ambiguity that should not be simply dismissed, there are difficulties with this interpretation. The greatest problem with Friedman's proposal is that it does not work well with the larger pattern found in Israelite society or in the Bible. The oracle makes much more sense if it is announcing that the normal societal expectation that favored the elder child was being challenged. Inasmuch as what has often been called the "underdog motif" is pervasive throughout Genesis's stories of brotherly struggle, it would be strange to find an oracle announcing the preeminence of an elder child.

Assuming that this oracle does indeed announce Jacob's and his progeny's preeminence over Esau and his descendants, one is still left with troubling questions. Why does Isaac not seem to know about or act on this oracle? Does Jacob know of this oracle when he gets Esau to sell his birthright in Gen 25:29-34? Does this oracle justify Rebekah's scheme to deceive Isaac in Gen 27 and trick him into blessing Jacob instead of Esau? These questions must be kept in mind as one proceeds through this narrative. The story continues by telling of the unusual birth in which Jacob the second born is gripping the heel of his elder brother, Esau, on the way out of the womb (Gen 25:26). This report puns on the name Jacob, which the writer understands to mean "one who pulls another down by the heel," a character trait that recurs later in Jacob's life. Directly after the birth announcement one finds a terse but important notice that "when the boys grew up, Esau was a skillful hunter, a man of the outdoors,[2] while Jacob was a quiet man, living in tents. Isaac loved Esau, because he was fond of game;[3] but Rebekah loved Jacob" (Gen 25:27-28). This certainly heightens the reader's suspense in that it contains several echoes of the

Cain and Abel incident, leaving one with a feeling of dark foreboding. In both stories there are two children who go into different occupations. In an inversion of Gen 4, Esau, the elder child, appears to be occupied with meat, which functions like Abel the younger son's offering. Esau's meat also earns him favor, in this case with Isaac. The additional detail that Rebekah favors Jacob gives the reader a hint that in this instance, too, the sibling rivalry will be mirrored by an adult rivalry, this time between a husband and a wife rather than between co-wives.

Esau Sells His Birthright and Blessing

The tale now moves quickly into the first of two episodes in which Jacob finds a way to dispossess his elder brother of his firstborn status. The initial episode, a mere six verses (Gen 25:29-34), is rather cryptic. Returning from the hunt famished, Esau finds Jacob cooking a red-colored stew. Esau crudely demands he be permitted "to wolf down some of that red stuff" (my translation of v. 30). Jacob agrees to feed him, but only if he first swears to sell Jacob his birthright. Scholars typically understand the birthright as a form of primogeniture, that is, the right to inherit a double share of the father's estate (Deut 21:15-17).[4] Esau is portrayed as someone with little concern for the future while Jacob is cleverly positioning himself. Strangely enough, Esau agrees to sell his birthright, after which Jacob serves him bread along with what is now described as lentil stew.

At least one purpose of this incident is to set up the excellent double pun in Gen 27:36, which plays not only on Jacob's name but also on the words for blessing and birthright, which contain the same three consonants in different order (blessing=ברך, birthright=בכר). "Esau said, 'Is he not rightly named Jacob? For he has supplanted me (literally, Jacobed me—ויעקבני) these two times. He took away my birthright (בכרתי); and look, now he has taken away my blessing (ברכתי).'" However, one issue raised by Gen 27:36 is that this verse implies that Esau felt cheated by the exchange of his birthright for the red lentil stew. While one cannot definitively prove it, it is possible that Esau thought he was purchasing something other than what he received on his plate. Esau, returning famished from the hunt and seeing Jacob's red stew, may have thought he was purchasing a blood soup, which would restore his waning life force.[5] Thus, he may indeed have had the wool pulled over his eyes in a way not unlike the ruse Jacob would later pull on Isaac, once again serving domestic fare as if it were something else.[6] Even if Esau knew what he was getting, it was a contract that was made under duress and would be enforceable neither by the legal standards of later rabbinic Judaism nor by most contemporary legal systems. This short passage raises several questions relevant to this examination of election, ones that will be reverberated more loudly as the Jacob narrative continues to unfold: (1) Does Jacob's behavior, even when it is of questionable legality and propriety, further his elect status? (2) Does the text view Jacob's behavior positively or negatively? (3) Is the text endorsing the notion that God in fact needs humans to bring the divine plan to fruition?

The Deception of Isaac

After Gen 26, a chapter that resumes the somewhat truncated Isaac story by further exploring how Isaac's very blessedness might lead to strife or blessing depending on how others treat him (Gen 26:10, 16, 22, 28, likely illustrating the principle announced in Gen 12:3 in action), the Jacob narrative resumes. Genesis 27 opens with the announcement that Isaac, believing he is on his deathbed, wishes to communicate his final blessing to his favored elder child, Esau. Esau is asked to hunt and prepare some game, food items that have made Esau Isaac's favored son (Gen 25:28), setting the scene for the transmission of Isaac's blessing. Rebekah, overhearing Isaac, puts into action a plan to deceive Isaac in order to ensure that her favored younger son, Jacob, rather than Esau, receives this blessing. While expressing worry that this plot may backfire, Jacob heeds his mother's advice and poses as Esau. Isaac senses something may be amiss, yet he does indeed bless Jacob. As Jacob leaves, Esau shows up only to learn that his sibling has once again outsmarted him. In a scene of great pathos, Esau pleads for a blessing, and he receives one that reads more like a curse.[7] Some commentators attempt to downplay the negative aspects of Esau's blessing by pointing out how similar the first line of Esau's blessing is to one part of Jacob's blessing in the original Hebrew (comparing v. 39b to 28a). But Gen 27:40 makes clear that Esau and his descendants will experience a difficult life and will be ruled by Jacob and his descendants at least for a time. The Hebrew Bible often employs only slightly variant phrases to describe vastly different outcomes (Gen 40:13, 19). The text is playing on the fact that often in life, so much turns on so little (thus the contemporary proverb, "life turns on a dime"). A slight variation in phrasing makes one blessing vastly superior to the other, just as a few short minutes determine who is the firstborn and who arrives first to be blessed.

Immediately following Isaac's blessing, Jacob is sent off to Mesopotamia in a set of two scenes whose artfulness is usually overlooked by source critics eager to rationalize this double explanation for Jacob's flight.[8] The first scene contains Rebekah's true motives. Rebekah learns that Esau is plotting to kill Jacob for his deceit (Gen 27:41-45). But if she told Isaac that she wished to send Jacob away because Esau was angry at him, Isaac might very well have ignored her plea and told her to live with the consequences of her deception. Thus, she informs Isaac that she is concerned about Jacob marrying the wrong kind of girl, that is, one from the local population (Gen 27:46). Isaac responds by sending Jacob off to Mesopotamia to take a wife from his kin (Gen 28:1-2). By employing this ruse Rebekah avoids a potential fight with Isaac and still gets her way, even managing to have Isaac authorize Jacob's flight to Mesopotamia. On top of this, Jacob receives yet another blessing from Isaac as he leaves home (Gen 28:3-4).

This episode is literarily quite rich, but a full treatment of its artistry is not appropriate in a study focused on the concept of election in the Hebrew Bible. For the purposes of this study the primary issue raised here is one broached earlier in the Cain and Abel as well as the Isaac and Ishmael stories, that is, is election in any way facilitated by human action? In this story the question has a unique twist. Unlike Sarai's suggestion that Abram procreate through Hagar, a remedy that is both legal and moral, here Jacob's and Rebekah's deceit that results in the theft of the blessing appears to be morally and legally problematic. This is so not only according to later rabbinic and Christian perspectives, which both struggle to justify Jacob's and Rebekah's behavior,[9] but possibly also from the viewpoint of the biblical text. After all, Esau is portrayed quite sympathetically, especially in comparison to Jacob, and Jacob is made to suffer for this deceit. Later passages like Jer 9:3 (Eng. 9:4) see Jacob as responsible for engendering a variety of negative characteristics in his descendants. This raises the following question: Does Gen 27 indicate that God's plans can even be fulfilled through wrongful human behavior? One's reply to this query is itself contingent on one's answer to a variety of other questions: (1) What is the relationship between the oracle Rebekah received in Gen 25:23 and the account of Isaac's deathbed blessing in Gen 27? (2) Is the blessing that Jacob receives in Gen 27 really equivalent to receiving God's blessing and thus attaining elect status? (3) Does Jacob's later life indicate he is indeed blessed, and does Esau's later life reveal his lower status? (4) If Jacob receives payback for the actions in Gen 27, can one assume that the narrator is condemning Jacob's and Rebekah's actions here?

One might argue that the oracle in chapter 25 is produced by a different author from the one who wrote chapter 27 and thus no attempt should be made to link these two passages together. However, traditional source critics such as Speiser attribute both to J.[10] Furthermore, since the canonical text is a literary whole, one naturally will read these two passages in relation to each other. But even if one assumes that Gen 25:23 is announcing God's election of the younger Jacob over his elder brother, Esau, it is not at all clear how or when this will come about. In fact, the oracle speaks more of the future progeny of the two siblings than it does of the actual brothers in the womb. It is certainly difficult to argue that the oracle explicitly authorizes Jacob's attempt to gain the birthright in Gen 25:29-34 and Rebekah's plan to deceive Isaac into giving Jacob Esau's blessing in chapter 27. On the other hand, in a canonical reading, this oracle provides a rationale for Rebekah's scheme in Gen 27. It is less clear that Jacob is acting on it when he obtains his brother's primogeniture in Gen 25:29-34 because we are not told that Jacob even knew of this oracle. Of course, the same holds for Isaac. Does he favor Esau in the face of a contradictory oracle from God, or does he lack all knowledge of such an oracle? All one can claim on the basis of the text is that Rebekah is putting into place a rational scheme to bring God's announced intentions to fruition.

Here one may be tempted to compare Rebekah's actions to Sarai's suggestion that Abram bring God's plan to fruition by procreating with Hagar. But as noted in the previous chapter, the Hagar incident itself is ambiguous. One can argue that just as Sarai's plan in Gen 16 backfired, so does Rebekah's plan here. Or alternatively, one can assert that while human actions always carry a variety of consequences with them, the Hebrew Bible frequently looks favorably upon characters who try to push destiny along, even if their attempts to do so sometimes go awry. Thus, Tamar in Gen 38 seems almost heroic for taking matters into her own hands. Although Moses kills the Egyptian taskmaster, forcing him to flee for his life to Midian, he ends up at Sinai where he receives his commission from God. Even the New Testament seems to endorse the notion that humans can on occasion force God's hand and that doing so can be good and even necessary (Luke 18:1-8).

One finds a spectrum of positions on this issue in the secondary literature. On one side, certain scholars are quite critical of the human actors in Genesis. For example, Laurence Turner analyzes the narratives in which humans try to interfere, either positively or negatively, with the divine plan in Genesis. He treats Jacob's and Rebekah's attempt to fulfill the oracle found in Gen 25:23 at length and reaches the following conclusions about all instances of human interference with divine proclamations, or what he calls "plot announcements":

> [H]uman attempts to frustrate the Announcements tend to fulfil them; human attempts to fulfil the Announcements tend to frustrate them. . . . the implication of all this is that the Announcements would have had a better chance of fulfilment if the human characters had done less to attempt to fulfil them and allowed YHWH to do more.[11]

A medial position is occupied by a scholar like Terence Fretheim,[12] who correctly notes that Turner's position is almost docetic and that it is out of tune with the fact that the biblical God tends to work through humans as they are rather than first perfecting them. He even seconds Hugh White's suggestion that Rebekah's subterfuge may serve as a positive model because it challenges the closed system of primogeniture, and Fretheim also shows sympathy for Rebekah's and Jacob's course of action.[13] However, Fretheim argues that first of all the ruse played on Isaac in Genesis 27 in no way contributes to God's ultimate blessing and election of Jacob, and secondly, it only brings about negative consequences for Jacob. Fretheim attempts to sustain his first point by claiming that what one finds in the Jacob cycle is a series of unrelated blessings. The first blessing in Gen 27:27-29 is a personal blessing that Isaac gives Jacob posing as Esau. Even the blessing Isaac gives Jacob as he leaves the land in Gen 28:3-4, which explicitly mentions the promises given to Abraham, Fretheim reads as only a commendation rather than an actual blessing. Fretheim believes that Jacob is blessed by God, but this only occurs in Gen 28:10-22 and 35:9-12 and is not in any sense connected to the two earlier blessings by Isaac. His second point, that Jacob experiences negative consequences from his deceit, utilizes much of the data gathered by Turner, who notes that Esau never serves Jacob, but the opposite may well have occurred (see Gen 33) and Jacob's life is not filled with blessing. After all he is on the lam in Mesopotamia and is afraid Esau will eventually kill him when he returns to Canaan.

The third position, probably the most widely held, is that Jacob is indeed God's elect and that his solo action in attaining the birthright, as well as his deception of Isaac at Rebekah's command, earn him both primogeniture and Isaac's blessing, thus fulfilling God's oracle from Gen 25. There are numerous factors to commend this third position, and one can do so even while granting the usefulness of some of Fretheim's and Turner's observations. To begin with, the text strongly implies that God's election of Jacob over Esau, something that in one sense had already occurred before their birth (as recognized by Paul in Rom 9:11-13), is indeed brought to fuller fruition through the actions of Jacob in Gen 25 and Rebekah and Jacob in Gen 27. Of course, one cannot know with certainty whether God would have found another way to accomplish God's goals if they had not acted at all. But it seems unlikely that God, as revealed within the pentateuchal narratives, would attempt to accomplish a major goal without working in concert with a human actor,[14] or that some way could be found to accomplish the goal of elevating Jacob over Esau that would not involve offending Esau and going against Isaac's wishes.

That negative consequences flow from Jacob's and Rebekah's actions, including the fracturing of the family unit that occurs when Jacob must flee for his life to Mesopotamia (Gen 27:41-45) as well as Jacob's having to suffer a ruse analogous to the one he employed on Isaac when Laban swaps Leah for Rachel (Gen 29:22-26), does not conclusively indicate that God disapproved of Jacob's and Rebekah's actions. After all, God created the same type of family strife in his decision to accept Abel's offering and reject Cain's. Furthermore, when Sarah suggested to Abraham that he drive Hagar and Ishmael out, an act that might be construed as immoral and most certainly resulted in long-term family scars, God tells Abraham to follow his wife's advice because the promise will be carried on through Isaac, not Ishmael (Gen 21:8-14). Finally, one should keep in mind that later in Genesis two other narratives seem to endorse the result of Jacob's behavior. In the first, initially one of Tamar's twins puts out a hand that receives a red thread (Gen 38:27-30), marking him as the firstborn (Gen 38:28). Clearly, the color red and the mention of a single extremity call to mind the earlier births of Esau and Jacob. However, in Tamar's case the red-marked child then retracts his arm, and the other child ends up coming out of the womb first. Here the elder red-marked child is already overtaken by his younger rival within the womb, perhaps signaling that such a reversal of fortunes is part of the nature of life. Toward the end of Genesis, a physically blind Jacob, calling to mind the state of Isaac when he gave his final blessing (Gen 27:1), rejects Joseph's attempt to imitate Isaac's preference for the elder when he gives the younger Ephraim primacy over his older brother Manasseh in spite of Joseph's plea (Gen 48:13-20). This passage strongly indicates that the narrator of Genesis and the character of Jacob himself affirm the correctness of what Jacob did those many years ago. With these facts in mind, it is possible to read Isaac's refusal to retract his blessing in Gen 27:33 ("Yes, and blessed he shall be!") less as an indication that blessings once spoken are irrevocable[15] than as evidence that Isaac came to recognize that Jacob's and Rebekah's actions were somehow merged with God's intentions, a fact he only glimpsed in the light of the way events transpired.

An additional point is that many modern interpreters seem a bit too sure that the Bible portrays Jacob in a strongly negative light. A good example is the following comment by Rowley:

> The character of Jacob is less exalted than that of Abraham, and if we were inclined to conclude from the story of the latter that God chooses them that are choice, we should be much more doubtful when we came to the story of Jacob. . . . Instead of looking behind for its causes, we should view it teleologically, and perceive that God was choosing an instrument fitted for his purpose. For the character that he came to attain Abraham was chosen; Isaac and Jacob less for themselves than for those who should come after them.[16]

However, one wonders whether the characteristics that Jacob exhibits might not have been viewed as assets in a culture like ancient Israel's, in which one might survive only by a bit of trickery.[17] While texts like Jer 9:3, mentioned above, and Hos 12:3 appear to play off the Genesis narrative in order to indict Jacob's descendants, they are likely inverting an image of Jacob's wiliness, which many Israelites may have held dear. Much the same can be said of the perception of Rebekah as pushy and deceptive.[18] Although many read her character in this way, within the biblical realm women who took matters into their own hands were often viewed positively. One only need mention Tamar in Gen 38, Moses' mother in Exod 2, or even Bath Sheba, who is a more ambiguous character, but ultimately one who triumphs through a bit of deceit (1 Kgs 1). Thus, Jacob's and Rebekah's behavior may have been much less troubling for the earliest biblical storytellers and their audiences than it would be for later biblical writers, not to mention for later Jews and Christians.

None of this is to gainsay the observation that Jacob receives payback for his actions. In fact, the bulk of his suffering comes after Gen 28:10-22, a text that even Fretheim believes finally confirms that God has now made Jacob the recipient of the patriarchal blessings. Thus, blessings do not insulate one from all future suffering. To attribute Jacob's later suffering primarily to his interference with God's elective plans seems to miss the point that God's elect tend to endure great suffering regardless of their previous behavior (Gen 4; 22). An additional issue is that while Jacob does indeed suffer in Mesopotamia, he becomes immensely blessed there as well. He not only acquires wives who soon bear the twelve sons who become the ancestors of the twelve tribes of Israel, but he also becomes wealthy. Laban openly tells Jacob that he has become blessed through Jacob's presence (Gen 30:27). Also important is that Jacob obtained this wealth by instituting an ingenious breeding plan to outsmart his manipulative and dishonest father-in-law, albeit by means of a divinely inspired dream according to one version of the events (cf. Gen. 30:25-43 to 31: 1-16). Clearly, human action helps bring God's promise to bless Jacob to fruition.

Although it is true that Jacob bows before Esau (Gen 33:3), rather than vice versa as expected from Gen 27:29, one must note that the oracle in Gen 25:23 made clear that it would reach fulfillment only in the far future when the progeny of the younger child would rule over those descending from the elder one. Indeed, Israel did rule Edom for a considerable time during the Israelite monarchy (2 Sam 8:14; 2 Kgs 8:20). And one must not forget that even during Jacob's lifetime, he returns to the land of Israel and receives confirmation that his children, rather than Esau's, have been chosen to inherit God's special land (Gen 28:13; 33:15; 35:12). The promises are complex in that they speak about events that will take place during the lifetime of the characters themselves as well as about events that will occur hundreds of years later.

While a small cottage industry has arisen attempting to correlate passages in the Bible with specific political events in Israel's history, such an approach has real limitations. Not only does much of Israel's history remain obscure but also over time a single passage may have been linked with a multiplicity of events.[19] More to the point, a problematic assumption drives this correlational method.

> The popularity of this form of interpretation is owing in no small measure to the pervasive modern perception, found even among the devout on occasion, that the category of the sacred is a mystification of social

> and political arrangements. Responsible interpretation, then, is the task of reducing larger spiritual structures to the institutional arrangements that not only accompany them, but account for them. That such arrangements are real, important and likely to be missed by religious traditionalists is to be granted. What must not be granted is this quasi-materialist presupposition that correlating the text with its social and political arrangements exhausts an interpreter's task.[20]

Turner, a scholar who focuses on the promises in relation to Jacob himself, argues that the text indicates the utter failure of the promises. However, he misses the fact that some of the promises could never be fulfilled literally. Thus when Gen 27:29 speaks of plural brothers bowing down to Jacob, obviously, this is impossible on the literal level of the story of Jacob and Esau. There are several possible explanations for the use of plural language here. Perhaps this blessing was moved from the Joseph story or is standard language of blessing that is not meant to be read in a literal fashion.[21] Alternatively, it could be reckoning with the fact that Esau is the ancestor of other rival peoples, such as the Amalekites (Gen 36:16), and thus, there are other relatives (often called brothers in biblical parlance) who will bow to Jacob.

Family Strife in Mesopotamia

Another aspect of the Jacob cycle needing attention is the other election of the younger over the elder sibling that occurs within this narrative, that of Rachel over Leah. When Laban switches brides on Jacob, he chastises him by saying that in his abode they do not elevate the younger over the elder (Gen 29:26), a phrase that calls to mind Jacob's offense against his brother, Esau. But in the end, Laban's plan to make Leah preeminent fails. Leah exhibits the characteristics of the non-chosen wife by easily giving birth to a number of children in rapid succession. On the other hand, Rachel is the classic barren wife who initially employs Sarah's methods by giving her maid Bilhah to Jacob to bear surrogate children for her (Gen 30:1-8). This is not the only human measure Rachel employs to conceive children, for she also uses magical/medicinal plants (Gen 30:14-15), after which she does conceive her first child. However, it remains unclear whether it was this herbal cure or Rachel's plea made earlier in Gen 30:1 having finally reached God (note Gen 30:22 speaks of God's remembering and heeding Rachel) that brought about a change in her condition.

Within this narrative one must not overlook the intense jealousy and the resulting strife between Rachel and Leah as Rachel strives for children, and Leah for Jacob's love. The twelve tribes of Israel are produced by means of this ongoing familial jealousy over Jacob's attentions. This sisterly rivalry is in turn mirrored in the strife between Jacob and Laban's family. Jacob's blessedness, which Laban recognizes (Gen 30:27), leads to greed on Laban's part. But Jacob outwits Laban and eventually accumulates vast holdings. In the end even Rachel and Leah become alienated from Laban's family, once more indicating that chosenness can bring blessing and strife at the same time.

The Question of Reconciliation

Perhaps the most novel aspect of this story is that it is the first of the rivalry narratives dwelling at length on the fact that the brothers meet years later, opening the path to possible reconciliation but also exploring the difficulties of overcoming long-standing family hatreds. The notion that the tension generated by divine favoritism can be mitigated or eventually overcome is a component of the election tradition that is deepened in each subsequent story. Thus when Cain kills Abel, he eliminates any chance for reconciliation. Turning to the Isaac and Ishmael narratives, one sees only a single verse that tells of a later meeting and perhaps hints that it was amicable (Gen 25:9). But here one finds two complete chapters dedicated to Jacob's encounter with Esau upon his return to Canaan (Gen 33–34). The question of how the narrative portrays the relationship between Jacob and Esau at the end of the story is important because it may shed light on how the final redactor of Genesis imagined the ways in which election might affect relations between the chosen and the nonchosen, or at least one possible model of such a relationship. In spite of the lengthy recounting of Jacob's and Esau's meeting—or perhaps due to it—there is disagreement about whether or not the text imagines a reconciliation occurring here. George Coats has argued rather convincingly that one major theme occupying the patriarchal narratives is that of strife and reconciliation. However, he sees reconciliation occurring only in the denouement of the Joseph story, and even there he does not believe it involves a complete cleaning of the slate that restores the characters to a perfect state of equilibrium.[22] Commenting on the Jacob narratives as a whole, he argues the following:

> God's chosen appears consistently as a figure embroiled in strife. And, moreover, the strife leads to separation that is not healed by reconciliation. . . . But perhaps the affirmation in all this strife and its corresponding lack of reconciliation is that God's blessing appears in spite of strife, as an alternative to reconciliation. If reconciliation occurs, so much the better (Gen 45:4-15). But blessing can emerge from relationships that cannot be reconciled.[23]

Others scholars, such as Levenson, see reconciliation in this narrative.

> Jacob and Esau have finally been reconciled—an astonishing turn when one considers the circumstances of their estrangement. . . . Indeed, as we have occasion to note, when he offers his brother a "present"—tribute with which to secure favor—he terms it his "blessing" (*birkātî*, [Gen 33:] v 11), as if offering to make restitution for the cause of estrangement. . . . Without ever giving up the birthright he assumed by deception, Jacob forgoes the hegemony it entails. Without reinstatement as the firstborn, Esau forgoes the vengeance that nearly destroyed the family.[24]

Unlike Coats, Levenson reads the text in a more holistic fashion that takes into account the terse priestly notice of Isaac's death and burial in Gen 35:27-29. This notice speaks of Esau and Jacob together burying Isaac, providing further support for Levenson's contention that Jacob and Esau eventually reconciled.

Of course, while these two scholars disagree, the contrast should not be drawn too starkly in that both believe that in some sense God's providential plan, or at least the part of it concerned with blessing, does reach fulfillment by the end of this narrative. Much of the argument seems to hinge on what reconciliation might mean. For Coats it appears to entail the notion that, ultimately, the brothers would live together rather than separately.[25] Yet even Coats, as will become clear below, does not think that reconciliation means that all past differences are resolved or that characters overcome all of their flaws.

One difficulty in interpreting the ending of this story is that it is relatively clear that Jacob remains quite suspicious of Esau's intentions toward him and there is some possibility that Esau might harbor ill will toward Jacob. Thus, Esau proposes what looks like a full reconciliation when he offers to escort Jacob and journey alongside him. Jacob responds courteously but somewhat disingenuously that he is overburdened with young children and animals and does not wish to delay Esau unnecessarily. However, Jacob tells Esau he will eventually meet him in Seir

(Gen 33:14), something that (as far as we are told) never occurs and, one suspects, a statement that Jacob had no intention of ever fulfilling. Esau also offers to leave some of his men as an (armed?) escort, a proposal Jacob also politely but firmly declines. While Esau appears generous here, one is left wondering why he is so intent on accompanying Jacob or providing him with an escort, as well as why he insists that Jacob should come to Seir to live with him (Gen 33:12-15).

Contrary to scholars like Coats, the fact that Jacob and Esau do not end up living together should not in itself be read as a sign that the narrator believes no reconciliation occurred. This is especially true in the case of this story inasmuch as both narrative and historical considerations appear to preclude such an outcome. Although living together is not only a possibility but a necessity for the brothers in the Joseph story, it is difficult to imagine how the Jacob story can end this way. Rather, Jacob alone must inherit the land of Canaan, and Esau, Edom's eponymous ancestor, must move on to Seir. Here it seems that there are levels of reconciliation, and as Westermann observes, "A reconciliation between brothers need not require that they live side by side; it can also achieve its effect when they separate and each lives his own life in his own way."[26] Thus, reconciliation neither signals a return to the *status quo ante*, nor does it magically erase the character flaws that people have exhibited all along. Rather, when reconciliation occurs in the Bible, usually the characters have matured, but they remain partially flawed. Jacob is still not totally honest with Esau about his intentions not to return to Seir with him. His obsequiousness is a ploy to end the encounter without offending Esau in a way that might have once more endangered Jacob and his family. Esau, too, may not be utterly changed. Surely, he is no longer the brute portrayed in chapters 25 and 27, but showing up with four hundred men (Gen 32:6; 33:1) and insisting that he escort Jacob to Seir (Gen 33:12-15) may well indicate that Esau is not all that savvy about how such a force would be perceived and/or that he might have continued to harbor ambitions of revenge against Jacob. Nevertheless, Esau appears to have mastered his envy of his brother's status in a way that Cain could not (Gen 4:7).

Concluding Remarks

Before turning to the final and most extended of the sibling narratives, the Joseph cycle, a brief summary of the issues raised by the Jacob and

Esau stories is in order. These stories raised or deepened the following points related to the concept of election:

1. The idea that the rivalry is not only between siblings but can be family-wide receives further validation here. Not only do both Rebekah and Isaac participate in such family strife by choosing a favorite child, but Jacob gets directly caught in similar familial dynamics in Mesopotamia. Here not only do Rachel and Leah jealously compete for his attention, but Jacob's feud with Laban and Laban's sons ends up alienating Rachel and Leah from their birth family.

2. The notion that human action may be required to bring the chosen one's election to consummation is here further reflected upon as well as morally complicated. It appears that at times even deceitful actions can be employed in bringing God's purposes to pass. While such deceit may lead to family strife and may result in the deceiver himself being deceived in hurtful ways, in this instance, the elect status of Jacob is further reinforced through his morally questionable behavior.

3. Once more it becomes clear that the selected child is put in grave peril that nearly results in his death, which in this case is averted only by Jacob's long exile, itself a symbolic death. Furthermore, Jacob's return to Canaan involves three potential mortal dangers, which he survives: Laban's possible revenge, which is only calmed by a divine warning Laban receives not to offend or harm Jacob (Gen 31:24, 29); Jacob's wrestling match with the night visitor at Penuel, who injures him; and his meeting Esau. Clearly, election involves suffering and humiliation, even if it often ends in exaltation.

4. The theme of reconciliation between the chosen and the non-chosen sibling is greatly deepened in this narrative and, as will be seen shortly, plays a central role in the Joseph narrative. Although the reconciliation here is not complete, the narrative envisions that the chosen and non-chosen lines can achieve a *modus vivendi* in which the chosen one offers the fruits of his blessing to the non-chosen and they each go on to fulfill their separate but ultimately intertwined destinies.

CHAPTER FOUR

JOSEPH AND HIS BROTHERS

While Joseph is the eleventh son born to Jacob, he is the elder son of Rachel, the second, younger but favored wife of Jacob. He is not only Jacob's favorite but also appears to be highly favored by God, as demonstrated by his beauty, his clear leadership qualities, his ability to have prophetic dreams, as well as his wisdom to interpret other people's dreams and dispense good advice. However, even though Joseph eventually exhibits all of these gifts, initially he misunderstands and misuses his chosen status. Only after a lengthy period of tribulation does he come to maturity and grow into his elect status. His brothers, too, grow and change over the course of the narrative.[1]

Joseph begins the story as someone who understands his father's tendency to favor him and the special gifts he has received from God primarily as signs that he will rule over his brothers, as evidenced by his rather immature conduct in relation to them. Not only does he bring back a negative report about how poorly some of them are doing their job (Gen 37:2), but he also taunts his brothers with his dreams, which he and they immediately understand as an adumbration of his future elevation over them, a rise in fortune that the brothers wrongly interpret as having only negative consequences for their lives. Of course, his brothers' hatred is further deepened by Jacob's favoritism and particularly by Joseph's tendency to flaunt his favored status. It seems quite improbable that Joseph is wearing the coat with long sleeves because it is cold out when he shows up to check on his brothers in Dothan in the middle of the day (Gen 37:17-23). It is much more likely that Joseph, like many a child who has been given a toy that his siblings have not received, is flaunting his favored status in front of his brothers for his own ego gratification. Thus, his brothers' initial hatred of him is readily understandable, although their actions against him, be it throwing him in an empty pit (Gen 37:24) or, worse yet, selling him into slavery (Gen 37:27), are clearly unjustifiable. All the characters in the early part of the narrative act from selfish motives, and each tends to react to the other party in the worst ways, giving little benefit of the doubt and leading to a growing mutual enmity that results in a huge family catastrophe.

This is true even of Judah and Reuben, characters who mitigate Joseph's fate by trying to save him from death. Reuben (the protagonist in the E account) initially appears as the least selfish actor in this drama in that he not only prevents Joseph's death, but also hopes to restore him alive to Jacob. However, a closer look at the larger narrative structure allows one to entertain the possibility that this act of kindness is driven by strong personal interests. One only needs to recall that in Gen 35:22 Reuben lay with Bilhah, one of Jacob's concubines, an incident that appears to have cost him his firstborn rights (Gen 49:4). It is conceivable that Reuben hoped to recapture his lost status by saving Joseph, Jacob's most beloved son, from the wrath of his brothers and restoring him alive to his father. Later in the narrative there is evidence that Reuben is indeed still trying to regain his father's respect and will go to great lengths to accomplish this (Gen 42:37).

Judah (the major actor in the J account of the story) can also be read as having a self-interested motive for his actions. Here one must note that while Judah is the fourth born, he is possibly the next in line, because not only has Reuben lost his status (as noted above) but so have Simeon and Levi through their violent actions in Gen 34 (as implied by Gen 49:5-7). If one reads Gen 37 as a literary whole rather than as two separate stories sloppily merged, it becomes clear that Judah must foil Reuben's plan to rescue Joseph and must do so in a way that eliminates Joseph if he hopes to attain preeminence over his siblings. Foiling Reuben's plan will ensure that Reuben will never regain his firstborn status. But even if Judah disrupts Reuben's attempt to save Joseph, this is not enough to establish Judah's position. With the first three of Jacob's children out of the picture, Jacob might well opt to choose Joseph as his primary heir inasmuch as he is the firstborn child of his favored wife Rachel. Thus, Judah needs to eliminate Joseph as well as earn the respect of the other brothers, which his plan accomplishes in one fell swoop.[2]

Jacob, too, exhibits rather immature or at least unwise behavior. Not only does he inflame the brothers by openly doting on Joseph, giving him special gifts and having him spy on his elder brothers (Gen 37:2-4), but even as he is aware of the brothers' jealousy of Joseph (Gen 37:10-11), he sends him unprotected into their arms (37:14). These facts combined with his obstinate refusal to be comforted over Joseph's death (Gen 37:35) indicate that he is far from a perfect human being. It soon becomes clear from the way the story continues that the various character weaknesses in Joseph, his brothers, and his father are not remedied quickly. Rather, all of them tend to act in selfish and self-serving ways rather than striving for the good of the larger family.

The Development of Joseph's Character

In Joseph's case, while he ends up in slavery in Potiphar's house (Gen 37:36; 39:1), his elect status propels him into the highest possible position he could occupy there (Gen 39:4). This narrative contains the beginnings of Joseph's transformation, but how much Joseph has changed is open to interpretation. The most common reading of the text sees a mature and morally upright Joseph wrongly accused of a sexual crime. But the text leaves enough interpretive space to suggest the possibility that Joseph here, too, continues to assume that he attained this position on his own and that his charisma was for no greater purpose than to live a comfortable life. After all, once in a position of some power in Potiphar's house, he makes no effort to contact his father. As James Kugel points out at length, the rabbis held Joseph partially culpable for Mrs. Potiphar's advances.[3] The ancient Jewish sages suggest that Joseph initially attracted the attention of Potiphar's wife because he was too busy preening himself.[4] The *shalshelet*, the extraordinarily long Masoretic accent mark over the first word in Gen 39:8, וימאן "he refused," is interpreted as signaling Joseph's ambivalence in rejecting Mrs. Potiphar's advances, pointing to a stream of interpretation that holds Joseph partially responsible for his second downfall. Even the biblical text leaves one wondering whether Joseph, who is in charge of Potiphar's house (Gen 39:4), knew that no servants were in the house on the day Potiphar's wife accosted the scantily clad Joseph. Did Joseph, flattered by all this attention, enter the house with the thought of consummating the relationship, but at the last moment change his mind and flee?

Certainly, it is no accident that Joseph's elect status puts him in the second highest rank in both Jacob's and Potiphar's houses (later he occupies this same position in Pharaoh's house too). Yet each time Joseph is in a high-status position a downfall occurs, first into a pit in the land of Israel, from which he is rescued only to be sold into slavery in Egypt, and then into a prison (the Hebrew of Gen 40:15 actually uses the same word found in 37:24, where it is translated as "a pit"), where he again rises to the top (Gen 39:21-23). While his tendency to rise is due to Joseph's intellectual, spiritual, and physical giftedness, his downfalls are also caused by these same gifts, or possibly by the misuse of them. On either reading this episode adds an interesting dimension to our survey of election. If, as on the more standard reading, Joseph was utterly innocent, this narrative suggests that giftedness, even if properly used, can attract the wrong type of attention and bring in its wake jealousy and danger for the chosen one. On the other hand, if Joseph contributed to his own downfall by not living up to his full potential, then this narrative once more demonstrates that the special attention God lavishes on the elect carries within it a danger for the chosen who are held accountable for even minor missteps.

Only after Joseph is in prison does he finally begin to use language indicating he is aware that his gifts come from God and are given to him so that he can be of use to others. Thus, his response to Pharaoh's two servants whose dreams he interprets is: "Do not interpretations belong to God? Please tell them to me" (Gen 40:8b). Similarly, in his dialogue with Pharaoh one chapter later, Joseph says, "It is not I; God will give Pharaoh a favorable answer" (Gen 41:16b). Although these can be interpreted suspiciously to suggest that Joseph has put himself in the place of God, the more likely sense is that Joseph is revealing that he is a skilled dream interpreter, even while acknowledging that this is a divine gift that entails responsibilities to God. It is significant that the seed that would eventually result in Joseph's change of fortunes is planted in prison when he acknowledges that any abilities he may possess come from God. Once he begins to use his gifts to help others who are in desperate straits he is on a path that eventually allows him to reap the benefits of his chosenness. This point is reinforced when Joseph continually invokes God's name in Pharaoh's presence (vv. 16, 25, 28, 32) and uses his gifts to save Egypt and much of the rest of the world from the coming famine (Gen 41:57, perhaps a fulfillment of Gen 12:3). Interestingly enough, even from this point Joseph's change in fortune is not immediate, but takes two years, inasmuch as Pharaoh's wine steward initially forgets the good turn Joseph had done for him along with Joseph's plea for his help (Gen 40:14-15; 40:23–41:1). Even when an elect character uses his gifts correctly, it does not always result in an immediately positive outcome. As we saw much earlier in the Abraham narrative, God's plans for the elect often require great patience and frequently entail some anguish and suffering.

The Joseph story strongly emphasizes the connection between election and service, stressing that election carries with it a duty to help others. But while the narrative views service as the fulfillment of election, election exists prior to any service and appears to abide even through a failure to perform such service. Thus, neither does Joseph earn God's favor through proper action, nor is his election canceled when he misunderstands and thereby misuses his special status. Rather, he always was God's specially elect one, due to God's mysterious choice of him as well as of his mother, Rachel, Jacob's favored younger wife. It seems likely that in at least one and possibly in two instances his failures led to various trials and tribulations that served as a type of punishment for misusing his divine favor, yet the narrator makes clear that he never lost his chosen status (Gen 39:2, 23).

Judah and Tamar: Genesis 38

Joseph appears much matured by the time he interprets dreams for Pharaoh's servants while in prison and even more so when he interprets Pharaoh's own dreams. However, the state of his brothers' moral and spiritual development is less clear. The tale of the brothers, or at least of Judah, the brother most often mentioned in Gen 37–50, resumes in Gen 38. While the widespread critical opinion is that this story is an intrusion interrupting the flow of the Joseph narrative,[5] scholars like Alter[6] and Levenson[7] have argued convincingly that this episode has significant connections to the Joseph narrative as a whole, as well as to the larger structure of the patriarchal stories. These include the use of the verbal root ירד (to go/bring down) in Gen 38:1 and 39:1; the expression הכר־נא (recognize now) in 37:32 and 38:25; the goat used in Gen 37 and 38 (as well as earlier by Rebekah to help Jacob steal Esau's blessing in Gen 27); the clothing used in a deceptive fashion in Gen 37, 38, and 39 (as well as in chapter 27); the twins born to Tamar in a fashion recalling Jacob's and Esau's births, as well as looking forward to the births of Joseph's two sons

Manasseh and Ephraim; and finally that Judah, after losing two sons, refuses to give up the third, just as Jacob initially refuses to surrender Benjamin after the loss of Joseph and Simeon (Gen 42:36-38).

The story of Judah and Tamar in Gen 38 appears to hint at Judah's lack of character development. Rather than seeing that the deaths of his first two sons were due to their faults, he attributes their deaths to his daughter-in-law Tamar. Furthermore, his sexual promiscuity, a character flaw he fails to recognize in himself but later projects onto Tamar, gets him into trouble. It seems likely the biblical author is indicating that both Judah and Joseph mature as characters through an incident involving charges of inappropriate sexual activity within the household where each lives. However, aside from the verse in which Judah admits that he, not Tamar, is more in the wrong (Gen 38:26), we are not left with a sure sense that he has overcome his previous deficiencies. It may even be that the text purposely juxtaposes the Judah and Tamar episode to the Joseph and Mrs. Potiphar story in order to draw a distinction between the morality of each character. Even if, as I have argued, Joseph may have contributed in some manner to his downfall in Potiphar's house, ultimately, he resisted engaging in illicit sexual activity, unlike his brother Judah. The technique of juxtaposing similar narratives in order to contrast characters occurs elsewhere in Genesis. Most prominently, one thinks of the way in which Abraham's hospitality in Gen 18 is immediately adjacent to Lot's less successful attempt at hospitality in Gen 19.

Joseph Reencounters His Brothers

When the story of the other brothers resumes in chapter 42, the language indicates that relations between Jacob and his ten sons continue to be frayed. Thus, Jacob rather rudely initiates the discussion about sending the ten brothers down to Egypt to buy grain when he asks, "Why do you keep looking at one another? I have heard," he said, "that there is grain in Egypt; go down and buy grain for us there, that we may live and not die" (Gen 42:1b-2). Furthermore, when the text notes that Jacob did not send Benjamin down to Egypt with the other brothers (Gen 42:4), it makes clear that Jacob continues to maintain a favorite son and that he may even suspect the brothers are implicated in Joseph's disappearance. Thus, the original point of contention that led the brothers to harm Joseph has not been alleviated. As in the episode of Cain and Abel, the brothers' plot to eliminate the chosen child has failed on all fronts. Clearly, neither Judah nor Reuben has succeeded in taking over Joseph's position. Rather, last-born Benjamin functions as the equivalent to Seth, the replacement for the dead brother. The story at the start of chapter 42 seems to be saying that while Joseph may have reached a new level of maturity, the three-way relationship between Jacob, Benjamin, and the other brothers indicates Jacob and his ten older sons are in the same state they were in at the end of chapter 37, or perhaps their relationship is even more fractured at this point in time.

The interaction between Joseph and his brothers resumes when they show up in Egypt and Joseph recognizes them, but they fail to recognize him. Of course, the brothers' bowing down to him immediately calls to mind his previous dreams (Gen 42:9). It is probable that before this point Joseph had already realized his dreams were not simply about his elevation over his brothers but were for some much greater purpose (Gen 41:57). After all, he is now vizier over all Egypt, and his battle for supremacy with his brothers must seem insignificant by this standard. Furthermore, the fact that he sends grain along with the money and provisions for their journey home (Gen 42:25) may demonstrate he has already begun to realize how his attaining such heights is part of God's plan to keep his estranged family alive. While the brothers were the ones who offered the original interpretation of the dream of the bowing sheaves as symbolizing their subordination, it may have actually foretold that when they were out of grain, Joseph would help sustain them.[8] Of course, Joseph's motives in how he treats his brothers are difficult to assess at this point in the narrative. Alter explores some of the possibilities: "Does Joseph now feel anger and an impulse to punish his brothers, or is he chiefly triumphant, moved to play the inquisitor in order to act out still further the terms of his dreams. . . . Is he moved chiefly by mistrust, considering his brothers' past behavior?"[9] Perhaps he is ready to forgive them but wants to know whether they have changed or would do the same thing once again. Alternatively, he may be concerned about whether the brothers might have already harmed or were planning evil against his full brother Benjamin, too. It may even be that many people in such a situation would have all these feelings and motives swirling around in their minds as they were flooded with a torrent of past negative and positive memories.

The brothers are not sociopaths, inasmuch as their guilty consciences begin to plague them immediately upon being accused of a differing crime of which they were innocent. This is why they mention the absence of Joseph when questioned harshly—indicating that psychically they sense their family is incomplete without him. "They said, 'We, your servants, are twelve brothers, the sons of a certain man in the land of Canaan; the youngest, however, is now with our father, and one is no more'" (Gen 42:13). Even more illuminating is the conversation they have once Joseph tells them, after three days in prison, that they must leave one brother behind and return with Benjamin in order to test their words.

> They said to one another, "Alas, we are paying the penalty for what we did to our brother; we saw his anguish when he pleaded with us, but we would not listen. That is why this anguish has come upon us." Then Reuben answered them, "Did I not tell you not to wrong the boy? But you would not listen. So now there comes a reckoning for his blood." (Gen 42:21-22)

When they arrive home to inform Jacob that Simeon is in prison in Egypt and will be freed only once they take Benjamin down with them (at least according to the E account), Jacob's already frayed relationship with his ten other sons reaches its nadir. When Reuben offers the lives of his own two sons as surety if he fails to bring back Benjamin safely (Gen 42:37), Jacob's response allows the deep family divisions to come into full view: "My son shall not go down with you, for his brother is dead, and he alone is left. If harm should come to him on the journey that you are to make, you would bring down my gray hairs with sorrow to Sheol" (Gen 42:38). This statement makes it perfectly clear that in Jacob's eyes he had only two children whom he considered his sons, and with Joseph gone, just Benjamin remains. From his perspective, the other ten sons are not his children in the way that Rachel's two are.

The Meaning of Chosenness in the Joseph Story

Although this favoritism is unfair, strangely enough the Bible does not appear to condemn it, despite the tendency by some recent commentators to read the stories of favoritism in Genesis as examples of how not to conduct your family relationships.[10] Toward the end of the Joseph story, Joseph in many ways appears to function as a stand-in for God, as he tests the brothers without their knowledge. Joseph has his brothers seated at a table in the order of their birth and then proceeds to serve Benjamin five times as much food as the other brothers (Gen 43:33-34). Clearly, Joseph is not striving to eliminate all favoritism and thus create an outcome in which everyone ends up on a level playing field.[11] Rather, he, like God, wants to see whether it is possible for a group of non-favored brothers fully to accept that the gifts people receive in life are never fairly distributed, especially the love and favor received from parents or from God. Each relationship is unique, and the Bible seems to say that some receive greater gifts in life than others (cf. Matt 25:14-30). The fact that God favors Joseph as Jacob does indicates that God loves in a way that humans do and points toward a theological explanation of the concept of Israel's election. If God's love is like human love in any way whatsoever, then it is unlikely that God has an identical love for all nations and all individuals. No human lover loves his or her beloved in the same way he or she relates to all other people in the world. Nor does one love other families as much as one's own. The truth is, it is unlikely any parent has an identical relationship with all of his or her children, or that children relate in identical fashion to their parents. In some sense God's special love for Israel reveals God's ability to connect to humans in a much more profound and intimate way than the assertion that God has a generic and equal love for all humans.

This is precisely the point made by Michael Wyschogrod in his book *The Body of Faith*, a probing theological reflection on Israel's bodily election.

> The choice, after all, is between a lofty divine love equally distributed to all without recognition of uniqueness and real encounter, which necessarily involves favorites but in which each is unique and addressed as such. If Abraham was especially loved by God, it is because God is a father who does not stand in legal relationship to his children, which by its nature requires impartiality and objectivity. As a father, God loves his children and knows each one as who he is with his strengths and weaknesses, his virtues and vices. Because a father is not an impartial judge but a loving parent and because a human father is a human being with his own personality, it is inevitable that he will find himself more compatible with some of his children than others and, to speak very plainly, love some more than others. There is usually great reluctance on the part of parents to admit this, but it is a truth that must not be avoided. And it is also true that a father loves all his children, so that they all know of and feel the love they receive, recognizing that to substitute an impartial judge for a loving father would eliminate the

> preference for the specially favored but would also deprive all of them of a father. The mystery of Israel's election thus turns out to be the guarantee of the fatherhood of God toward all peoples, elect and nonelect, Jew and gentile.[12]

While it may be difficult to acknowledge that one's parents might love one more or less than another sibling, this is precisely what Judah does when he pleads with Joseph to release Benjamin and offers himself as a replacement.

> Then your servant my father said to us, "You know that my wife bore me two sons; one left me, and I said, Surely he has been torn to pieces; and I have never seen him since. If you take this one also from me, and harm comes to him, you will bring down my gray hairs in sorrow to Sheol." Now therefore, when I come to your servant my father and the boy is not with us, then, as his life is bound up in the boy's life, when he sees that the boy is not with us, he will die; and your servants will bring down the gray hairs of your servant our father with sorrow to Sheol. For your servant became surety for the boy to my father, saying, "If I do not bring him back to you, then I will bear the blame in the sight of my father all my life." Now therefore, please let your servant remain as a slave to my lord in place of the boy; and let the boy go back with his brothers. For how can I go back to my father if the boy is not with me? I fear to see the suffering that would come upon my father. (Gen 44:27-34)

Judah's language strongly echoes Jacob's description of his special relationship to Rachel's two sons at the end of chapter 42. Although Judah may think that Jacob's favoritism is unfair, he has come to recognize that it is a fact of life he must respect. This surely shows some growth in Judah's character, even if (as argued below) the brothers still exhibit certain character deficiencies at the end of the narrative.[13]

Once Judah has proved that he has indeed matured enough to accept life's unfairness, Joseph not only reveals himself, but he articulates a profound insight into the concept of election.

> Then Joseph said to his brothers, "Come closer to me." And they came closer. He said, "I am your brother, Joseph, whom you sold into Egypt. And now do not be distressed, or angry with yourselves, because you sold me here; for God sent me before you to preserve life. For the famine has been in the land these two years; and there are five more years in which there will be neither plowing nor harvest. God sent me before

> you to preserve for you a remnant on earth, and to keep alive for you many survivors." (Gen 45:4-7)

Joseph makes clear that the purpose of his election was not so that he could lord it over his brothers, but so that he could be in a position to save their lives. Both Joseph and his brothers initially misunderstood the true meaning of Joseph's elect status. While such election is indeed unfair, it is an inherent part of God's merciful plan to preserve Jacob's whole family, as well as much of the rest of the world (Gen 41:57; 50:20). This story articulates a theology of election that illuminates not only the relations among Joseph and his brothers, and by extension between the later tribes of Israel who are represented by their eponymous ancestors, but also between Israel and the other nations of the world. Israel's election is bound up with Israel's special responsibilities of divine service, which are of benefit for the world as a whole.

Divine Providence

The theme of God's providence, which is interwoven with the idea of election in this story, is found not only in these few verses in chapter 45, but also a number of times (in more cloaked ways) earlier in the story, as well as in Gen 50. This deserves attention inasmuch as the idea of such providence may illuminate the meaning of election. Earlier in the narrative one finds strong hints of providence in the strange way that events are linked together by an unlikely set of circumstances. One thinks particularly of the man in the field who knew where Joseph's brothers were (Gen 37:15-17). Had this man not been there the plot would have never unfolded. Was this man a divine figure? It is not uncommon for an angelic being to be called "a man" in the Hebrew Bible (e.g., Gen 18:2, 16; 19:1). One also thinks of how each event in Joseph's life leads to the next and how the story is framed by three sets of dreams. More subtle than these facts is the function of three recurring word pairs found throughout the Joseph story: recognition/non-recognition (נכר/ לא נכר), remembering/forgetting (נשׁה or זכר/שׁכח), and knowledge/not to know (ידע/ לא ידע). Not only do Jacob and Judah recognize the clothing accoutrements presented before them in chapters 37 and 38, but Joseph recognizes his brothers, though they fail to recognize him, in Gen 42:7-8. In this very scene Joseph's recognition is linked to his remembrance of his earlier dreams (Gen 42:9). But the trope of remembering and forgetting has already been broached in Gen 40:23, when Joseph begs Pharaoh's chief steward to remember him when he is released from prison. Of course, the cupbearer forgets, and in an interesting twist, Pharaoh's dreams spark a sudden remembrance of Joseph, just as later the recognition of his brothers causes Joseph to remember his own dreams. When Joseph speaks of the famine, he notes that the years of plenty will soon be forgotten (Gen 41:30). He names his firstborn child Manasseh, punning on the Hebrew root נשה, "to forget," proclaiming that God has made him forget all his troubles and his father's house (Gen 41:51). While the word for remembering is used only for Joseph in chapter 42 (v. 9), it is clear that when Joseph deals with the brothers harshly, it reminds them of their wrongful act, which they recall in vivid detail (42:21-22).

One finds the root "to know" (ידע) and its negative "to fail to know" (לא ידע) in several places—including but not limited to Judah's encounter with Tamar (Gen 38:16); the description of Potiphar, who is said to lack all knowledge of how Joseph runs his house (Gen 39:6); the confession of the brothers about their wrongful treatment of Joseph (Gen 42:23); the brothers' bewilderment over how the money ended up in their sacks (Gen 43:22); and most important, Joseph's questioning his brothers about whether they knew he could divine the future (Gen 44:15). Finally, in Jacob's response to Joseph he uses this root twice to tell Joseph he is intentionally switching the blessings of Ephraim and Manasseh (Gen 48:19).

I would contend that there is a connection between the ubiquity of these three word pairs and the fact that God is rarely overtly active in this story. The lack of the same direct divine intervention in human affairs that occurs elsewhere in Genesis might lead one to assume the Joseph story is driven by a set of rare coincidences. However, these key word pairs hint to the reader that one should look back on the events in one's memory and recognize how God's providential hand has been guiding life's events, acknowledging God as the source of one's blessing—much as Joseph himself eventually does (Gen 45:4-11).

While it is important to take full account of the notion of God's providence in the Joseph story in particular, and in the patriarchal stories in general, some qualifications need to be made about the Hebrew Bible's use of this concept. There appears to be a tension between Gen 45:5-8, in which Joseph tells his brothers that God, not their actions, brought him down to Egypt, and Gen 50:20, in which Joseph claims that the brothers' evil actions were in some way brought to a good end by God. Most likely this tension reflects a source critical problem (45:1-8=J; 50:15-21=E), although one can read the way the redactor deployed these sources as itself literarily significant. When Joseph first reveals himself to his brothers, the redactor uses the source that takes a stronger view of divine providence, thus reducing the sense of the brothers' guilt and enhancing the power of this scene of reconciliation. By using the materials from the other source at the end of the narrative to depict a greater balance between divine action and human action, the redactor leads one to imagine that while an initial reconciliation did occur, normal feelings of the long-standing family rift eventually resurfaced, revealing that the reconciliation between Joseph and his brothers was far from total.

There is indeed more of a reconciliation in this instance than in the Jacob and Esau narrative (since the brothers ultimately do once more live together); however, issues from the past continue to cloud the relationship between Joseph and his ten brothers. In the end, Joseph's brothers still reveal some dishonesty in dealing with him in that they apparently fabricate a speech that Jacob supposedly made in order to shield themselves from what they believe will be Joseph's coming revenge (Gen 50:15-17). This may be a further manifestation of the possibility that the brothers never really accepted Joseph's offer of reconciliation. A careful look at Gen 45:14-15 reveals that when Joseph embraces Benjamin weeping on his neck, Benjamin responds in kind. However, Joseph then turns to his brothers and kisses each of them and weeps upon them, but they only speak to him in response.[14] Perhaps Joseph's attempt at reconciliation, like that of Esau before him, is doomed because the brothers' guilt over previous misdeeds leaves them suspecting the sincerity of Joseph's offer to let bygones be bygones.

While some scholars see Joseph as a complete saint throughout the narrative,[15] others like Coats point to a Joseph who matures but remains flawed in the end.[16] Even after he put his brothers through a grueling test, he appears to remain somewhat hurt by their past deeds (Gen 50:19-20). Coats seems closer to the truth, yet one wonders whether his understanding of Joseph at the end of the narrative is not reading a modern concern for balanced power in all relationships into an ancient text that did not share such concerns. After all, Joseph once more speaks tenderly toward his brothers, assuring them of his support and good intentions toward them (50:21). In any case, Coats is surely correct that an imperfect relationship between Joseph and his siblings does not mean that no reconciliation has occurred. Reconciliation does not necessarily entail full erasure of the past or newly perfected characters. Rather, it involves a commitment to live the relationship differently than one did in the past.[17]

The evidence presented here, along with that found in many other biblical texts such as the plague narratives (cf. Exod 7:13; 8:15, 28; 9:12; 10:20), clearly demonstrates that the Hebrew Bible did not have a single coherent view of divine providence and its relationship to human action. Rather, the biblical authors struggled to give due to both aspects, sometimes laying the stress more on the human side, sometimes more on the divine one. Furthermore, even when one speaks of the Bible subscribing to divine providence, it is essential to keep in mind that, aside from a limited number of certain apocalyptically oriented prophetic fragments (Isa 24–27; 66; Zech 12–14) and rare late books like Daniel, the biblical authors' views of providence did not usually encompass the full-blown idea that all history was being orchestrated toward some final consummation.[18] Generally, God's providential actions are explored through his actions in relation to Israel and the other nations she interacts with, and the focus is less on some final consummation than on God's ongoing relationship with the world, as seen through his providential care for his special people Israel.

The Joseph Narrative and Other Stories of Sibling Rivalry

The Joseph story has very strong connections to the three other stories of sibling rivalry in Genesis. Not only are the texts dealing with Cain and Abel, Isaac and Ishmael, Jacob and Esau, and Joseph and his brothers all linked in a number of ways, but there also appears to be a step-like structure in which certain themes are deepened in each succeeding story. One way these four stories are connected to one another is by means of an interlocking rotation between stories involving a single mother who bears rivalrous children and those involving rival wives who bear rival children. Thus, one first has the instance of Eve bearing Cain and Abel, followed by Abraham, who fathers Ishmael by Hagar and Isaac through Sarah. Then Rebekah bears Jacob and Esau (returning to the Eve pattern), only to have Jacob involved with two rival wives (reaching back to the pattern two generations previously). The fact that both Judah and Joseph produce sets of rival brothers, each from a single woman in the generation after Jacob (i.e., Peretz and Zerah from Tamar; Manasseh and Ephraim from Asenath), hardly seems accidental.

Often such patterns run even deeper. For example, the twin births of Jacob and Esau and of Peretz and Zerah involve an extremity, the color red, and a reversal of primacy between the children. Of course, in a more subtle way the Cain and Abel story also invokes the color red in Abel's innocent blood. Such repetitive patterns create a haunting effect in which the narratives keep rubbing up against one another. Furthermore, questions raised in one narrative are revisited and posed differently or in a more sustained fashion in a later narrative. One thinks of the way in which the Cain and Abel narrative raises the issue of whether election is initiated by humans or by God (Gen 4:3-5), and how in the Abraham cycle the question is less about the initiation of election than whether humans can contribute to the consummation of God's elective plan (Gen 16; 22). This question is posed more starkly in the Jacob cycle, where one is asked to entertain whether even possibly unethical human actions might contribute to the fulfillment of God's designs for humanity (Gen 27). The Joseph story perhaps ups the ante even more by exploring whether even violent actions that are explicitly condemned may be at the same time a necessary part of God's providence.

Thus, the continued meditation on certain issues or motifs can express deep theological significance, as Levenson has shown in his investigation into the theme of the death and resurrection of the beloved son, a pattern found in all four of these rivalry stories. I suspect another trope that not only plays an aesthetic role but also is of special theological significance in the Genesis narratives explored here is the image of seeing God's face. In the first story of Cain and Abel, God is reported to have looked upon Abel and his sacrifice but not upon Cain and his sacrifice (Gen 4:4-5). Moreover, part of Cain's punishment is to be hidden from the face of God (Gen 4:14). In Gen 16:13-14, in verses that may have been displaced from the now second Hagar story, describing her discovery of a well (Gen 21:19), Hagar encounters an angel and has her eyes opened. Here she describes God as אל ראי, "a God of seeing." Furthermore, the well also bears the word "seeing" in its name, באר לחי ראי meaning something like "well of the living one who sees me." Strangely enough, Isaac's near sacrifice ends with the report that Abraham called the place Adonai-yireh (literally "the Lord will see"), which is then used to explain a common proverb, "on the Mount of the Lord there is vision" (Gen 22:14 NJPS). Jacob's closest encounter with death occurs when he returns to Canaan and he must once more meet Esau. Not only does he wrestle all night face-to-face with a shadowy divine figure at a place named Peniel (or Penuel), meaning "the face of God" (Gen 32:30-31), but the word "face" is used a number of times when Jacob speaks of appeasing Esau. The first three letters of the word "face" (פני) are used four times alone in Gen 32:21 (Eng. 32:20) and later Jacob tells Esau that seeing his face is like seeing the face of God (Gen 33:10). In the Joseph narrative one hears the brothers attribute the following statement to Joseph: "You shall not see my face unless your brother is with you" (Gen 43:3, 5; 44:23). The very strong emphasis in these narratives on seeing, especially on seeing God's face, is too frequent to be coincidental.[19] While the Joseph story lacks an explicit reference to seeing God, it may well imply it, inasmuch as Joseph himself often functions as a stand-in for the Deity. If this idea is correct, the Joseph narrative may be hinting at a connection that runs through the stories of Jacob and Esau, and Isaac and Ishmael, and all the way back to Cain and Abel. That is, if one hopes to see God's face and thus receive God's blessing, one must be reconciled with one's brother.

In addition to its connections to the sibling stories within Genesis, the Joseph tale shares an unusual number of affinities with the narratives surrounding King David's family, commonly called the "Succession Narrative" or "Court History" (2 Sam 9–1 Kgs 2). As several scholars with keen literary sensibilities have noticed, there are a host of motifs and verbal links between the narrative dealing with the question of which child will succeed King David and the Joseph story. Thus, both stories have a Tamar who is involved in an inappropriate sexual act and never has sex again, both have a friend who is around the protagonist immediately before he sleeps with the Tamar character (i.e., Hirah in Gen 38:12, and Jonadab in 2 Sam 13:3), both mention the unusual word for the garment Joseph received from his father (a כתנת פסים Gen 37:3; 2 Sam 13:18), both have an incident occurring at a sheepshearing festival (Gen 38:13; 2 Sam 13:23-29), both contain the identical expression "lie with me" in a scene involving an inappropriate sexual advance rebuffed by the other party (Gen 39:7, 12; 2 Sam 13:11), and both revolve around rivalries between various brothers, in which the eldest living son of the most recent wife ends up ruling over his siblings. More subtly, the method of characterization is similar in striking ways. To begin with, human actions drive both plots, but the outcomes are described in providential terms (Gen 45:5-8; 50:15-20; 2 Sam 17:14). Also, both narratives contain characters that are morally complex. These are just a few of a long list of potential parallels.[20]

There are also occasional references to other sibling stories such as the link between the woman of Tekoa, who mentions two sons who had a mortal encounter in the field (2 Sam 14:6), calling to mind Cain and Abel. Her concern that she might lose both sons to the single crime is reminiscent of Rebekah's comment in Gen 27:45. There is also the fact that a rape occurs in Genesis, leading to the fall of two brothers, Simeon and Levi, and one occurring in 2 Samuel that also leads to the eventual fall of Amnon and Absalom. Finally, one thinks of the strong resemblance between Rebekah's manipulation of Isaac in Gen 27 and Bath Sheba's participation in the plot to convince the doddering King David that he had promised the throne to Solomon, her son (1 Kgs 1).

What is one to make of all these interconnections? From a historical perspective we are left to choose among the following options: one corpus was dependent on the other (although which way such dependence might run is disputed); perhaps both corpora were produced at a similar time or possibly by a similar writer or school; both may draw on a common set of stock motifs out of which they are weaving their tales; or there may be a complex redactional relationship between them in which each story over time was drawn into tighter relationship with the other.[21] For this study it is not necessary to figure out the exact relationship between these two masterworks. In what follows, the focus will be on the theological implications of these manifold connections.

Theological Reflections on the Sibling Rivalry Stories

Certainly one implication is that while election may be initiated for mysterious reasons by the Deity, the way in which such election unfolds is ultimately bound up in a complex set of human motives and actions that are done freely by humans, but nevertheless orchestrated by God to bring his plans to fruition. Thus, Reuben Ahroni's statement about the Jacob cycle can be applied more broadly to all the sibling stories, including those from 2 Samuel:

> However, the Biblical doctrine with regard to human freedom seems to hinge upon a dialectical tension. On the one hand, the Scriptures stress the absolute sovereignty of God, his omnipotence and foreknowledge. Hence, human fate and destiny are divinely determined. But, on the other hand, the Scriptures equally insist that God's foreknowledge does not preclude human freedom: man is endowed with the power of self-determination and he is possessed of the ability to choose between conflicting courses of action.[22]

While all human actions bring consequences in their wake, they often contribute to the divinely ordained plan, frequently in rather ironic ways. Thus, many of David's and Jacob's troubles arise from their personal failings, particularly from their inability to control their children's behavior in relation to each other. In both extended narratives about the family life of major Israelite ancestors, deceitful and/or wrongful actions do at times appear to be legitimated explicitly and do in some instances bring about God's purposes. Here one thinks of the ways in which Rebekah and Bath Sheba manipulate their spouses along with Tamar's deception of Judah. Furthermore, Hushai defeats Absalom's plans through an outright lie. In the wake of this deception the text reports: "For the LORD had ordained to defeat the good counsel of Ahithophel, so that the LORD might bring ruin on Absalom" (2 Sam 17:14). This is reminiscent of Gen 45:5 and 50:20, verses suggesting that God's plan is advanced through the evil actions of Joseph's brothers.

Another major element tying the Joseph story not only to the stories surrounding the succession to David's throne, but also to the other sibling rivalry stories in Genesis and elsewhere in the Bible, is that all these stories follow a common pattern in which the elder brother (or multiple brothers in the case of Joseph and Solomon), whom one would usually expect to be favored by the rule of primogeniture, seems to be overshadowed by the second born. Thus Abel, Isaac, Jacob, Joseph, Moses, David, and Solomon are all younger siblings who eventually eclipse their elder sibling or siblings.

This commonly occurring trope is obviously making an important theological point. One element of this point is that God appears to favor individuals not favored by human convention. But why does a highly tradition-bound culture like that found in much of the Hebrew Bible contain images of a deity who does not abide by the norms held dear by the community, and even enshrined within its own divinely ordained laws (Deut 21:15-17)? One likely explanation for this unusual state of affairs is that the Hebrew Bible time and again reveals God's power by showing how human attempts to control outcomes are subtly subverted by God. This recurring literary pattern might be labeled the Bible's "underdog motif." It shows up in many places in the Hebrew Bible aside from stories of brotherly struggle. Thus, the prominence of several different women in the beginning of the exodus story indicates that God frequently uses the powerless to overcome the powerful. The Bible enjoys stacking the deck against God's plans in order to highlight God's victories all the more. God gives all the advantages to those opposed to his plan, but his plan always prevails, frequently even by means of resistance to it or through those who seem to be totally marginal and powerless.[23]

However, the question remains as to why a society would enshrine such a motif as a central part of its identity. Here it seems difficult to escape the conclusion that this motif's prominence is in good measure driven by Israel's perception of herself in relation to her older, venerable, and more dominant neighbors, Egypt and Mesopotamia. This should not be all that surprising inasmuch as various biblical thinkers (such as the Priestly writer of Gen 1) regularly reacted against Mesopotamian and Egyptian religious ideas. Thus, it seems that at least part of the stress on the underdog motif, particularly the way in which younger brothers supersede their elders by divine choice, is connected to Israel's sense of her late-born status. Rather than seeing this as an impediment to her divine election, as one would expect according to the rule of primogeniture so prominent in the ancient Near East, Israel views her late-born status as evidence of her worthiness to become God's chosen people.

Another facet of these stories in which the younger sibling comes to outshine his elder brother(s) is that in a number of them the younger sibling who eventually triumphs is portrayed as a character who, at least for a time, is seriously flawed. Here one thinks of Jacob, Joseph, David, and Solomon, as well as possibly Isaac and Moses. The emphasis of these stories on the upsetting of human expectations by noting God's mysterious election of the youngest child, even when he is flawed, must certainly reflect a deep-seated Israelite perception that their nation is blessed, but has not earned this blessedness primarily through merit. The ability to sense one's chosenness and also to see one's character flaws is perhaps one of the greatest achievements of the Israelite religious mind. It creates a sense of ultimate meaning for one's nation, but it does so in ways that mitigate movement toward an unfettered imperialism and triumphalism. This sense of undeserved chosenness is explored in all the above sibling stories but particularly emphasized within the Joseph tale, perhaps the single most sustained meditation on this topic in the Bible. The story of Joseph and his brothers affirms that God does indeed mysteriously favor some over others. Yet it also proclaims to the elect and the non-elect that the divine favor bestowed in election is not to be used for self-aggrandizement. Rather, election reaches its fruition in a humble, yet exalted, divine service that benefits the elect and the non-elect alike.

Finally, one must note that many of these stories probe the emotional life and the behavior of the non-elect in relation to the elect, most especially when jealousies become inflamed over such favoring. The Bible recognizes that some are chosen and others are not, and that even among the chosen, some are elevated over others. It also acknowledges that this situation is fraught with grave dangers for everyone involved. The stories explored above present a variety of possibilities, some tragic (Cain and Abel), others more hopeful (Joseph and his brothers). In at least one instance, that of Esau, it is possible to read the text as indicating that the wronged sibling, while initially inflamed with intent to murder his brother, was ultimately more prepared to work for a fuller reconciliation than was the favored Jacob. In any case, the sibling narratives as a whole suggest that, while difficult, those not chosen can learn to accept and live with the mysterious unfairness inherent in a world shaped by God's gracious love.

Section 2

Chapter Five

Promise and Covenant

That the notion of election is both central and pervasive within the Hebrew Bible is reinforced upon realizing that a number of other prominent theological motifs, such as the promises to the patriarchs and the ideas of covenant and commandment, are themselves inextricably intertwined with the fact of Israel's chosenness. The first of these, the promise theme, is a crucial framing device within the patriarchal stories, several of which received extended treatment earlier in this book. Thus, God's promises to Abraham first mentioned in Gen 12:1-3, 7 initiate Abraham's and his descendants' special relationship to God. Elements of these promises echo like a regular refrain throughout Genesis (Gen 15:4-5, 16-21; 17:20; 22:15-19; 24:60; 27:28-29; 28:3-4, 13-15; 35:9-12; 48:15-16). The promises themselves are a complex composed of at least three distinct elements, the promise of progeny, of blessing, and of land. There are other occasional components such as inheriting the gates of one's enemies (Gen 22:17; 24:60) or having God's continuous presence (Gen 28:15). God articulates many of them, but several are on the lips of various human beings (Gen 24:60; 27:28-29; 28:3-4). A number of scholars think that the current compound form of these promises is due to an extended process of coagulation in which older elements like the promise of progeny may have been linked together with younger ones such as the promise of land, yet in the current canon these ideas are now inseparably fused into a coherent whole.[1]

A quick examination of these promise texts in Genesis and elsewhere in the Hebrew Bible reveals that the promises contain a profound articulation of Israel's self-understanding of her divine election. In a very real sense, Gen 1–11 represents God's failed attempt to create a working relationship between humans, nature, and himself. In the wake of this failure God moves from a plan in which he demands equal obedience from all humans to a two-tiered plan in which most people are held to a minimal religio-moral standard (which later Judaism came to conceive of as the seven Noahide commandments that all Gentiles must observe), and one man's extended family is given a special place in the divine economy requiring that its members maintain a higher religio-moral standard.[2] As Gen 12:2-3 makes clear, Abraham's and thus Israel's election is closely bound up with God's larger plan to bring blessing to the whole world, even while God's purposes in choosing Abraham and his descendants are not exhausted by this linkage.[3]

> I will make of you a great nation, and I will bless you, and make your name great, so that you will be a blessing. I will bless those who bless you, and the one who curses you I will curse; and in you all the families of the earth shall be blessed.

It seems quite likely from the heavy use of the root for "bless" (ברך), employed five times in verses 2-3, that Abram and his descendants are the ones who will undo the earlier divine curses connected to human evildoing (Gen 3:17; 4:11; 5:29; 8:21; 9:25). The use of the word אדמה (earth) at the end of Gen 12:3 calls to mind the curses that both Adam and Cain brought upon the earth (Gen 3:17; 4:11). The promise of a great name for Abram (Gen 12:2) may suggest that Abram's obedience to God will succeed where those who sought to make a name for themselves by building a tower (as an assault on heaven) failed (Gen 11:1-9). Noah is invoked as one who will provide comfort from the curse (Gen 5:29), but the fact is that after the flood God merely promises not to curse the ground again due to human misbehavior (Gen 8:21). Yet Ham's behavior (Gen 9:22) along with the Tower of Babel incident indicate that the human-divine rift remains unhealed.

Clearly, Abram is part of a larger divine plan that will bring blessing to the whole world, yet the exact meaning of the *niphal* of ברך (bless) used in the all-important final clause of Gen 12:3 remains hotly debated.[4] Is this rare verbal form best translated as a passive and rendered as "all the families of the earth will be blessed" by or through Abram, his name, or his descendants? Or should one look to the alternate places in which this similar blessing is rendered by the *hithpael* (Gen 22:18; 26:4), opting for the reflexive, "all the families of the earth will bless themselves" by/through Abraham?[5] The two renderings imply two differing scenarios. If one reads this verb as a reflexive, the sense communicated may be something akin to members of the Gentile nations saying, "May you be blessed like God blessed Abram." If one opts for the passive meaning, this seems to imply the stronger notion that Abram's family will be a conduit through which blessing will pass to the other nations of the world, or possibly that the other families of the earth will receive blessing in direct proportion to how these nations treat Abram and his chosen descendants. Although the immediate context of Gen 12 focuses more on assuring Abram than on the place of the nations in God's plan for Abram,[6] this latter theme is developed in greater depth elsewhere in Genesis.

Neither translation of Gen 12:3 makes it absolutely clear how the families of the earth might be blessed or bless themselves through Abram and his descendants, but passages later in Genesis suggest that part of this blessing comes about through mediatorial services rendered by Abraham and Israel. This is made rather explicit in a divine speech that reveals God's motivation for telling Abraham that he is about to destroy Sodom and Gomorrah.

> The LORD said, "Shall I hide from Abraham what I am about to do, seeing that Abraham shall become a great and mighty nation, and all the nations of the earth shall be blessed in him? No, for I have chosen him, that he may charge his children and his household after him to keep the way of the LORD by doing righteousness and justice; so that the LORD may bring about for Abraham what he has promised him." (Gen 18:17-19)

In this passage God, either having an internal dialogue with himself or possibly talking to the other divine beings who go on to Sodom in verse 22, initially suggests he was going to destroy Sodom and Gomorrah without notifying Abraham. However, he convinces himself that this is a wrong course of action apparently because to do so would impede the mission of Abraham and his future descendants to do righteousness and justice. This speech evokes Gen 12:3 when it links God's decision to tell Abraham about the coming destruction of Sodom to the fact that through Abraham and the nation that will grow from his progeny, blessing will extend to all the nations of the world (Gen 18:18). As the story unfolds, Abraham questions God's justice, strongly implying that at least one part of Abraham's and his descendants' duty is to call God to account if he is acting unjustly. Further proof that Abraham's election entails an intercessory role can be gleaned from Gen 20:7, 17 in which he intercedes for Abimelech and his larger household. Thus, at least one part of Abraham's and later Israel's elective service involves functioning as a mediator pleading for God's mercy, even for those who do not deserve it on the basis of their own behavior, as Abraham does on behalf of the residents of Sodom.[7]

The idea that Israel's elective status might imply a mediatorial role is further developed when one examines certain covenantal texts, a theological complex with close ties to the promise passages and the theme of Israel's election. The various biblical covenants that God makes with the people of Israel are a formalization of God's promises to Israel's ancestors as well as of Israel's self-understanding that they are God's chosen people. Note the language employed by the following passage, which serves as preface to Israel's acceptance of the Sinai covenant and the commandments it entails.

> Now therefore, if you obey my voice and keep my covenant, you shall be my treasured possession out of all the peoples. Indeed, the whole earth is mine, but you shall be for me a priestly kingdom and a holy nation. These are the words that you shall speak to the Israelites. (Exod 19:5-6)

Here God conceives of Israel as a priestly people, a concept that entails her functioning as a mediator of the divine to the world as a whole.[8] If one takes such language as more than mere metaphor, it implies that Israel not only intercedes for the nations, but she is also the means by which God's blessings radiate out to the larger terrestrial world.

Having highlighted the universal implications of Israel's election, that Israel serves a mediatorial role between the Gentile nations and God, I must add a cautionary note, lest this important side of election theology totally eclipse other elements of this theology. In particular, I am concerned about a Christian tendency to reduce Israel's election to her service to the larger world. I think here not only of Rowley's statement that "Israel's election was to service"[9] but also of the seminal and very influential article by Hans Walter Wolff titled "The Kerygma of the Yahwhist."[10] In this article Wolff puts tremendous weight on the final clause in Gen 12:3, often translated "in you all the families of the earth shall be blessed." Wolff seems to read this clause in a manner that turns it into an explanation for Israel's election. Clearly, New Testament understandings of Christ's death and resurrection as providing a way for Gentiles to become a part of God's elect people are the driving force behind the Christian tendency to read the promise texts generally, and Gen 12:1-3 in particular, in a way that emphasizes Israel's service to the nations. While such readings are theologically understandable once one reads Genesis in the light of various New Testament ideas, one must still reckon with the meaning of these texts within the Hebrew Bible's theological universe. Even if Christians wish to link the Old and New Testaments into a theological unity, they *need not* do so in a manner that damages the theological witness of the earlier materials by reading various Old Testament texts in ways that dissolve the ongoing importance of the historic people of Israel, replacing a supposedly disobedient Israel with the later church (an idea Paul warns against in Rom 11:28-31).

Genesis 12:3 indicates that God's promises have implications for the larger world, but their central focus is on Abraham and his chosen descendants, the people of Israel. A careful look at all of Gen 12:1-3 suggests the nations being blessed or blessing themselves is an effect or consequence (albeit an important one) of God's electing Israel. But that is not the same as saying it is a reason or an explanation of the purpose of Abraham's and thus Israel's election. The same is true when one examines the divine dialogue in Gen 18. It affirms that Abraham and by extension his descendants may play an intercessory role. But that does not mean that the purpose of Israel's chosenness is exhausted by or reducible to this role. While Exod 19 strongly suggests that Israel plays a priestly mediatorial role, the passage highlights the fact of Israel's special closeness to God. God's special love for Israel, brought into full view when he freed them from Egypt and brought them to Sinai (Exod 19:4), is at the forefront. This topic will be discussed at greater length in chapter 9, "Prophecy and Election," but for now it is sufficient to note that the total purposes of Abraham's and thus Israel's election are never fully articulated within the Hebrew Bible. In any case, God's choosing Israel involves a mysterious act of divine love that precedes any call to service and persists even when Israel fails to respond to God properly. Most important, in all of these texts Abraham and his chosen descendants, the people of Israel, remain God's elect, affirming an enduring distinction between God's chosen people and the other nations of the world.

Covenant and Election

Having briefly touched on one aspect of the relationship between covenantal ideas and notions of election (i.e., Israel's role in mediating the divine to the world), we now return to the intersection between covenantal and election theologies in a more sustained fashion. Unsurprisingly, this is a very fruitful area of discussion inasmuch as the various streams of covenantal theology reflect Israel's attempt to explore the implications of her divine election. A point less often noticed, which will provide a focal point to the discussion below, is that certain tensions within the notion of covenant bear a striking resemblance to tensions within the sibling stories explored in chapters 1–4. Furthermore, some of the ways these covenantal tensions are eased within the larger canonical framework also are remarkably analogous to the solutions offered within the sibling stories.

Usually, scholars begin analyzing the idea of covenant by noting that there are two very broad categories of covenants in the Hebrew Bible, those between human individuals and/or nations (e.g., Gen 21:27), and those between God and human individuals/nations and/or the whole human community. For the purposes of this theological discussion it makes sense to focus on the latter type in which God is a partner in the proceedings. Divine/human covenants also fall into two distinct patterns. Thus, scholars describe some of these covenants as conditional, indicating much of the burden falls on the humans involved, while others are frequently labeled unconditional, meaning most, if not all, of the obligations fall upon God.[11]

Typical examples of unconditional covenants are the Noachic (Gen 9:8-17) and Abrahamic covenants (at least in Gen 15) in which the obligations fall primarily, if not exclusively, upon the Deity. Thus, they tend to occur in promise or oath form. Alternatively, in those that are called conditional, such as the covenant at Sinai, the obligations fall much more heavily upon the human side of the partnership, which must take on the yoke of the commandments (Exod 19:4-6; Lev 26; Deut 28). That is, in an unconditional covenant God accomplishes his purposes with little to no human input while a conditional covenant requires human actions to bring it to fruition. In some sense, these two major streams of covenantal theology resemble the tension in the sibling stories between those places in which divine election occurs in a mysterious and arbitrary fashion driven solely by God's fiat (e.g., God's choosing Abraham parallels the unconditional covenantal theology) and those passages in which divine election seems inextricably bound up with human actions (e.g., Jacob's gaining the birthright and blessing parallels the theology of conditional covenants).

Interestingly enough, the streams of conditional and unconditional covenantal theology become murkier the more one examines them, just as it is frequently difficult to discern whether election is driven more by divine action or by human response. Even in the Abrahamic covenant (and perhaps in the Noachic one as well), human behavior energizes and seals the covenant that previously was only an incomplete promise. Thus, some view Abraham's fulfillment of the circumcision commandment in Gen 17 along with his obedience to God during the *Akedah* ("the binding of Isaac") as necessary to bring the Abrahamic promises to fruition.[12] Such a reading is strongly supported by Gen 22:15-18 as well as Gen 26:2-5.[13] Even God's covenant with Noah was understood to contain an implicit demand for a proper human response; otherwise it became null and void.

> I will utterly sweep away everything from the face of the earth, says the LORD. I will sweep away humans and animals; I will sweep away the birds of the air and the fish of the sea. I will make the wicked stumble. I will cut off humanity from the face of the earth, says the LORD. (Zeph 1:2-3)

In this prophetic text, which builds on the language of the flood narrative, not only does God nullify his supposed unconditional eternal promise never again to destroy the world completely, but he actually goes a step further by indicating that this time he will even annihilate the fish that were spared in Noah's flood. Similarly, in 1 Sam 3 God nullifies what appeared to be an unconditional promise to Eli's family of eternal priesthood due to the abuse of priestly privileges by Eli's sons.

On the conditional side, the Sinai covenant as presented in different pentateuchal sources implies a greater element of mysterious divine action than scholarship has often recognized. To begin with, Israel is redeemed from Egypt and brought to Sinai due to God's attachment to this people, even though Israel has not yet accepted the full array of commandments given at Mount Sinai. The text makes crystal clear that God had already elected Israel as his people early on in Exodus (note God's reference to Israel as "my firstborn son" in Exod 4:22-23). Equally important, in the eyes of the biblical writers (as well as of most postbiblical Jews) the Sinai commandments are not best described as a set of demands that conditionalize Israel's relationship to God. Stressing the conditionality of this covenant leads one to ignore the fact that receiving the commandments was the greatest possible divine gift. Many critics who describe the Sinai covenant in purely conditional terms focus only on its accompanying obligations rather than seeing that God, acting out of divine love for Israel, is offering her a manual of instruction to live in right relationship to the divine. In fact, this element of divine grace becomes predominant even in the Sinai covenant inasmuch as God shows a willingness to reanimate this covenant with an undeserving Israel after the golden calf incident.

An additional nuance in the Bible's covenants occurs in the language surrounding God's promise of eternal dynasty to David and his progeny. Although most scholars place the Davidic covenant preserved in pre-exilic texts such as 2 Sam 7 into the unconditional category of covenants and see it as related to the ancient Near Eastern covenants of grant,[14] it may actually occupy some middle ground between the conditional and the unconditional. In its original form, the promise to David guarantees that he will always have a descendant on the throne, but disobedience brings negative consequences to the reigning monarch.

In any case, this pre-exilic Davidic theology coexisted with other more conditional streams of biblical theology, at times peacefully, at others not (Jer 7). However, the shock of the exile appears to have led to new reflections on the nature of God's covenantal relationship to Israel and her reigning monarch. Thus, certain texts like Jer 7, Ps 132, and 1 Kgs 2:4; 8:25; 9:4-5 (the latter, likely postexilic additions to the Deuteronomistic History)[15] appear to turn the somewhat ambiguous Davidic covenant into a much more conditional one. I say more conditional because, as indicated above, even the earlier forms of the Davidic royal theology included some stipulations and some type of punishment.[16] Still, it is clear that over time the specific stipulations and the blessings and curses from the Sinaitic traditions began to pervade the royal theology. While 2 Sam 7:14-16 and Ps 89:20-37 tell us that if certain Davidids fail to act properly they will be punished, but the dynasty will endure eternally, 1 Kgs 2:4; 8:25; 9:2-9; 2 Kgs 21:7-8; and Ps 132:11-12 make eternal dynastic succession contingent upon obedience to the commandments of God. In the words of Jon Levenson:

> The subordination of the Davidic covenant to the Sinaitic in 1 Kgs 8:25, therefore, must be seen as a reinterpretation of the pristine Davidic covenant material, a reinterpretation that reflects the growing canonical status of the Sinaitic traditions that will become the Pentateuch. 1 Kgs 8:25 is the vengeance of Moses upon David, of the "kingdom of priests" upon the hubris of the political state, for it resolves

> the clash between the two covenants in favor of the Mosaic one. The entitlement of the house of David is no longer indefeasible; it is contingent upon observance of the *mitsvot*.[17]

The theological move to conditionalize those less conditional covenants strongly suggests Israel's elect status hinges finally on Israel's obedience to God.

On the other hand, a countermovement within the Hebrew Bible emphasizes the notion that humans do little or nothing to influence God's elective actions. Thus, one finds certain late biblical texts that imagine God's acting unilaterally at some point in the future, indicating that in the end election may require less human response than it did in the past (Jer 31:31-34; Ezek 20:33-44; 36:16-32). While one might object that these passages still speak of humans responding to God, in these texts a proper human response to God is ensured in that God will remake human nature (Ezek 36:26 speaks of God's conducting a spiritual heart transplant on the Israelites) or fully reveal himself to them (as in Jer 31:34). Removing the possibility of any willful human rebellion seriously calls into question the possibility of any real human contribution to the covenantal relationship.

Even as certain exilic theologians were gravitating to these two opposite poles, either heightening God's graceful action or alternatively emphasizing the importance of human actions to heal the divine/human rift, others were seeking to synthesize the insights of both positions into a new theological framework. In particular one thinks of Deut 4:25-31 (cf. Lev 26:40-45; Deut 30:1-14). In this text as well as in Deuteronomy and the Deuteronomistic History as a whole, if Israel is ever to be reconciled with God, she will need to obey the Sinai commandments. Failure to do so will result in a punishment of exile and death as explicitly stated in verses 25-26:

> When you have had children and children's children, and become complacent in the land, if you act corruptly by making an idol in the form of anything, thus doing what is evil in the sight of the LORD your God, and provoking him to anger, I call heaven and earth to witness against you today that you will soon utterly perish from the land that you are crossing the Jordan to occupy; you will not live long on it, but will be utterly destroyed.

Upon initial inspection it appears that in this text the conditional theology of Sinai has fully trumped any notion of an unconditional covenantal relationship between God and Israel. But note the way the passage continues in Deut 4:30-31:

> In your distress, when all these things have happened to you in time to come, you will return to the LORD your God and heed him. Because the LORD your God is a merciful God, he will neither abandon you nor destroy you; he will not forget the covenant with your ancestors that he swore to them.

Here the endurance of God's unconditional promises to the patriarchs is emphasized, introducing a permanent note of unconditioned grace into the heart of the Sinai theology. While Israel may have violated the Sinai covenant, this has not severed the relationship between God and Israel because the unconditional nature of the divine promises made to the patriarchs means that the relationship between Israel and God is unbreakable. As verse 29 notes, Israel as God's eternally elected people has an open invitation to repent and again be obedient to God's law: "From there you will seek the LORD your God, and you will find him if you search after him with all your heart and soul." Hence the two streams of covenantal theology, the conditional and the unconditional, are synthesized in such a way that each qualifies and limits the other. Obedience to Sinai is preeminent in terms of consummating the relationship between God and his chosen people, but the unconditional promises to the patriarchs are preeminent in terms of how the relationship began and why it can endure human disobedience. This type of synthetic covenant theology may be a further reflection of Deuteronomy's attempt to articulate a covenantal theology modeled on a relationship bound by love, a notion explored further in the next chapter. For such relationships involve a complex admixture of unconditional and conditional elements.

The attempt to produce a single coherent covenantal theology from a variety of distinct streams of tradition can be seen clearly in the later biblical period. As Brooks Schramm points out in reference to Neh 9–10, a text likely from the latter part of the fifth century B.C.E. or later, over time the strong distinction between the unconditional covenant with Abraham and the conditional one with Israel at Sinai began to dissolve.

> The internal logic of Nehemiah 9–10 is something like this: God made a covenant with Abraham, a covenant which God faithfully keeps in spite of Israel's persistent disobedience, but Israel's access to this covenant is only through Sinai, through the observance of command-

> ments. *The Abrahamic and the Sinaitic are therefore conceived as one covenant. The Abrahamic aspect of the covenant ensures its endurance, while the Sinaitic aspect is that which "energizes" it.*[18]

Of course, Neh 9–10 is in many ways simply engaging in a holistic reading of the pentateuchal narrative. After all, in Exod 4:22, long before Israel has accepted the commandments at Sinai, God refers to Israel as "my firstborn son," indicating that Israel is already God's special people. Yet in Exod 19:5 God tells Israel, "If you obey my voice and keep my covenant, you shall be my treasured possession out of all the peoples," indicating that Israel fully becomes God's people only after accepting the commandments at Sinai. The easiest way to make sense of this tension is to read these as two movements in a single covenant as Neh 9–10 does.[19]

There is a striking resemblance in the manner that the Hebrew Bible productively mediates the tension between the unconditional and the conditional streams of covenantal theology and the way that the sibling stories attempt to balance the respective human and divine roles in the elective process. The sibling stories see the notion of election as one that is begun by a mysterious divine process (such as God's choosing Abel, Abram, Isaac, Jacob, or Joseph), but somehow this process is brought to fruition through the human response of characters who react to the divine in appropriate ways (thus, Abraham passes the test through his obedience to God's command to sacrifice Isaac, Jacob offers Esau his blessing back in the form of a gift, and Joseph ultimately overcomes his estrangement from his brothers and saves their lives). So too, one finds texts like Deut 7:7-8 indicating that election originates in the mystery of God's love for Israel, and yet this relationship is fully realized only through obedience to God's laws given at Sinai (Deut 7:9-16).

Reflections on the Later Christian Appropriation of Israel's Covenantal Theology

While the early Christian appropriation of election theology will be discussed in more detail in the final chapter of this book, at this point it may be useful to at least outline what strategies Paul employed with these covenantal texts in the early Christian period. Faced with his unique set of circumstances, Paul opted to negate the notion that the covenantal relationship between God and his chosen people could be fully consummated only through obedience to the laws of Sinai. Instead he stressed the priority and unconditionality of the Abrahamic covenant, which, whether he intended to or not, had the effect of relegating the Sinai covenant and its demands to a secondary status (Rom 4; Gal 3–4). Paul here understands divine election as a mysterious divine process, strongly deemphasizing the notion that humans are co-partners in the elective process (Rom 9:6-29).[20]

Paul faced a crisis similar to those biblical writers who survived the destruction of Jerusalem in 587 B.C.E. He also had to explain why things went wrong with the divine plan, and he too drew the conclusion that human disobedience was at the root of the problem. Most interesting is that the radically differing proposed solutions involved attempts to come to terms with the tension between God's conditional versus his unconditional relationship to his chosen people. While the exilic community left a place for divine grace in allowing that the covenant between God and Israel could not be broken, most texts continued to advocate that this relationship could be reanimated and consummated only by Israel's obedience to the Sinaitic covenant. On the other hand, Paul chose to highlight the alternative vision of texts like Jer 31:31-34; Ezek 20:33-44; 36:16-32 as well as other more apocalyptic passages such as Isa 66 in which God remakes humans and human history, thus accomplishing his goals with little, if any, human input.[21] Paul is likely driven to this view not only by the current historical situation in which the Romans seem unconquerable from a human perspective, but also by his understanding of and emphasis upon the unconditional nature of God's covenant with Abraham. In particular, Paul comes to believe that the Abrahamic promise that all the families of the earth are blessed through Abraham means that the Gentiles, through faith in Jesus as the Christ, can join the people of God. Thus, Paul elevates those streams of covenantal theology that are unconditional over those that are conditional, most particularly the Sinai covenant. In a real sense he ended up undoing the theological synthesis found in texts like Deuteronomy and created a new synthesis in which the conditional covenantal streams connected to Sinai were marginalized and the unconditional Abrahamic (and Davidic) streams were elevated to a new preeminence (Rom 4).

Further evidence of the early Christian tendency to emphasize the unconditional nature of God's relationship with the human community may be seen in the fact that Paul and other New Testament writers tend to highlight the roles of Abraham and David while often ignoring (or at times even denigrating) the role of Moses (2 Cor 3). In Rom 4 not only does Paul utilize Abraham and David in his explanation that the Gentiles are included in the Hebrew Bible's promises, but here he elides Moses altogether. In Gal 3–4 the idea that God gave the law at Sinai appears to be challenged, thereby devaluing its significance. This theological maneuver, while likely grounded in Paul's religious outlook, may have gained further impetus from the strange fact that the gospel spread quickly among Gentiles but was not well received by the Jewish community. An emphasis on the unconditional covenants and especially on God's covenant with Abraham would allow early Christians to link Gentiles to certain of God's promises in the Hebrew Bible, while severing these promises and the early Jesus movement from the vast majority of the Mosaic obligations.

The exilic community's theological response to the events of 587 B.C.E. and that of the early Christian community as found in Paul and the Gospels are attempts to reactualize the biblical heritage each community inherited by productively reexploring the possible implications of certain deep theological tensions in the light of pressing new realities. As will be seen in the final chapter of this book, the early rabbis were also engaged in the task of reevaluating the meaning of Israel's election in the wake of the destruction of the Second Temple in 70 C.E., and their understanding of election theology bears a number of disjunctions from (but also some striking resemblances to) the theology developed by Paul and other New Testament writers.

CHAPTER SIX

ELECTION IN LEVITICUS AND DEUTERONOMY: LAW AND HOLINESS

In order to further unpack the connections between promise, covenant, and election, it will be useful to briefly explore ancient notions of law and holiness and their relationship to the concept of election. Some of the most developed reflections on this topic can be found in the Priestly writings in the Pentateuch as well as in the book of Deuteronomy. While these two schools of thought have much in common, there are also substantial differences in their religious worldviews. These two unique views of Israel's theological self-understanding came to serve as the basis for further unfoldings of the notion of election that developed in the later biblical and postbiblical periods.

Turning to the Priestly corpus,[1] some elements of the Priestly school's view of Israel's election have already been discussed in passing, but not as part and parcel of the larger Priestly theology. Thus, most scholars attribute a number of the promise passages throughout Genesis (e.g., Gen 17:15-22; 28:3-4; 35:11-12) to the Priestly writers. And several covenantal texts, including the first biblical covenant made between God and Noah (Gen 9:1-17) as well as one version of the second divine/human covenant made between God and Abraham (Gen 17), come from this school's hand. However, as one can gather from even a cursory reading of the Pentateuch, these promise and covenant texts reach fruition only after the people of Israel are redeemed from Egypt and accept the fuller covenantal relationship with its extensive set of commandments that God offers Israel at Mount Sinai.

Although conducting a detailed analysis of the Priestly legislation is beyond the scope of this survey, an overview of the Priestly concept of election can be gleaned by outlining this school's view of holiness and its understanding of Israel's covenantal responsibilities toward maintaining such holiness. In the Priestly literature Israel is told time and again to maintain a state of holiness (Lev 11:44; 19:2; 20:26). The concept of holiness in the Hebrew Bible cuts across the Western dichotomy of the spiritual versus the material. One's physical state has implications for one's spiritual state and vice versa.[2] A spirituality that is distinct from the body and the material world, a widespread idea today, is difficult, if not impossible, to find within the Hebrew Bible. Similarly, there is little evidence in these pentateuchal texts for a dichotomy between what today we call ritual versus moral behavior. Thus, maintaining a holy state involves both body and spirit in adhering to God's commandments—commandments that involve civil, criminal, ritual, and moral dimensions of life. Leviticus 19 opens with the command that Israel be holy like God, and within this chapter one finds legislation from each of these spheres.

In Priestly texts, Israel is commanded to be holy because the most holy God lives in proximity to the people of Israel (Num 35:34; Ezek 20:41). Israel's failure to maintain the proper level of holiness will eventually cause God to abandon his dwelling place, the Israelite shrine or temple, thus leaving Israel vulnerable to attack from external forces (Ezek 8–11).[3] Through maintaining a proper state of holiness, Israel continues to be protected by the divine presence that abides in her midst (Pss 46; 48).

In the Priestly theology, Israel functions as a mediator for God's holiness by creating an environment in which the Deity will become manifest. This requires that Israel construct a shrine and its utensils according to a precise model revealed by God to Moses (Exod 25:9, 40; Num 8:4).[4] It also necessitates that various ritual procedures be executed correctly. God's environment was affected not only by the actions or inactions of various cultic officials, but also by any Israelite who even accidentally committed a breach of the laws of holiness.[5] On this basis ancient Israel recognized and accepted a type of communal responsibility that held individuals culpable, at least at some level, for the misdeeds of other Israelites. Israel was held communally accountable for maintaining a fit environment in which God could manifest himself and through his presence on earth radiate blessing to the whole terrestrial world. Maintaining the proper environment entailed three basic responsibilities:

1. The community as a whole was obligated to make every attempt to avoid behavioral lapses that might result in polluting themselves, their land, or God's sanctuary. This vigilance included being watchful of even accidental lapses.

2. If a breach occurred, the community as a whole must first determine what offense was committed and then identify the sinner who committed it, if at all possible.

3. They must make sure that every breach is atoned for properly. This may require a sacrificial act, a fine, a confession, or some combination of these. In more severe cases it requires the removal of the individual offender from the group by either excommunication or execution.[6]

The rationale behind this elaborate system is summed up quite nicely by the following quotation:

> One becoming impure as the result of an offense against the deity introduced a kind of demonic contagion into the community. The more horrendous the offense, the greater the threat to the purity of the sanctuary and the surrounding community by the presence of the offender, who was a carrier of impurity. This person required purification if the community was to be restored to its ritual state, which, in turn, was a precondition set down by the resident deity for his continued presence among the people. The deity had made a vital concession to the Israelites by consenting to dwell amidst the impurities endemic to the human situation (Lev. 16:16). If his continued residence was to be realized, YHWH required an extreme degree of purity (Exod. 25:8).[7]

When the purity of God's environment was violated, it could lead to a swift and severe reaction by God against the individual offender (Lev 10:1-7) or sometimes against the nation as a whole (Josh 7). This was not an arbitrary punishment.

> There is a reason for YHWH's wrath. It was not mere displeasure at being disobeyed. His wrath was a reaction based on a vital concern, as it were, for his own protection.[8]

From a Priestly perspective, Israel's election is quite literally an election for divine service. The people of Israel living in the land of Israel become responsible for maintaining the proper environment for God to dwell among them (Num 35:34). In this theology, Israel protects the

Deity from offenses to his holiness, yet in so doing, Israel, and by extension the entire world, enjoys God's presence and the blessing that accompanies it. Israel's special calling involves a profound amount of commitment and self-sacrifice. While requiring Israel to maintain her distinction from the other nations of the world, her enforced separation is beneficial to the world as a whole.

Here is another instance in which one finds distinctions among the elect. Although all Israel is responsible for keeping a heightened level of purity (meaning both moral and ritual purity), there are indeed gradations of holiness as one approaches closer to the divine presence. Thus, one finds a ring-like structure in Priestly texts in which God occupies the holy of holies, with the high priest at the next level of holiness. Then come the other priests who work in the sanctuary, followed by the Levites who maintain, move, and guard God's sanctuary. Finally, one has the other Israelite tribes along with anyone else residing in the larger area of God's holy presence, which suffuses the land of Israel. It should be noted that P's scheme reflects elements of election theology found elsewhere in the Bible. While all Israel is chosen, at times certain Israelites are specially designated for leadership positions. Thus, the high priest here is akin to the figure of Joseph in Genesis, Moses in Exodus, or Samuel and David in 1–2 Samuel. While in some respects this scheme is hierarchical and exclusionary, in other ways it is quite inclusive. Since holiness is a quality Israel must maintain, even aliens living in the land are included in aspects of the legislation (Lev 17:15-16; 19:33-34). Certain P texts appear to permit something akin to conversion. Exodus 12:48-49 goes so far as to permit a resident alien to participate in the communal Passover ritual as if he were a native Israelite, as long as he and the males in his family are willing to be circumcised.

Those who describe P's hierarchical and exclusionist tendencies in purely negative terms tend to overlook certain very positive features of this theology. Firstly, the Priestly writers of the Hebrew Bible did a great deal to democratize various theological ideas. Thus, Lev 19 begins with a call for *all the congregation of the people of Israel* to be holy as God is holy. Now every Israelite must maintain not only a higher level of ritual purity but also higher standards of behavior toward one another and toward those in the immediate orbit of the Israelite community because they live in close proximity to the divine presence (Lev 19:9-18, 33-34). Furthermore, it may well be that the heavy emphasis within various strata of the Hebrew Bible on Israel's responsibility to care for the poorest and most marginalized elements of their own society flows from an idea that P highlights. There is a widespread awareness in the ancient Near East that the king was especially charged with maintaining and protecting the rights of the disenfranchised, such as widows and orphans (2 Sam 14; Ps 72:12-14). The king is considered God's representative on earth and thus he, like God, is obligated to protect the weak and the poor. It seems possible that once Israel came to see herself as a royal nation this awareness carried in its wake the notion that every Israelite was now responsible to care for the dispossessed within their society.

Even more important is the fact that the P school produced the most important biblical basis for guaranteeing the fundamental dignity and uniqueness of each human being. This is the notion that all humans are created in the image of God (Gen 1:27; 5:1; 9:1-6).[9] Inasmuch as all humans are created in God's image, when one treats another person with dignity one honors God, and when one degrades another human being one damages the divine image (Prov 19:17; 17:5; Matt 25:31-46). P develops this notion further after the flood, where it is linked not only to the prohibition on murder but also to the recognition that God has a covenantal relationship with all of humanity (Gen 9:1-17). Before labeling Israel's conception of herself as a priestly people distinct from other nations as a regressive and elitist notion that should be rejected, one must reckon with the fact that it was this very feature that yielded Israel's unique insight that Israelites of all societal strata bore responsibility to create a just society and that P is the very author who gave Western civilization the idea that we are all created in the divine image. It seems that P contains one of the deepest biblical expressions of biblical universalism precisely because of his profound insight into Israel's unique identity, not in spite of it. Contrary to the common belief that Israel only develops a sense of universalism through a weakening of her particularistic identity, here (and elsewhere in the Hebrew Bible as will be seen later in this book), universalism is found in a text that affirms Israel's unique sense of chosenness.

Election in Deuteronomy

When one looks at the concept of holiness and Israel's self-understanding of her election in Deuteronomy, one finds a somewhat different picture.[10] The most important distinctions include the following: much less emphasis on the role of priests and Levites and much greater cultic participation by laypeople, the allowance of non-sacrificial slaughter, differing rationales for certain central commandments like keeping the Sabbath, the nature of God's presence in the temple, and perhaps most important, the way in which Israel's holiness is described. Deuteronomy makes clear that priests do not function as the centerpiece of Israelite worship, in effect democratizing the cult. Thus, tithes and the offering of the firstborn (Deut 14:22-29; 15:19-23) are shared with clergy but no longer belong exclusively to them for their temple service (as in P=Num 18). While sacrifices are mentioned, they play a much more muted role.[11] Laypeople get a much larger share of them, and profane slaughter is now permitted (Deut 12:8-27). Commandments are sometimes explained in more "humanistic" terms, such as when the observance of Sabbath is grounded in the memory of God's redemption of the people from slavery in Egypt (Deut 5:15), rather than in the cultic imitation of God's rest during creation (Exod 20:11). Deuteronomy prefers to speak of the temple as the place in which God will choose to place his name (Deut 12:5, 11, etc.), possibly an attempt to avoid the more immanent Priestly notion that God might actually dwell in the temple.[12] Finally, the holiness of the people of Israel living in the land makes the land holy, and this holiness is less something the people must strive to attain (as in Lev 19:2) than something that they are inasmuch as God chose them. Thus, the word "כי which introduces both Deut 7:6 and 14:2 suggests . . . Israel is to obey *because* they are the chosen treasure."[13]

Another distinction concerns the status of the land in relation to the people of Israel. In P, the land itself is holy, and it requires those in it to act in proper ways. In Deuteronomy, holiness resides more in the Israelite people than in the land itself. The land becomes holy by virtue of the elect Israelites living in it. Thus, Deuteronomy allows aliens residing in the land to eat carrion, while Leviticus prohibits this (Deut 14:21; cf. Lev 17:15). In P texts, anyone in the land of Israel must observe the most basic rules of holiness because the land is holy in and of itself.

A number of scholars, following the lead of Moshe Weinfeld, have described the religious outlook of the authors of Deuteronomy as advocating a desacralizing or even a secularizing and/or humanizing tendency.[14] Others have argued, persuasively in my opinion, that it is more accurate to attribute the shift in Deuteronomy to a differing conception of God and God's holiness.[15] In many ways the spiritual outlook of Deuteronomy is more human-centered, less hierarchical, and more tolerant, yet there are ways in which it is more rigid. Because Deuteronomy sees the people of Israel as a holy people chosen by God, the book draws lines between those who are ethnically Israel and those who are not in much starker ways than one finds in the Priestly texts (in which aliens living in the land are required to observe certain commandments, and if they wish to be circumcised, they can closely join themselves to God's people). While aliens are mentioned in Deuteronomy, evidence suggests that in a number of such passages this refers to dispossessed Israelites from other tribes and not actual foreign-born persons, as the same term implies in Priestly texts.[16] In any case, Deuteronomy is the text most concentrated on wiping out the pre-Israelite inhabitants of the land, and it also contains a list prohibiting certain other foreign groups from joining God's people (Deut 23:4-9, Eng. 3-8). Another interesting point is that while Deuteronomy sees Israel as God's special people, it is much less clear than in P texts what role this people is to play in relation to the larger terrestrial world. Although this at times leads to a kind of ethnic triumphalism (Deut 28:7-14), in fairness, there is room left for other nations to play their legitimate roles in the larger divine drama (Deut 2:1-25).[17] Some texts in Deuteronomy and the Deuteronomistic History appear to go so far as to grant legitimacy to the gods of the other nations of the world (Deut 4:19; 29:25 [Eng. 29:26]; 32:8-9; Judg 11:24). Such passages affirm that the other gods exist, but prohibit Israel from worshiping gods allotted to the Gentiles.

Most important, a number of texts check an easy triumphalism with the admonishment that Israel has not yet lived up to her potential.

> When the LORD your God thrusts them out before you, do not say to yourself, "It is because of my righteousness that the LORD has brought me in to occupy this land"; it is rather because of the wickedness of these nations that the LORD is dispossessing them before you. It is not because of your righteousness or the uprightness of your heart that you are going in to occupy their land; but because of the wickedness of these nations the LORD your God is dispossessing them before you, in order to fulfill the promise that the LORD made on oath to your ancestors, to Abraham, to Isaac, and to Jacob. Know, then, that the LORD your God is not giving you this good land to occupy because of your righteousness; for you are a stubborn people. Remember and do not forget how you provoked the LORD your God to wrath in the wilderness; you have been rebellious against the LORD from the day you came out of the land of Egypt until you came to this place. (Deut 9:4-7)

Here the undeserving Israelites benefit from two factors: the evil of the Canaanites and the meritorious behavior of their ancestors, that is, the patriarchs (cf. Deut 10:15). But this does not mean that Israel is not God's chosen people. In fact, Deuteronomy is one of the biblical books that brings election theology to a new level of sophistication with its psychologically penetrating meditations on various issues connected to the topic (e.g., Deut 7–10). Furthermore, D also helps create a theological vocabulary to name God's favoring of Israel, as demonstrated by D's use of the verbal root בחר (to choose), which is employed to describe God's election of Israel.

In one particularly moving passage from Deut 7 that is excerpted below, God's election of Israel is again linked with his promise to the patriarchs. But here one finds an additional motivation that picks up on Hosea's language of love: God chose the people of Israel because he fell in love with them.

> For you are a people holy to the LORD your God; the LORD your God has chosen you out of all the peoples on earth to be his people, his treasured possession. It was not because you were more numerous than any other people that the LORD set his heart on you and chose you—for you were the fewest of all peoples. It was because the LORD loved you and kept the oath that he swore to your ancestors, that the LORD has brought you out with a mighty hand, and redeemed you from the house of slavery, from the hand of Pharaoh king of Egypt. (Deut 7:6-8)

Here election is grounded in the mystery of divine love. In neither of the two above-cited passages is Israel's election based on her current spiritual state. The notion that Israelites are God's elect but have not yet demonstrated their right to the title by acts of obedience is a nice counterpoint to the Joseph story in which Joseph's tendency to misuse his elect status leads to his suffering but in no way means he is less elect (Gen 39:2-4, 21-23). Deuteronomy's view of election strongly centers on God's grace as well as on Israel's responsibilities to respond to this grace in a way that she has not heretofore. In some sense the blessings and curses found in Deut 28 reflect the two potential outcomes of Israel's election, blessing for obedience and curse for disobedience, with no real middle ground.

One may draw the following conclusions from this brief comparison between the Priestly conceptions of election and those found in Deuteronomy:

1. While the question of Israel's relationship to "the other" will receive extended treatment immediately below in chapters 7–8, one can see a clear contrast in how P and D each define Israel over against non-Israelites. Priestly texts are more inclusive of those non-Israelites living in the land of Israel, although such inclusiveness is double-edged. For those interested in joining themselves to the people of Israel it offers an avenue to participate in Israel's religion, although it is perhaps overstated to say it allows for full conversion. Those aliens and foreigners not interested in Israelite religious practices are still obligated to follow certain cultic rules and regulations as long as they reside in the land of Israel. Whether this general religious approach is called tolerant depends greatly on whether one is speaking of aliens and foreigners who are eager to follow Israelite practice or of those who are forced to abide by such practices even if they personally would have preferred not to observe such rules.

Deuteronomy is less inclusive of foreigners and aliens, but once again, it is difficult to assess if it is more or less tolerant of foreigners in its religious outlook. By excluding them it also excludes aliens residing in the land of Israel from having to observe purity-based regulations. It also appears to offer less space for foreigners to integrate themselves into the Israelite community. However, unlike P, Deuteronomy explicitly admits that at least some other peoples have a relationship to God, and it appears to legitimize a multiplicity of human religious systems.

2. Priestly texts conceive of holiness as something humans continually need to strive to attain. Israel may be chosen, but she is not automatically holy by the simple fact of election. These texts prescribe behaviors and link these behaviors to the call for Israel to become holy. Thus, Lev 19 opens with a call to become holy followed with instructions on how one does this, and Lev 20:22-27 proceeds to do the same in reverse order. By contrast, Deuteronomy sees all Israel as elect and thereby as holy by divine fiat (Deut 14:1-2). The task of the Israelites is to avoid engaging in behavior that might bring punishment to God's already holy people.

3. Both P and D are attempts to construct an ideal Israelite society, and they spend little energy on questions surrounding the implications of Israel's election for the larger world. Contemporary scholars interested in such ideas must deduce how each theological school might understand Israel in relation to the other nations of the world from texts that do not focus on this issue. With that in mind, one can argue that P views Israel as having a special status that carries with it special obligations, but these

grow out of an implicit assumption that Israel's service benefits the larger terrestrial world. Thus, the people of Israel serve as God's cultic functionaries maintaining his presence on earth. The language used to describe God's choice of Israel is one of holiness and separation but not one that dwells on God's emotional attachment to Israel (Lev 20:24-26).

Deuteronomy's theology appears to lack P's implicit notion that Israel's service to God benefits all nations. However, this may be explained by a number of factors. There is some evidence that the book was produced as the platform for Josiah's attempt to declare his independence from foreign interference. If the text did serve to shore up Judean nationalism, this might explain its tendency to focus more squarely on the implications of God's election for Israel as a nation. One should keep in mind that it may have been this deep concern with reforming and reinvigorating Israel's religious heritage that led the authors of Deuteronomy to engage in a very extended and probing meditation on the concept of election in which the love images employed by Hosea are explicitly linked to the notion of God's election of Israel (Hos 1–3; Deut 7:6-8; 10:15). Furthermore, Deuteronomy's movement toward democratizing the cult and the book's possible hesitancy to employ P's conception of God's presence in the temple may have involved a rejection of the notion that Israel's service helped maintain the cosmos. It may be that D's theology sees Israel's service in terms of Israel being an exemplar of true rather than idolatrous worship of God (Deut 4:6-8). In any case, whatever superiority Israel might have, according to Deuteronomy, stems not from Israel's behavior, but from a mysterious divine choice that is grounded in God's love for Israel and her ancestors. Deuteronomy's whole tone suggests an Israel chastened by her failures.

4. Both P and D affirm God's relationship to non-Israelites, but in distinct ways. P not only stresses that *all* humans are created in God's image but also develops the idea that God made a covenant with *all* of humanity after the flood. D, on the other hand, explicitly recognizes that God has allotted territories and even other deities to non-Israelites.

5. P and D represent two different streams of covenantal theology. P tends to stress the notion that God separated Israel from the nations for a divine service that carries in its wake benefits for the larger world. Deuteronomy perceives election as something grounded in God's mysterious love for Israel, without regard for any service she is to perform for the nations. In many ways, these two theologies of election are woven together into a new unity within Deutero-Isaiah (Isa 40–55), a text that

will receive much attention in chapter 9, "Prophecy and Election." This prophet of the exile (along with his counterpart Trito-Isaiah=56–66), who puts tremendous emphasis on the idea of Israel's election, regularly speaks of God's unfailing love for Israel (Isa 49; 54; 62). This, combined with the strong use of language that speaks of God's choosing Israel (Isa 42:1; 43:1; 44:2), is surely a further heightening of Deuteronomy's election theology. At the same time Deutero-Isaiah regularly pictures Israel's election as having implications for the larger terrestrial world (Isa 42; 49). This outward-looking view of Israel's election may well be a heightening of P's notion of Israel as a priestly nation. Interestingly enough, the centerpiece of Deutero-Isaiah's theology is a notion that both P and D affirm: in spite of Israel's failings that resulted in her exile, she remains God's chosen people (Lev 26:43-45; Deut 4:25-31; Isa 43).

Introduction to Chapters 7–8

Israel and the Other

Israel's chosenness raises a host of complex issues about Israel's understanding and treatment of non-Israelites. While this topic has been broached in passing in earlier chapters, it is fraught with complexity and therefore deserves extended discussion. Thus, the next two chapters are dedicated to a careful analysis of the status of non-Israelites within various legal, narrative, and so-called historical texts drawn from the Hebrew Bible. This particular discussion sets out to clear up numerous widespread misperceptions concerning the implications that Israel's election has for "the other." A brief preface to the topic is in order before launching into the detailed textual discussions contained within the next two chapters. This will provide the reader with an overview of the wider scholarly conversation surrounding this aspect of election theology and in the process elucidate some of the major confusions and misunderstandings raised by certain recent interpreters.

In particular, a number of contemporary thinkers, secularists as well as Jewish and Christian scholars, have issued a forceful call to repudiate the idea of chosenness because, so they claim, such an idea inherently leads the elect to devalue and ultimately maltreat those not belonging to the chosen group.

> As a way of working out and consolidating one's religious identity, the wholesale slaughter of people (whether in *herem*, crusade, or *jihad*) is exactly what it seems to be, no more and no less. The pressure that builds up naturally in the idea of election is here unleashed, and the idea is given its fullest expression. The Conquest tradition is the primary

> expression and fulfillment of the idea—the *Urtext*. The biblical idea of election is the ultimate anti-humanistic idea.[1]

Thus did Jeremy Cott, in an article published more than two decades ago, starkly pose the dilemma faced by anyone who seeks to use the Bible as a moral and spiritual guide today. How can one possibly maintain that the conquest tradition, which relates that God called for the annihilation of every Canaanite man, woman, and child, is an authoritative part of Scripture on a par with other items such as the Ten Commandments or the story of the exodus? The logic behind Cott's statement, at first blush, seems quite compelling. Its central premise, which almost all contemporary theologians and biblical scholars would endorse, is that genocide is morally wrong and could not be a practice decreed by God. Furthermore, the command to commit genocide appears to conflict with other basic biblical concepts, such as the notion that the biblical God is a just God, not one who punishes the innocent along with the guilty. Building on the premise that genocide is morally unacceptable, Cott argues that not only are the conquest tradition and the idea of Israel's election interrelated, but that the slaughter of the Canaanites prescribed in the conquest tradition is in fact the culmination of the notion of election. If Cott is correct on this latter point, one must reject not only the conquest tradition but also the idea of Israel's election.

While Cott is to be commended for looking at some of the most troubling biblical texts in an unflinching manner, a number of his assumptions are problematic; moreover, those assumptions appear to have become accepted premises in other recent scholarly treatments of Israelite religion. The central problem with Cott's thinking is its assumption that election theology inherently leads to destructive violence directed against those not elected. Cott explains this tendency by referring to modern psychological notions about insecurity and scarcity: "The problem of election . . . is the problem of scarcity, the sense that there is not enough to go around. By scarcity we mean insecurity."[2] In his view, election theology is an outgrowth of the most primitive human instincts.

The essential components of Cott's argument have recently reappeared in the highly popular book by Regina Schwartz, *The Curse of Cain*. Like Cott, Schwartz asserts that Israel's election spells violent destruction for all non-Israelites: "The Other against whom Israel's identity is forged is abhorred, abject, impure, and in the 'Old Testament' vast numbers of them are obliterated."[3] Schwartz also attributes the rise of such ideas to an immature and dangerous psychological process that should be outgrown and abandoned. Reprising Cott's terminology, she writes, "The very idea that identity is constructed 'against' suggests scarcity, as though there were a finite amount of identity itself, and so a space must be carved out for it and jealously guarded, like finite territory."[4] Other recent scholarship has also associated the notion of Israel's election with a violent and intolerant attitude toward all non-Israelites, grounding this assertion less in psychological than in sociological and ideological terms. Thus, Gerd Lüdemann asserts that "as Israel is the holy people, chosen by YHWH, it must totally avoid contact with other peoples; political neutrality and religious tolerance are excluded."[5]

The problem with this line of thinking is that it fails to recognize that ancient Israel's exclusivism did not generally lead to the idea that all those excluded should be annihilated. Cott, Schwartz, and Lüdemann seem unaware that the Israelite idea of election presupposes three rather than two categories: the elect, the anti-elect, and the non-elect. The elect are God's chosen people, Israel. The anti-elect are those few groups who are deemed to be enemies of God and whom Israel is commanded to annihilate. Texts that mandate Israel's behavior toward the anti-elect pose a serious challenge to any biblical theologian or scholar and will be treated in detail in chapter 7. But if one hopes to understand what Israel's election theology implied for non-Israelites, one must recognize that most texts that affirm Israel's elect status view the vast majority of foreign individuals and nations as members of the non-elect rather than the anti-elect. These non-elect peoples were always considered fully part of the divine economy, and in a very real sense, Israel was to work out her destiny in relation to them, even if in separation from them. The failure by certain recent scholars to distinguish between the non-elect and the anti-elect leads them to misunderstand and ultimately to reject the notion of election on false grounds.

This is not, however, to say that such scholars utterly reject the biblical vision of relations between Israelites and non-Israelites. All three of the above-mentioned scholars recognize that many texts in the Hebrew Bible treat foreign individuals and nations with great tolerance, but they tend to attribute such texts to an alternate stream of Israelite religion that rejects the idea of Israel's special election. Thus, Cott argues "that there is, in biblical religion, a distinct theology of the stranger that is, in spirit, the exact opposite of the idea of election."[6] Furthermore, there is a tendency to blur the biblical distinction between the non-elect and the anti-elect by measuring all biblical texts on a scale ranging from "inclusive" to "exclusive," associating inclusivism with a tolerant universalism and exclusivism with an intolerant particularistic nationalism.[7]

Although this whole way of conceiving things is flawed,[8] here my concern is to demonstrate that both those texts that are labeled as "exclusive" as well as those regarded as "inclusive" flow from the particularistic notion of Israel's election. Texts dealing with the non-elect, which will be examined in chapter 8, display a broad spectrum of attitudes ranging from the more inclusive to the more exclusive. Furthermore, it is not always easy to discern which texts are ultimately more tolerant. This is so for two reasons. First, texts that are more inclusive are rarely as inclusive as those who hold them up as models claim. Even when such texts speak favorably of certain outsiders, or at times go further and permit specific individuals or groups to attach themselves to Israel, they continue to assert that God has indeed specially chosen the people of Israel. Second, the more exclusive texts are not always as intolerant as those who vilify them suppose.

Cott, Schwartz, and Lüdemann assess various biblical passages from a modern political and psychological viewpoint, but they utterly fail to reckon with the larger biblical framework in which those passages are set. If we are to make fair judgments about the biblical idea of election and what it implied about the treatment of aliens and foreigners, we must address these issues in the larger context of the theology of Israel's election. Treating the texts in a holistic fashion ameliorates some aspects of the most morally troubling texts, those that call for the annihilation of the anti-elect. While such texts remain problematic, a fuller understanding of their place in the Israelite theology of election reveals that they are of some religious value.

Thus, the task of the two following chapters will be a modest attempt to bring some much-needed clarity to the question: How did Israelite culture conceive of and treat non-Israelites? In order to do justice to this rather complex topic, I will devote chapter 7 to the treatment of the anti-elect and chapter 8 to the treatment of the non-elect.

CHAPTER SEVEN

THE ANTI-ELECT IN THE HEBREW BIBLE

The most difficult problem raised by the concept of election in biblical literature is not the issue of why some are elect and others are not, or of how the elect and non-elect should interact with each other, but the notion that certain individuals, families, groups, or nations constitute a category best labeled "the anti-elect." The anti-elect include those who are viewed as so evil or dangerous that warfare against them may include a call for their annihilation, as well as either the destruction of their livestock and other possessions or the dedication of these items to the Deity. Although the statement by Cott (quoted in the introductory remarks above) grievously misconstrues the biblical notion of election by erasing the category of the non-elect and assuming that all non-elect people are anti-elect, it forces the reader to acknowledge a set of deeply troubling texts in the Hebrew Bible. While I intend to argue that a variety of factors ameliorate some of the problematic aspects of these texts, they remain troubling for those in the Jewish and Christian traditions.[1] On three points, however, I part company with Cott, Schwartz, Lüdemann, and others who make similar arguments. First, I believe that the relevant texts deserve a more sympathetic reading; second, although a more sympathetic reading cannot erase all of the troubling aspects of these texts, the call to jettison the concept of election by linking it solely to these troubling texts is equally problematic; and third, later Jewish tradition has found ways to tame and defang such texts even while retaining the integrity of the canon.

Three groups of people in particular fit my definition of the anti-elect in the Hebrew Bible: the Amalekites, the Canaanites, and less obviously, the Midianites. The last group is clearly on the margins of the category of the anti-elect. The Midianites are often portrayed positively in the biblical text, and according to certain sources, Moses' father-in-law is himself a Midianite (Exod 2:15-22; 18:1; Num 10:29; but cf. Num 12:1 and Judg 1:16; 4:11). Other passages number the Midianites among Israel's potential enemies, although not among the anti-elect (Gen 37:36; Judg 6–7). In Num 25 and 31, however, the Midianites incur treatment reserved elsewhere for the anti-elect. Thus, in Num 31 Israel executes the Lord's vengeance by combating Midian (Num 31:3), and while all things Midianite are not initially destroyed, eventually all humans, except for virgin women, are killed. Furthermore, the treatment of captured animals and plunder resembles the policies of the sacral warfare practiced against the Canaanites. One difference in Israel's policy toward the Midianites that distinguishes it from the anti-Canaanite polemic, is that the decree of war against the Midianites is phrased as retaliation for a specific Midianite wrong against the Israelites (Num 31:16). This justification for Israelite hostility toward Midian recalls the justification for Israel's enmity toward the Amalekites (Deut 25:17-19), a group that will receive attention further below. Thus, the evidence for the anti-elect status of the Midianites is inconclusive. Not only does the Bible contain conflicting testimony about the treatment of the Midianites; even the harsh treatment meted out to them in Num 31 is not a clear-cut indication that they have joined the anti-elect, for some Midianites are spared. Although in certain texts the Midianites are treated in ways resembling the anti-elect, this group's ambiguous status within the Bible makes it a poor case on which to ground a comprehensive discussion of the anti-elect.

Israel's Anti-Canaanite Polemic

The largest set of texts dealing with a group of anti-elect people centers upon the numerous passages that describe the elimination of the Canaanites. While much of the book of Joshua is devoted to these matters, biblical passages relevant to the Canaanite problem appear in Deuteronomy, Judges, and elsewhere. These texts pose serious issues for any interpreter who wishes to argue that the models of conduct endorsed by God in the Hebrew Bible should indeed shape our moral universe.

Certain mitigating factors, however, must be kept in mind as one seeks to understand these challenging texts. First, even the harshest texts are more nuanced and ambiguous than some would concede. Thus, while Josh 10 implies that all Canaanites were eliminated in one fell swoop, all Canaanites were not in fact killed. Not only do Rahab and her extended family survive (Josh 2), but so do the Gibeonites (Josh 9), as well as other groups (Josh 13:1-7; 16:10; 17:12-13). Furthermore, within the text of Joshua itself the rules of warfare are modified. In Josh 6, all enemy property is to be destroyed or dedicated to God, but in Josh 8:2, the people are permitted to keep some of the spoils. Lawson Stone has argued that the redaction history of Josh 1–12 indicates that later tradents, likely unaware that these accounts were more fiction than fact, were so troubled by this rhetoric that they softened the anti-Canaanite polemic. These tradents added the occasional notice to explain that the Canaanites were only annihilated because they rebelled against God and failed to sue for peace (see Josh 11:19-20).[2]

Amid these accounts of Israelite behavior toward non-Israelites, an Israelite household, Achan and his family, are treated like the anti-elect once they violate God's rules concerning warfare (Josh 7). The fact that many Canaanites are not destroyed while some disobedient Israelites are executed supports Lori Rowlett's assertion that the book of Joshua is primarily concerned not to maintain ethnic boundaries but to create communal order by stifling dissent during a period of instability.[3] In other words, ethnicity does not exclusively determine who belongs to the anti-elect and must therefore be annihilated.

Of course, Joshua is not the only text in the Bible to comment on the problem of the Canaanites. Passages in Genesis portray the Canaanites in somewhat more positive terms. These texts provide an alternative model in which Canaanites live side by side with Israelites.[4] In Gen 34, for example, Jacob criticizes his sons Simeon and Levi for their behavior when they kill all the inhabitants of Shechem in retaliation for the rape of Dinah, their sister. And in Gen 23 and Gen 38,[5] Israelites and Canaanites interact peacefully.

More important yet is that textual as well as archaeological evidence indicates that the Canaanites were probably never purged in a genocidal campaign by Joshua. The early chapters of Judges concede the Israelites' failure to drive out the native population, and the Deuteronomistic History as well as texts like Hosea and Jeremiah attribute the downfall of both Israel and Judah to the fact that they adopted various forms of illicit worship practiced by the natives they failed to eliminate. The archaeological evidence does not support, nor do any of the theories current among contemporary critical historians accept, the mass destruction of Canaanites by Israelites as advocated repeatedly by Deuteronomy and described frequently in Joshua.[6] Many scholars endorse some form of the peasant revolt model proposed by George Mendenhall and elaborated by Norman Gottwald and assume that the majority of ancient Israelites were themselves the descendants of Canaanites.

That these narratives have little basis in actual history does not mean that they can be dismissed as unproblematic. Biblical texts that contain a rationale and a program for something akin to genocide still demand a reckoning, even if these ideas were never fully actualized in the biblical period. Such texts continued to enjoy authority in religious communities, and there have been times throughout history when members of those communities have appealed to Scripture for the authority to marginalize, dispossess, and sometimes annihilate certain groups. For example, Heinrich Bullinger (1504–1575), a Swiss Reformer, cited biblical precedents when justifying the right to fight an all-out war to defend true religion against idolaters: "The magistrate of duty is compelled to make war upon men which are incurable, whom the very judgement of the Lord condemneth and biddeth to kill without mercy. Such were the wars Moses had with the Midianites, and Josue with the Amalechites."[7] William Gouge (1578–1653), an English Calvinist, turned to the same source to justify war against Catholics: "Papists are to Protestantes as Amalekites to Israelites."[8] That Native Americans were also at times figured as Canaanites certainly contributed to their harsh mistreatment. Thus, Cotton Mather, in his "Soldiers Counselled" (1689), speaks of the Native Americans as "Amalekites annoying this Israel in the wilderness"; such rhetoric would be reinvigorated in the following century, when the Native Americans became allied with French Catholics, themselves viewed as the Antichrist.[9]

The long shadow cast by the biblical anti-Canaanite polemic on subsequent history cannot be lightened, and a plain-sense reading of these texts indicates that God seems to have endorsed genocide on certain occasions. But it is essential for a biblical scholar to evaluate the biblical text in its own historical context, uncolored by its career in postbiblical history. The question that remains is this: If these anti-Canaanite texts are more imaginative than historical, as the literary and archaeological evidence suggests, why did ancient Israelite thinkers generate and continue to be preoccupied by such ideas? One explanation is that texts that call on Israel to kill all the Canaanites were likely produced during a period of instability and powerlessness. Some regard these texts as a legacy from the time of Josiah's attempted reformation and believe that they were designed to propagate a newly unified sense of identity during a politically insecure period, and were possibly addressed to members of the Israelite community whose dissent could threaten a fragile order.[10] Others think that these texts may represent an exilic attempt to comprehend Israel's failure to maintain possession of the land that, according to tradition, it had received from God. Alternatively, this harsh rhetoric might have arisen among the exiles as a strategy for maintaining Judean social and religious identity by constructing that identity in contrast to either the Babylonians among whom the exiles lived or the Judeans who were not removed from the land.[11]

The Amalekites as the Demonic Other

Perhaps even more troubling than the anti-Canaanite polemic are the texts that deal with the Amalekites (Exod 17:8-16; Deut 25:17-19; 1 Sam 15), the enemy whose demonization in biblical literature left a lasting impress on the Jewish religious imagination. While some have compared the anti-Canaanite polemic to certain Nazi policies, no biblical text ever advocated the pursuit and slaughter of Canaanites who lived outside Canaan or fled its bounds. The condemnation of the Amalekites, however, is phrased in terms of a cosmic battle between Israel's God, YHWH, and Amalek that will last throughout time (Exod 17:14-16). Furthermore, the fact that the evil Haman, the mortal enemy of the Jews in the book of Esther, is textually and genetically linked to Agag, the king of the Amalekites (see Esth 3:1; 1 Sam 15:8), may hint that even if this enemy appears outside the land of Israel, he is to be destroyed. Thus, unlike the anti-Canaanite polemic directed solely against Israel's neighbors in the land, the condemnation of Amalek acquires within biblical tradition an aura that may vaguely recall certain features of genetically based Nazi racism, even though Israel's policy toward Amalek falls far short of Nazi policies and has an altogether different character.

Later streams of Jewish tradition preserve some elements of this troubling idea even while other parts of the tradition attempt to mitigate it.[12] In the Passover Haggadah one finds the following statement: "For it was not one man only who stood up against us to destroy us; but in every generation they stand up against us to destroy us, and the Holy One, blessed be he, saves us from their hand."[13] Although their response is not completely rational, even today many Jews strongly identify with the feeling that the various groups who have persecuted them over the last several thousand years are somehow akin to one another. This sentiment has to some degree been reinforced by the Shoah (Holocaust). After all, Haman's hatred of the Jews and the reasons he gives to the king for their destruction (Esth 3:1-11) sound uncannily similar to much anti-Semitic rhetoric in its postbiblical and more modern forms.

The recycling of elements of biblical anti-election theology, while troubling, also helps to reveal why those elements appeal to the religious imagination and how they function within it. Fundamentally, the idea of Amalek is an attempt to make some theological sense of recurring historical evils. While such theologies are potentially dangerous, they also serve a purpose by helping communities survive and explain troubling historical events. In Judaism, the theological idea that massive historical evils perpetrated by individuals and groups who harbor an irrational hatred of Jews and Judaism are part of a larger cosmic pattern has helped the community make sense of tragedies and thus continue to survive. Christianity, too, has preserved elements of the theology of the anti-elect, which it received through late biblical apocalyptic prophecy, where the elect and the anti-elect are set against each other in mortal struggle on a cosmic scale. In fact, such dualistic apocalyptic notions were absorbed more readily by early Christianity than by rabbinic Judaism, and ancient Christianity in turn appears to have bequeathed this powerful notion to Western civilization, where it remains active even today. Such ideas, while rightfully disturbing, should not simply be dismissed as some primitive holdover. Although the notion of the anti-elect contains a demonic potential, it is essential to recognize that the same notion expresses a profound religious yearning for God's justice to prevail over evils so irrational that they seem demonic.

Jewish Attempts to Mitigate the Theology of the Anti-elect

In conjunction with this presentation of the major texts and issues that embody the Hebrew Bible's notion of the anti-elect, as well as some factors that might mitigate its harshness, it may be of some use to see how postbiblical Jewish thinkers dealt with this disturbing idea. In fact, elements of arguments that I have advanced above were already formulated in texts from antiquity. The following passage from the Wisdom of Solomon demonstrates that by the second century B.C.E., ancient exegetes were troubled by the annihilation of the anti-elect and sought ways to make ethical sense of this idea:

> Those who lived long ago in your holy land you hated for their detestable practices, their works of sorcery and unholy rites, their merciless slaughter of children, and their sacrificial feasting on human flesh and blood. These initiates from the midst of a heathen cult, these parents who murder helpless lives, you willed to destroy by the hands of our ancestors, so that the land most precious of all to you might receive a worthy colony of the servants of God. But even these you spared, since they were but mortals, and sent wasps as forerunners of your army to destroy them little by little, though you were not unable to give the ungodly into the hands of the righteous in battle, or to destroy them at one blow by dread wild animals or your stern word. But judging them little by little you gave them an opportunity to repent, though you were not unaware that their origin was evil and their wickedness inborn, and that their way of thinking would never change. For they were an accursed race from the beginning, and it was not through fear of anyone that you left them unpunished for their sins. (12:3-11)

Here one finds a list of atrocities committed by the Canaanites that justifies their eventual destruction. This passage also contains an interesting attempt to explain a tension within the anti-Canaanite polemic: that although the Canaanites deserved to be destroyed, they were not all killed at once. Wisdom of Solomon attributes this delay to an act of divine mercy that allowed them time to repent, thus softening the harshness of their later annihilation. Immediately afterward, however, the passage turns back from the topic of God's mercy to the question of Canaanite behavior and adds a new element, the notion that the Canaanites were inherently evil. The text introduces this idea by alluding to Gen 9:20-27, which identifies Canaan and his descendants as the ones who received Noah's curse and perhaps also Ham's predisposition to sexual immorality. Wisdom of Solomon is clearly pursuing a variety of strategies to ameliorate the ethical qualms raised by the troubling notion of the divine command to annihilate the Canaanites. Some of these exegetical and interpretive moves are in tension or even in contradiction with others. On the one hand, the Canaanites are demonized, thus justifying their immediate extermination. On the other hand, God mercifully delayed their destruction in order to give them time to repent. Thus, the conflicted text reveals that at an early stage, ancient interpreters were already disturbed by the moral problems raised by the killing of the Canaanites and sought ways to mitigate or resolve those problems.

Jewish thinkers continued to wrestle with these troubling texts, and important streams of later Jewish tradition substantially softened the anti-Canaanite and anti-Amalekite polemic. Consider the following statement from the great Jewish philosopher Moses Maimonides (1135–1204):

> In a war waged against the seven nations or against Amalek, if they refuse to accept terms of peace, none of them is spared, as it is said: "But of the cities of these peoples . . . thou shalt save alive nothing that breathes" (Deut 20:16). So, too, with respect to Amalek, it is said: "Blot out the remembrance of Amalek" (Deut 25:19).[14]

In this short passage, Maimonides, building on midrashic antecedents,[15] creatively (mis)reads the biblical text and interprets it to mean that even the Canaanites were offered a chance for peace and were only annihilated if they failed to surrender. Furthermore, he moves Amalek into the same category as the seven Canaanite nations, thereby allowing that they may be spared too. Other streams of Jewish tradition resolve the moral problem posed by the command to kill the Amalekites by reading it in a spiritualized fashion, as a call to eradicate evil from the world or as an indication that humans must resist their own evil impulses.[16] These post-biblical traditions demonstrate that even while the Jewish and Christian traditions grew out of and appropriated the Hebrew Bible, they often subdued problematic elements of the biblical tradition through a variety of interpretive strategies. This is not to say that later Jewish and Christian traditions contain only statements that ameliorate these troubling texts. It does mean, however, that neither Judaism nor Christianity simply inherits and utilizes the biblical text in uncritical fashion. This process of critically appropriating and reshaping tradition has its roots in the biblical text itself.[17] Over time, the theology of the anti-elect was thus tempered to a large degree.

Concluding Reflections on the Bible's Anti-elect Theology

None of the above arguments, however, should be taken to indicate that the call for the destruction of the anti-elect is, on a deeper reading, no longer morally and religiously problematic. Even if one could argue decisively that such texts were never actualized in Jewish history, one must acknowledge that the genocidal aspects of these texts do at times bear an uncomfortable resemblance to racialist ideologies and at times they have been cited to justify group persecutions. While one must not sidestep the truly disturbing nature of these texts, I would argue strongly against taking what some would see as the next logical step, that is, abandoning the concept of Israel's election. As Cott indicates in the quotation that opened the "Introduction to Chapters 7–8," some believe that the notion of election inherently and inevitably leads to "the wholesale slaughter of [innocent] people."

But there are two problems with this assertion. First, it is not at all evident that the anti-Canaanite polemic must *of necessity* be actualized in history just because it is part of Scripture. This is true in the biblical period, in which textual and archaeological evidence strongly suggests it was never fully actualized and may not have been actualized at all, as well as in later Jewish tradition, for many Jewish exegetes were morally troubled by the theme of the destruction of the anti-elect and sought to limit its potential for harm. Second, even if the notion of election and the anti-Canaanite polemic are sometimes linked in the biblical text, it is dubious to assert that the anti-Canaanite polemic is either the most central feature of the theology of Israel's election or the inexorable consummation of that theology. In a great number of biblical texts, the notion of election recurs without occasioning the call for a holy war against the anti-elect, or anything like it.[18] More important, as we will see in the following chapter, the same theology of election that sometimes called for the wholesale destruction of the anti-elect elsewhere gave rise to some of the most sensitive ideas concerning the treatment of aliens and foreigners found anywhere in the ancient world. Election did not simply imply that every non-Israelite was doomed for destruction. Far from it. The vast majority of non-Israelites are better labeled the non-elect, and they often assumed a very important and positive place in Israel's understanding of the divine economy. It is to this group that we now turn our attention.

CHAPTER EIGHT

THE NON-ELECT IN THE HEBREW BIBLE

The previous chapter on the anti-elect has demonstrated that harsh treatment was indeed prescribed for some non-Israelites (as well as certain Israelites like Achan in Josh 7), and that even if some of the relevant passages may be more mythic than historical, the Hebrew Bible contains ideological components that resonate with the modern war crime of genocide. These facts might lead one to assume that ancient Israel's strong sense of group identity led her to mistreat anyone outside the group. Yet this is not at all the case. Rather, the Hebrew Bible presents an exceedingly complex set of views on the way Israelites relate to those who are best referred to as the non-elect. This term enables us to identify the large set of individuals, groups, and nations who are neither members of the people of Israel, God's elect, nor are they counted among those who are utterly beyond the pale of divine and human mercy in the Israelite imagination, the anti-elect.

The non-elect are treated in a host of passages, sometimes in ways that are troubling, but often in ways that are surprisingly positive. In fact, many non-Israelites serve as moral models to ancient Israel. Furthermore, positive images of "the other" found in certain biblical passages are frequently held up as exemplars for the proper treatment of "the other" today. While the relevant texts vary in their portrayals and descriptions of the legal status of non-elect individuals and groups, there is no warrant for arguing, as do Cott, Schwartz, and other recent writers, that the least exclusivistic of these passages are opposed to or have transcended Israel's particularistic theology of election. Rather, the biblical spectrum of views on the treatment of non-elect outsiders, ranging from the more inclusive to the more exclusive, developed out of and remains deeply connected to Israel's sense of her own election. One cannot take a shortcut through these theological problems by associating election with certain passages that treat "the other" negatively and disassociating it from those that treat "the other" positively, for these are two sides of the same coin. When one grasps that all of these texts are expressions of Israel's theology of election, it soon becomes clear that many of the more exclusive passages are not as intolerant as they first appear, and many of the more inclusive passages are not as tolerant as some believe.

The Non-elect in Legal Texts

Take, for example, the Hebrew Bible's view of individual resident aliens. Often they receive positive treatment, as evidenced in many narrative and legal contexts. But more interesting is that one sometimes finds this to be the case even in places where one might least expect it. Not a few scholars of the various legal corpora in the Hebrew Bible have argued that the Priestly groups responsible for large portions of the Pentateuch and Ezek 40–48 were highly ethnocentric and intolerant of non-Israelites.[1] And yet one finds the following text in the midst of the P corpus:

> When an alien (גר) resides with you in your land, you shall not oppress the alien. The alien who resides with you shall be to you as the citizen among you; you shall love the alien as yourself, for you were aliens in the land of Egypt: I am the LORD your God. (Lev 19:33-34)

And while Deuteronomy stresses the necessity of annihilating the native inhabitants of the land of Canaan, it includes pointed injunctions to love resident aliens and to guard their rights (Deut 10:19; 24:17-22). Special protection for resident aliens appears in Israel's oldest legal code, the Covenant Code (Exod 22:20 [Eng. 22:21]), where such protection is also linked to Israel's experience of what it means to be in such a vulnerable position.

A similar complexity surrounds the status of certain foreign nations that Israel might be expected to treat in the harshest possible manner. For example, it seems quite logical that a nation like Egypt, which enslaved and oppressed the Israelites for a long period of time, would be treated with special contempt. But surprisingly, one finds in Deut 23:8-9 (Eng. 7-8) a call for the Israelites to recognize that the Egyptians once played host to the Israelites and thus deserve a minimal level of kindness in return. Similarly, the book of Deuteronomy warns Israelites to respect the borders of Edom, Ammon, and Moab, nations that were not infrequently Israel's enemies or the allies of her enemies (2 Kgs 3; Pss 83; 137; Obad 1), because Israel's God had assigned these lands to them (Deut 2:1-20).

Clearly, the texts that deal with the non-elect are far from systematic; biblical books that from our modern Western viewpoint are at times quite positive toward certain aliens and foreigners seem quite regressive in other ways. Although such tensions can sometimes be attributed to a divergence in the sources behind the current text, in other examples a single source tenders divergent opinions. Thus, the Priestly author of the Holiness Code (Lev 17–26), while showing intense deference to the rights of resident aliens as indicated by the command to love them (19:33-34), makes clear that distinctions remain between true Israelites and resident aliens (25:39-48). Similarly, within Ezek 40–48, a set of exilic or early postexilic Priestly additions to the book of Ezekiel that many see as relatively unified, one finds a passage that inveighs against the admission of foreigners to the temple precincts (Ezek 44:5-9), and yet another that provides for the allotment of land to resident aliens and their treatment as natives (47:21-23). In Ezra, a postexilic text generally viewed as among the least tolerant and most exclusive books in the Hebrew Bible,[2] a passage such as 6:21 (cf. 2 Chr 30:18-19; Neh 10:29 [Eng. 10:28]) seems to leave a loophole by which certain outsiders wishing to join God's people may be admitted.

Readers of the Hebrew Bible must consider a number of particulars if they hope to gain a fair understanding of how foreigners and aliens were treated within its world. First, several different Hebrew terms are applied to non-Israelites, and even a single Hebrew word may carry distinct meanings in different contexts, or may change in meaning over the long historical period during which the biblical text assumed its canonical form. Aside from the word גר, frequently translated as "resident alien," the following terms also occur: תושׁב, "temporary resident" (Gen 23:4; Lev 25:35; Num 35:15); זר, "strange person," which can denote a non-priest (Num 3:10, 38), a non-Levite (Num 1:51; 18:4), or more generally, a non-Israelite (Isa 1:7; Jer 5:19);[3] and נכרי or בן נכר, "foreigner" (Deut

17:15; Exod 12:43). In addition, many other non-Israelites are identified by their ethnicity. Some are more closely related to Israel through geography or (imagined) ancestry, while others remain much more distant kin in the Israelite imagination.[4]

Christiana van Houten has made a plausible case that the biblical term גר slowly evolved as it moved from its earliest uses in Exodus through its later uses in Deuteronomy and Leviticus:

> The laws dealing with the alien developed and became more inclusive. What began as an appeal for justice for the alien in the Covenant Code (Exod 23:9) comes to be understood as a legal principle in the Priestly laws: "There shall be one law for the alien and the native born." This then opened the door for the inclusion of the alien into all the rights and privileges of Israelite society. . . . Although this tendency has not been perfectly linear, it is still possible to conclude that the alien who began as an outsider and an object of charity has come to be included, if willing, among the people of Israel.[5]

The Non-elect in Narrative Texts

One must bear in mind that narrative materials present a variety of portraits of foreigners unmatched by the legal corpora; a number of these portraits are remarkably positive toward certain foreign individuals or groups. Some of these passages raise the possibility that certain foreign-born individuals or groups could be more easily integrated into Israelite society than comparable legislative texts suggest.

Foreign figures who are treated with great respect include, among others: Melchizedek, king of Salem (Gen 14:17-20); the pharaoh who ruled during Joseph's lifetime; the daughter of the succeeding pharaoh, who saves Moses' life (Exod 2:5-10); Jael, wife of Heber the Kenite, who kills Israel's enemy Sisera (Judg 4); Hiram, king of Tyre, who facilitates Solomon's construction of the Jerusalem temple (1 Kgs 5); the Queen of Sheba, who testifies to Solomon's wisdom and Israel's great fortune (1 Kgs 10); the widow from Zarephath, who shelters Elijah (1 Kgs 17); Job, the wise and righteous man from the East; Cyrus, king of Persia, who conquers Babylon and decrees the return of the exiled Judeans to their land (Isa 45:1-4; 2 Chr 36:22-23); the non-Israelite sailors in Jonah's boat who pray, sacrifice, and make vows to the Lord (Jonah 1:14-16); and also the inhabitants of Nineveh, moved to sincere repentance by Jonah's words

(Jonah 3). Sometimes foreign individuals, clans, or groups are closely attached to or even merged with the people of Israel. Among these are such well-known figures as Rahab the Canaanite (Josh 2); Ruth the Moabitess; Reuel, Jethro, or Hobab the Midianite, who becomes Moses' father-in-law (Exod 2:16-22; 18:1-12; Num 10:29-32; Judg 1:16); and other, perhaps less familiar, figures such as Uriah the Hittite (2 Sam 11–12) and Naaman, the Aramean general, who worships the God of Israel though remaining a resident of Aram (2 Kgs 5).

All of these texts belie the widespread assumption that Israel's sense of her own election inherently led Israelites to express contempt for the non-elect peoples. Indeed, a number of texts in the Hebrew Bible appear to be challenging Israel to recognize that the non-elect often have much to teach the elect about how one should act in the world and serve God. Moreover, several of these characters are juxtaposed to Israelites who are shown to be sorely lacking. Thus, Naaman is set against Gehazi, Elisha's greedy and disobedient servant; the intoxicated Uriah is implied to have more sexual self-control than does the sober King David; and Abimelech, king of Gerar, appears to be more pious and God-fearing than Abraham (Gen 20). Through these contrasts, the narrators of the Hebrew Bible call into question the idea that one can enjoy the status of the elect without fulfilling the responsibilities of the elect, or that the non-elect cannot act in accord with God's will.

Perhaps even more interesting is that several non-Israelite characters in the Hebrew Bible actually articulate God's saving actions to the sometimes erratic and unfaithful Israelites. Furthermore, at least on one occasion, a non-Israelite delivers a set of stunning affirmations of Israel's election and its implications for Israel and her enemies. Thus, characters like Jethro, Rahab, and Naaman (Exod 18:10-11; Josh 2:9-11; 2 Kgs 5:15) all proclaim the unique power of Israel's God in contexts in which at least certain Israelites seem to doubt God and his saving abilities. Perhaps most unusual is Balaam, a foreign prophet hired by Balak the Moabite king to curse Israel. Instead of delivering curses, Balaam prophesies four separate oracles, each highlighting aspects of Israel's specially elect status. Here a non-Israelite notes that Israel is a unique people not like the other nations of the world (Num 23:9), a nation who is blessed with an irrevocable blessing (Num 23:19-23), a people that will triumph against its mortal enemies (Num 24:8, 17-24). The fact that Israelite texts employ non-Israelites in this unusual fashion suggests that Israel is aware that certain non-Israelites may have greater insight into God's plans for Israel than many Israelites do. Far from being derogatory toward outsiders, these texts indicate that Israel needs the theological insight of non-Israelites to help her realize her unique status and fulfill her destiny.

Questions Surrounding the Assimilation of Foreigners

As briefly noted above, a number of the narratives surrounding certain non-Israelites raise the complicated question of conversion. It is difficult to discern whether it was possible for a non-Israelite to join the people of Israel in the biblical period, because the terms involved in such an analysis are themselves slippery and problematic. Clearly, it would be wrong to speak of conversion to Israelite religion as an open possibility for much of the biblical period.[6] Shaye Cohen has argued at length that the whole notion of Judaism as a religion probably developed in the Hellenistic era at the earliest.[7] Before this time, Jewish identity was marked by ethnic or tribal affiliation rather than a religious affiliation. When we speak of conversion today, we presume an abstraction called a "religion," comprising a series of beliefs connected to particular practices, an abstraction that did not exist during much, if any, of the period of time described in the Hebrew Bible. Thus, groups—such as the Gibeonites (2 Sam 21:1-14)—and individuals—such as Uriah the Hittite—who sought to attach themselves to the Israelite people in antiquity frequently maintained their foreign identities. It seems possible that, on the individual level at least, total assimilation might indeed occur over several generations, as children grew up and married Israelites. The notice concerning Rahab's family in Josh 6:25, however, suggests that some groups of foreigners remained ethnically separate even while living among the people of Israel. Thus, in many instances it is more accurate to speak of individuals or groups attaching themselves to God or God's people rather than using the term "conversion" and all that it implies.[8]

A related issue is whether such assimilation was easier for foreign women seeking to join ancient Israel than it was for foreign men. While rabbinic Judaism eventually developed a matrilineal system in which the mother determined the religion of the child, there is substantial evidence that, in ancient Israel, the religion of the father and husband may have been determinative for the status of the family unit as a whole. Thus, the patriarchs all marry Mesopotamian spouses; Judah marries a Canaanite woman (Gen 38:2); Joseph, an Egyptian named Asenath (Gen 41:45); and Moses, a Midianite or Cushite woman (Exod 2; 18; Num 12). Although never clearly stated, it appears that the text views all of these women favorably, perhaps suggesting that they obtained Israelite credentials simply by marrying an Israelite man. Later, Ruth the Moabitess marries an Israelite man and gives birth to King David's ancestor, in spite of the prohibition in Deut 23:4-7 (Eng. 3-6). Furthermore, the legislation in Deut 21:10-14 permits Israelites to take brides from among the women captured in war; and in the account of the blasphemer in Lev 24:10-23, he is introduced as the son of an Israelite woman and an Egyptian man. This individual is referred to not as an Israelite, but as the son of an Israelite woman, perhaps revealing that he was not actually part of the people of Israel. These passages indicate that the progeny produced by an Israelite man marrying a foreign woman could be considered fully Israelite while those of an Israelite woman intermarrying with a foreign man might not be.

The objection can be raised that a number of texts condemn the practice of Israelite men marrying foreign women, including Exod 34; Deut 7; 1 Kgs 11; Ezra 9–10; Neh 13; and Prov 1–9. There are many possible explanations for the tensions between texts that appear to condone or endorse marrying foreign women and those that unconditionally condemn the practice. One solution is that these divergent passages come from different times, and that authors of earlier texts were, on the whole, more open to the assimilation of foreign women than were the authors of later texts. Another possibility is that these tensions reveal a heated religio-political debate about Israelite identity, a clash between those who advocated a more liberal view of Israelite identity and those who advocated a stricter construction. One unusual nuance is that the book of Deuteronomy contains some of the strongest prohibitions against foreign marriage (Deut 7:1-6; 23:2-9 [Eng. 3-8]), and yet this same book permits marriage between Israelite men and captive women (21:10-14). One might argue that Deuteronomy never intended that this legislation be applied to the Canaanites, who are singled out for destruction in Deut 7, but rather to enemies living outside Canaan. But it is harder to believe that the author would not have envisioned marriages between Israelites and Ammonite and Moabite captives, given the frequent battles between these peoples and Israel.[9] The rabbis resolved the possible contradiction between the laws of Deuteronomy that prohibit marriage to an

Ammonite or a Moabite (Deut 23:4-7 [Eng. 3-6]) and the narrative of Ruth's marriage to Boaz (Ruth 4) by arguing that the text in Deut 23 applied only to males, inasmuch as it uses the masculine grammatical form.[10] It is not impossible that the rabbis' solution may have fleshed out the actual intent of the law and that, as suggested above, women from the non-elect nations could indeed assimilate more easily than males from those same nations.[11]

Yet another possible explanation for the apparent tensions over the legitimacy of marriage between Israelites and non-Canaanite foreign women is that while the authors of Deuteronomy and the Deuteronomistic History recognized the legal right of Israelite men to take foreign captives as brides and thus developed regulations for the practice, they also had serious reservations about taking foreign brides in other circumstances, particularly in the case of politically motivated marriages between Israelite kings and foreign women. This would explain the prohibition against the king who would "acquire many wives" (Deut 17:17), as well as the criticism directed toward Solomon, who did just that (1 Kgs 11). After all, in the minds of the authors of Deuteronomy and the Deuteronomistic History, precisely this custom of sealing foreign alliances by marriage, a custom espoused by Ahab as well as by Solomon (1 Kgs 16:31-33), led to the cardinal sin of cultic syncretism.[12] It may be that this condemnation of royal behavior was extended to the general populace in the postexilic period by Ezra (9–10), Nehemiah (13), and the authors of Prov 1–9 for a variety of possible religio-political reasons, which I list here briefly, in anticipation of further discussion below. Perhaps the community was now more vulnerable to external cultural forces; perhaps marrying foreign women may have increased the divorce rate among the returnees, thus threatening social stability (Mal 2:10-16) and possibly also Judahite control over the temple; perhaps the Persian government wished to consolidate its provincial political control within a well-defined ethnic group; or perhaps those returning from exile either wished to achieve political control or felt that they alone had remained true to the religion of their fathers.[13]

Grappling with Exclusivist Passages

In any case, it should now be clear that the biblical evidence for the treatment of aliens and foreigners in ancient Israel is highly complicated and requires more nuanced treatment than it usually receives. Reckoning with this complexity is made more difficult by the frequent scholarly propensity to place the relevant texts into a simplistic schema that values each text in proportion to its conformity to our Western notions of pluralism. Thus, as noted above, it is now quite commonplace in the critical literature to find assertions that texts like Ezra 9–10 and Neh 13 represent the most ethnocentric passages in the Hebrew Bible. These texts are frequently associated with a Second Temple priestly party affiliated with the groups that produced the final editions of Leviticus and Ezekiel. Texts such as Isa 56 and Ruth supposedly represent a more inclusive strand of the tradition. And between these poles lies Deuteronomy, which contains both tolerant and intolerant passages.

Such schemata tend to distort the texts and do a disservice to those seeking to understand each passage within its context. Texts such as Isa 56 and Ruth may be more inclusive than Ezra and Nehemiah, but they are far from universalistic or non-ethnocentric. While 2nd and 3rd Isaiah will receive extensive discussion in the following chapter, "Prophecy and Election," Schwartz is surely correct when she likens Isa 56 to the book of Ezra: "However narrowly or broadly conceived, Ezra and Isaiah are bent on delimiting community, and whenever a 'people' are circumscribed, someone is left out."[14] Indeed, Ezek 40–48, a text often aligned with Ezra and Nehemiah as advocating a narrow definition of Israelite identity in contrast to the "more tolerant" Isa 56, may embody a much broader definition of Israel. As H. G. M. Williamson notes, the book of Ezekiel as a whole sees Israel as the union of many factions: those who went into exile and those who stayed behind, those from Judah and those from the north. This "view of Israel as the single people of God"[15] is in marked contrast to the position taken by 2nd and 3rd Isaiah, whose "Israel" denotes either just the exiled community or the subset of this community who remained true to YHWH (along with those few Gentiles who might join this remnant community). The truth is that not only does Ezek 40–48 envision a larger group of native Israelites in its vision of the ideal community, but as noted above, it too permits resident aliens to join this community even while excluding foreigners (Ezek 47:21-23; 44:5-9).

Just as some contemporary scholars exaggerate the inclusive tendencies of texts like 3rd Isaiah, so do some scholars misrepresent texts like Ezra and Nehemiah, evaluating them in the harshest possible terms and displaying little sympathy for those confronting the historical situation described in the texts. Thus, D. J. A. Clines is "outraged at Ezra's insistence on racial purity, so uncongenial to modern liberal thoughts."[16]

Going even further, Lüdemann declares that "the Nazis shamelessly directed ideas which were similar to those developed by Jews under Ezra and Nehemiah."[17] A cursory look at the relevant texts might lead one to sympathize with Clines's and Lüdemann's utter revulsion at Ezra's marriage policies, although their attempt to equate them with modern racism or, worse yet, with Nazism is grossly unfair. On closer examination, however, the responses of Clines and Lüdemann are not only anachronistic; they also do an injustice to the complexity of the historical situation faced by figures like Ezra and Nehemiah. Biblical thinkers, the authors of Ezra and Nehemiah among them, did not utilize modern notions of ethnicity and race at all. To equate Ezra's policies with Nazism obscures the fact that Ezra's and Nehemiah's ideas were not racially motivated and that neither ever advocated anything even slightly resembling the Nazis' systematic annihilation of certain ethnic groups. Their agenda was light-years away from genocide. They were not trying to eliminate a threatened minority. They were trying to preserve a threatened minority.

When we raise the question of the exact nature of the historical situation faced by Ezra and Nehemiah, it becomes clear that statements like Clines's and Lüdemann's fail to reckon with how enigmatic these texts are and how little scholars actually know about their contexts. For example, scholars remain divided over whether the so-called intermarriage crises that Ezra and Nehemiah faced were in fact identical. Nehemiah 13 is more likely dealing with the threat of intermarriage between Israelites and foreigners; Nehemiah himself is disturbed to find Tobiah "the Ammonite" living in the temple compound while Israelites are marrying women from Ashdod, Ammon, and Moab (Neh 2:10; 13:1-14, 23-31).[18]

The case of Ezra is more ambiguous primarily because of questions surrounding the meaning of Ezra 9:1-2 and 10:44. Determining the precise significance of Ezra 9:1-2 is difficult for several reasons. To begin with, these verses are themselves attempting to make sense of a variety of possibly conflicting pieces of biblical legislation (Deut 7:1-6; 23:4-9 [Eng. 3-8]; and possibly Lev 18; 19:19; with imagery drawn from Isa 6:13) by combining them in a new way that likely subverts at least the plain meaning of Deut 23:8-9 (Eng. 7-8).[19] Some have argued that the grammar of Ezra 9:1 indicates that the so-called "peoples of the lands" committed abominations like those of the previous Canaanite inhabitants. If this interpretation is correct, the verse refers not to actual Canaanites or to other foreigners, but to Judeans who had stayed behind and/or inhabitants of the territory of the long-extinct northern kingdom.[20] On the one hand, it is reasonable to suppose that Ezra is describing a split between differing groups claiming to be Israel, namely, those who returned from Babylon and others who stayed in the land; on the other hand, the fact that Ezra 9:1-2 includes Ammonites, Moabites, and Egyptians among the "peoples of the lands" who provided brides for Israelites, as well as the identification of those brides as "foreigners" (נכריות [Heb.], 10:14, 17, 18, 44), probably indicates that Ezra is also dealing with intermarriage between Israelites and foreigners.[21]

These difficulties are compounded by the ambiguity of the last verse in the book of Ezra (10:44), which appears to describe how those Judean men who were supposed to separate themselves from their foreign wives and children actually responded to Ezra's pleas. Unfortunately, this verse is so cryptic that interpreters continue to disagree over its content. Some argue that it signals Ezra's success in driving out these unwanted women, while others claim that in spite of Ezra's efforts, the verse reveals that his plan was never implemented.[22]

These literary and historical uncertainties frustrate the interpreter. It is well-nigh impossible to draw moral and theological conclusions about the positions reflected in the books of Ezra and Nehemiah without a clear picture of their socio-historical situation. For example, scholars have long disagreed about whether Ezra indeed reached Judah before Nehemiah did, as the canon asserts. In fact, matters are so murky that some wonder whether "Ezra is indeed a historical person and not merely a fictional priestly double of Nehemiah."[23] The cryptic nature of the texts and our ignorance of the history of the period render any attempt to place these texts in their socio-historical context extraordinarily hypothetical.

This very lack of knowledge has enabled certain other scholars to paint a much more sympathetic portrait of Ezra and Nehemiah as they confronted the intermarriage crisis. For example, Joseph Blenkinsopp points out that economic factors may very well have aroused Nehemiah's concern over marriages between priests and non-Judean families. He observes that because "daughters could in certain circumstances inherit, exogamous marriage could lead to alienation of family property."[24] Furthermore, Blenkinsopp notes that too frequently scholars neglect the "point that Nehemiah's religious measures were part and parcel of a larger objective, namely, the survival of a *people*."[25] And Williamson contends that texts like Mal 2:10-16 may indicate that the offending marriages took place after certain returnees divorced their original wives, perhaps in an attempt to boost their social standing in their new place of residence.[26]

If Williamson's conjecture is correct, Ezra's and Nehemiah's policy of breaking up such marriages may have been a legal maneuver of last resort to force certain men to take responsibility for their original families, as well as to preserve a struggling community. Daniel L. Smith-Christopher probably goes the furthest of any interpreter in drawing a fully sympathetic portrayal of those biblical figures who took what today is often labeled as an exclusivist stand on issues of community identity:

> To be troubled by what appears to be "exclusivism" on the part of Haggai, or to feel a need to put an acceptable face on the separation of the marriages of Ezra-Nehemiah, is to misunderstand profoundly the nature of group solidarity and survival of minorities.[27]

All of the reconstructions presented above—even those that are less critical of or indeed quite sympathetic toward figures like Ezra and Nehemiah—share one curious feature. Each implies that while Ezra's actions may be justified by a sociological explanation, they were less than ideal solutions to the problems he faced. This comes through quite strongly in Williamson, who makes a valiant effort to rationalize Ezra's actions but ends up labeling them as racist.[28] And although neither Blenkinsopp nor Smith-Christopher says so explicitly, one senses that they see Ezra as choosing a lesser evil, whereas a text like Isa 56 represents a nobler solution altogether.[29] This very point deserves further reflection.

It is likely that during the Second Temple period, the question of who represented the "true Israel" sparked fierce debates. But it is unlikely that *any* party to those conversations would have denied that the concept of "Israel" was grounded in familial and corporeal ideas. As I have discussed above, the question of whether it was possible for non-Israelites to join Israel is best phrased not in terms of religious conversion, but in terms of adoption into a tribe. The question of membership in the "true Israel," rather, was reformulated to include issues of behavior and practice. Was a genealogical connection to the Jewish people sufficient to make one part of the elect? Or was only a smaller subset of those born to Israel—that is, those who were properly observant and pleasing to God—truly elect?[30] At this time, the already ancient notion of a "remnant" began to influence the theology of election in important ways;[31] such thinking eventually gave rise to certain currents in early Christian theology (e.g., Rom 9:6-8, 27; 11:2-5).

Those who wished to limit membership in the people of Israel, either by excluding individuals of Israelite birth who were thought to have fallen away into sin or by preventing outsiders from assimilating through marriage or some other means, did not necessarily act out of malice toward those excluded from Israel.[32] Rather, groups advocating either of these views were attempting to preserve the integrity of the elect so that they could function as God's priestly people. They believed that if Israel failed to maintain sufficient obedience within her own ranks to the divine imperatives she had received, or if Israel became a homogeneous mixture of elements from several nations, God's wider purpose in electing Israel would have been defeated.

Christian Exclusionary Rhetoric

It is true that Christians, on the basis of certain prophetic texts that speak of a possible change in the relationship between Israel and the nations in the eschaton, eventually came to believe that God called Gentiles as well as the physical descendants of Abraham, the Jews, to join the people of God.[33] However, even these early Christian understandings defined community in ways that would be considered equally intolerant by the standards of modern universalism. Modern Christian scholars like Blenkinsopp and Williamson ultimately judge Ezra's and Nehemiah's response to the crisis of intermarriage as a necessary evil that could be remedied only by the advent of Christianity and its receptivity to converts. Yet a number of early Christian authors cite Ezra approvingly as they define their own communities in exclusionary terms. In the Christian case, this exclusion is less genealogical in orientation. Nevertheless, Christian exclusionary rhetoric has the similar effect of labeling nonbelievers as morally and even ritually tainted and of banning marriages between Christians and nonbelievers, although in one famous passage, such marriages are (with some reluctance) permitted to continue if they were initiated before one partner became a Christian (1 Cor 7:12-16).

Thus Jerome, in discussing a New Testament passage that he believes prohibits Christians from marrying heathens (2 Cor 6:14–7:1), actually cites Ezra's exclusivism as a *positive* exemplar: "And Ezra checked an offence of this kind against God by making his countrymen put away their wives."[34] Similarly, Cyprian invokes Ezra in support of Paul's prohibition of marriage between Christians and heathens: "Also in Esdras, it was not sufficient for God when the Jews were laid waste, unless they forsook their foreign wives, with the children also whom they had begotten of them."[35] In fact, early Christians drew a line from Abraham through Ezra to Paul in order to strengthen their arguments against intermarriage, as Christine Hayes makes clear: "Paul and the church fathers are clearly heir to and continuators of a tradition of interpretation that viewed sexual unions across group boundaries as utterly prohibited from pre-Mosaic times and as a desecration or even defilement of that which is most holy to God."[36] Furthermore, it is likely that this prohibition undergirded the Theodosian Code (a Latin compilation of imperial laws promulgated in 438 C.E.), which prohibited Jewish/Christian intermarriage on pain of death (3.7.2).

It is crucial to note that even though Ezra and Nehemiah compare the foreign wives to the sinful anti-elect, they never call for the deaths of those women or of the husbands who betrothed them. But the Theodosian Code does. It is less surprising that ancient Christianity moved in this virulently intolerant manner insofar as its constitution of "the other," unlike the earlier biblical and later rabbinic understandings, usually assimilated all of the non-elect to the category of the anti-elect. This classical Christian propensity to reduce the theological landscape to the binary opposition of elect versus anti-elect (albeit a tendency that grew from the soil of early Jewish apocalyptic texts exhibiting dualistic ideas), along with the modern Christian tendency to ignore how particularistic and exclusivistic early Christianity really was, has continuing effects.[37] It has led many Christian and secular critics to misrepresent Israel's treatment of "the other" and to malign the concept of election in ancient Israel and in Judaism. Once one grants that "non-elect" is not equivalent to "anti-elect" in the conceptual world of the vast majority of texts in the Hebrew Bible, it is possible to see that Ezra's and Nehemiah's exclusion of foreign women is not at all a judgment that such women are damned. Rather, as correctly noted by Blenkinsopp, these marriage policies were an attempt "to maintain the characteristic way of life, the religious traditions, even the language of a community, against the threat of assimilation."[38] Such texts are ultimately animated by the notion that God's larger salvific plan for the world would come to naught if the people of Israel lost their uniqueness.

In sum, while Christian scholars have every right to argue that later Christianity devised a solution to the problem of intermarriage with foreigners superior to that implemented by Ezra, they can do so with integrity only if they acknowledge the following four points. First, rabbinic Judaism itself found a similar way to convert spouses who were seeking to join the people of God. Second, ancient Christianity shunned the unconverted "other" in ways different from, but highly analogous to, those found in texts like Ezra and Nehemiah. Third, Christianity, while appearing to be highly open and tolerant, harbored a strong tendency to consign all nonbelievers to the category of the anti-elect, who would remain damned unless they converted.[39] New Testament texts highlight certain late biblical apocalyptic ideas that erode the distinction between the anti-elect and the non-elect, thus losing sight of the widespread biblical notion that the non-elect could have a positive place in the divine economy on their own terms (Rev 20:15). Finally, early Christians did not see themselves as universalists who accepted all human beings because of their common descent from Adam, but rather as particularists who thought they found in Jesus a new way to link believing Gentiles to Abraham and, through him, to God's elect people (Rom 4). Indeed, eventually the church would claim to be "Israel" itself. This is not to imply that Jews and Christians have identical understandings of election. Chapter 11 below is dedicated to demonstrating the unique ways each tradition adopted the Hebrew Bible's ideas of chosenness. But it does mean that Christians should recognize that those who attack election because it is a particularistic idea that is inherently exclusivistic are attacking a core belief of both Christianity and Judaism.

Concluding Reflections

I hope to have shown that the implications of the Hebrew Bible's notion of election for non-Israelites are considerably more subtle and complex than is often recognized by critics today. In particular, great mischief results when scholars and preachers conflate the Hebrew Bible's understanding of election with the Christian category of salvation, implying that the non-elect are damned. Just as damaging is the equation of the election of Israel with modern racialism—a gross anachronism that cannot withstand critical scrutiny. None of this is to say that election does not pose serious challenges to modern critical interpreters. Clearly, some aspects of election theology are morally problematic and need to be critiqued. However, attempts to marginalize or jettison the idea of election by linking it to a small-minded ethnocentric hatred of those not chosen are intellectually ill-conceived. Such attacks have failed to see that some of the most tolerant and intolerant biblical ideas flow from the same election theology. Furthermore, as will be demonstrated in the next chapter, the highest flights of Israelite universalism are achieved not through a weakening of Israel's particularistic identity, but through a deepening of Israel's sense of her unique identity.

CHAPTER NINE

PROPHECY AND ELECTION

Unsurprisingly, the theology of the prophets, men who regularly cajoled Israel to live up to her deepest calling, is deeply suffused with elective ideas. Various prophetic authors invoke aspects of election theology, often reshaping and developing it along the way. Scholarship has long recognized the important role played by early literary prophets like Amos, Hosea, and Micah in the development of Israel's covenantal theology. Thus, although these early prophets did not work within the framework of the full-blown covenantal theologies that one finds in texts like Leviticus and Deuteronomy, they helped lay the groundwork for many concepts that Leviticus and Deuteronomy (as well as later prophets like Jeremiah) eventually brought together into a larger covenantal theology.

For example, Amos never uses the term "covenant" to describe Israel's relationship to YHWH, yet many rudiments of this concept are present.[1] One only need to call to mind that the use of ידע (to know) in Amos 3:2 almost certainly comes from Near Eastern treaty language.[2] This treaty language would eventually come to have tremendous influence upon the shape of Israel's covenantal theology, especially as it is formulated within Deuteronomy.[3] Furthermore, the way that Amos 4:6-11 describes sending a set of warning punishments in hopes of stirring the Israelites to return to God has a striking similarity to God's actions in Lev 26:14-33.[4] Similar uses of judgment language with strong covenantal overtones can be found in Hos 4 and in the lawsuit language in Mic 6.[5] When one turns to later prophets such as Jeremiah and Ezekiel who draw aspects of their theology from earlier prophets as well as from the thinkers who would eventually produce Deuteronomy and Leviticus, these covenantal tropes become highly developed (Jer 7; 26; Ezek 18; 20).

Inasmuch as covenant and election are frequently intertwined, it should come as no surprise that many prophets also played a pivotal role in the development of Israel's election theology. Early Israelite prophets may have been the first to develop and in any case greatly expanded upon the notion that God's choice of Israel was ultimately grounded in God's mysterious love for his special people. Here one thinks particularly of Hosea, who speaks of God's relationship to Israel in a variety of familial metaphors of love, particularly that of a husband's love for his wife even when she betrays him (Hos 1–3) and of a father's love for his son even when he is disobedient (Hos 11).

These familial love metaphors are returned to and further deepened in many later prophetic books. The prophet Jeremiah, picking up on Hosea's terminology, proclaims: "I remember the devotion of your youth, your love as a bride, how you followed me in the wilderness, in a land not sown" (Jer 2:2). Like Hosea's imagery, the wayward wife imagery at times slides into father and child imagery, such as in Jer 3, which opens with the charge of Israel acting as an unfaithful wife but then shifts to God as father and Israel as his rebellious children (Jer 3:4, 14). This heartrending love language reaches a fever pitch in Jer 31 in which God proclaims his everlasting love to Israel (Jer 31:3). One finds a differing but related use of such familial imagery in Ezekiel, a prophet who depicts Israel's infidelity to her God in graphic or even pornographic terminology (Ezek 16; 23). Ezekiel describes God's permanent attachment to Israel not in terms of God's eternal love and mercy toward his people, but as flowing from the need to prevent his holy name from being profaned (Ezek 36:16-36). Ezekiel is a priest with a highly transcendent understanding of God. While deemphasizing God's mercy and love, Ezekiel heightens the notion of God's unbreakable connection to Israel regardless of how offensive Israel's past behavior has been. Clearly, a prophet's larger theological presuppositions affect the way he expresses his particular theology of Israel's election. Nevertheless, it is difficult to read very far into any prophetic text without finding an affirmation of Israel's elect status. This is true throughout the prophetic corpus down to its closing (Mal 1:2).

One could argue that the trajectory begun in the book of Hosea reaches its zenith in certain oracles from the later chapters of Isaiah generally attributed to an anonymous exilic prophet or prophets. In 2nd and 3rd Isaiah (Isa 40–55=2nd Isa; 56–66=3rd Isa), time and again God declares that his unbreakable relationship to Israel is based on his eternal love for her (Isa 43:4; 54:8, 10; 63:7, 9). At times these texts depict God groping for language that reaches even beyond human love: "Can a woman forget her nursing child, or show no compassion for the child of her womb? Even these may forget, yet I will not forget you. See, I have inscribed you on the palms of my hands; your walls are continually before me" (Isa 49:15-16).

Aside from these familial metaphors, other election-oriented metaphors developed within the prophetic corpus include: farmer and vineyard (Isa 5:1-7; Jer 2:21), sheep and shepherd (Jer 23:1-4; Ezek 34:1-31), potter and clay (Jer 18:1-11; Isa 64:7-8 [Eng. 8-9]), and master and servant (Jer 30:4-11; Isa 41–49).[6] Furthermore, at least one prophetic book, Jonah, contains a narrative that, in part, explores elements of Israel's election theology.[7]

Pressing questions remain over exactly how much these prophetic meditations on election influenced the elective theologies found within the Pentateuch, as well as how much various passages in Jeremiah and Ezekiel drew upon pentateuchal sources. In any case, it is a certainty that by the late pre-exilic period the notion of election was quite pervasive in both prophetic and pentateuchal sources, and on a canonical reading the election theologies of these two collections mutually illuminate each other. In fact, one could argue that had the idea of Israel's election been less developed, the group who went into exile may never have survived the exile intact. After all, belief that God had an unbreakable connection to his beloved people Israel provided hope to the exiles that they would again be restored to their homeland. As one can see from texts like 2nd Isaiah, the idea of election provided much of the rationale for embarking on the long return journey from Babylon to Zion. Unsurprisingly, election theology continued to play a central role in much of the theological ferment that occurred during the Second Temple period.

Tensions Within Prophetic Election Theology

One of the most fruitful ways to illumine the election theology found within various prophetic texts is to examine some of the major tensions within this corpus, paying particular attention to the manner in which modern critical scholarship has dealt with these tensions. As will be seen, contemporary scholars have sometimes misunderstood the biblical text by imposing modern and/or Christian assumptions onto it. Here I will explore three interrelated sets of issues surrounding election theology in the Hebrew Prophets under the following headings: The Scope of Election: Particular or Universal?; Election and the Eschaton: The Nations Inside or Alongside Israel?; and finally, The Purpose of Election: Instrumental or Intrinsic?

The Scope of Election: Particular or Universal?

As noted in the introduction to this book, until quite recently biblical scholarship has often uncritically absorbed the strong preference of modernity for all things universal and derided any idea that smacked of particularism. This has led to an unfortunate propensity to highlight any biblical passage that appears to emphasize such universalism, often leading to misunderstandings of such passages as well as doing serious injustice to the vast bulk of the more particularistic material found throughout the Hebrew Bible and the New Testament. This scholarly distortion is evident in discussions of Israelite prophetic texts that were produced over a range of time. Thus, most scholars believe Amos contains the oldest written collection of prophetic oracles from the biblical period, and unsurprisingly, one finds a number of scholars who assert that Amos transcended Israel's particularistic understanding of Israel's election. Of course, others have rejected a universalist reading of this prophet. The debate is framed by the following two passages from Amos:

> Hear this word that the LORD has spoken against you, O people of Israel, against the whole family that I brought up out of the land of Egypt: You only have I known of all the families of the earth; therefore I will punish you for all your iniquities. (Amos 3:1-2)

> Are you not like the Ethiopians to me, O people of Israel? says the LORD. Did I not bring Israel up from the land of Egypt, and the Philistines from Caphtor and the Arameans from Kir? (Amos 9:7)

The first text is an extraordinarily blunt critique of those Israelites who had mistakenly come to understand election as nothing more than a special entitlement. Amos reminds his audience that although the people of Israel have a unique relationship with God, any privilege this entails carries with it a higher level of responsibility. In any case, this text is a critique of certain distorted views of election, albeit one that heightens the particularity of Israel's election.

Amos 9:7 is much more enigmatic. Several recent scholars have argued that in this latter text Amos shatters the notion that Israel is God's only elect people. Thus, Brueggemann's emphasis on God's concern with the downtrodden leads him to assert that the biblical God "is a God who characteristically enacts exoduses, and who does so in many places, perhaps everywhere." Furthermore, he claims that Amos 9:7 shows that "the Exodus memory is left intact for Israel's affirmation, but the exclusiveness between Israel as an Exodus people and YHWH as an Exodus God is broken."[8] Similarly, John Collins makes the following observations about Amos 9:7:

> It is clear from this passage that the Exodus from Egypt was commemorated in the cult at Bethel, against which Amos directed much of his preaching. Amos does not question the Exodus itself, but he radically relativizes it by suggesting that other peoples have parallel experiences. . . . Amos, then, lends no support to particularist Israelite interpretations of the Exodus. His God is the God of all peoples, and is responsible for everything that happens in history.[9]

Each of these interpreters is correct in highlighting the radical language employed by the verse, but their arguments seem overstated when Amos 9:7 is read as part of Amos as a whole, not to mention when it is read in relation to the Bible's larger theological framework, a point astutely made by Levenson.

> But, most importantly, can we be confident that Amos's telling the Israelites that they are (or have become) like other nations is not yet another of his verbal assaults upon them? Elsewhere in the Hebrew Bible, when Israelites become like other nations, they are seen to be failing in their divinely assigned mission (e.g., 1 Sam 8:4-22). Here, too, Amos may be telling his Israelite audience that they are no different from other nations (including the odious Philistines) who have benefited from YHWH's universal superintendence of history and yet fail to recognize him and to honor his moral claims upon them.[10]

Inasmuch as Amos regularly utilizes sharp rhetorical attacks, it seems likely that Amos is calling his audience to behave like God's elect rather than simply saying Israel is mistaken about her claims to be God's special people. Such a reading is supported by the vast bulk of Amos's preaching, which is indignant that the Israelites, a people who have an ongoing relationship with God, have acted so corruptly. In this more likely reading, the apparent contradiction between Amos 3:1-2 and 9:7 is easily explained as representing two differing, but related, critiques of God's wayward people. Thus, Amos, and I would contend other Israelite prophets as well, when faced with possible abuses of the notion of election tended not to discard or denigrate it, but to remind the people of Israel of the fuller meaning of election and call Israel to fulfill her vocation.

The scholarly debate concerning how universalistic or particularistic Israel's prophets were is perhaps most clearly attested in the vast array of scholarship that has been focused on 2nd and 3rd Isaiah. These texts have received extensive attention for a number of reasons, most particularly because Christians link several key passages within these collections to certain central Christian beliefs. These include the notions that certain texts such as Isa 53 foretell the vicarious atoning power of Jesus' death and resurrection, as well as the belief that some verses in these collections authorize Israel (which in Christian terms came to mean the early church) to missionize the Gentile nations. This latter issue, whether these texts ever endorse a call to missionize the Gentiles, will receive attention in this section of our discussion.

In terms of the issue of universalism versus particularism in 2nd and 3rd Isaiah, much turns on how one should go about making sense of two very complex collections of oracles, each of which appears to contain internal tensions on exactly this issue. Thus, even a quick survey of 2nd and 3rd Isaiah reveals some passages that seem quite inclusive and open to foreigners (Isa 42:6; 44:5; 49:6; 56:1-8) and others that proclaim ever more loudly God's special love for Israel in highly particularistic terms that are frequently negative toward the other nations of the world (Isa 40:17; 43:3-4; 60:1-16). While some tensions can be explained by a historical critical approach that argues that 3rd Isaiah may be a composite collection of materials written after 2nd Isaiah, even within the relatively unified 2nd Isaiah there are many dissonant notes. At times the text contains seemingly contradictory exclamations right next to one another. In Isa 45:22, for example, YHWH proclaims: "Turn to me and be saved, all the ends of the earth!" However, the very next verses announce that the whole world not only submits to God, but that the nations who are responsible for Israel's low state will be shamed while Israel triumphs (Isa 45:23-25). In Isa 49:23, foreign kings and queens are described as licking the dust of the former exiles' feet, while in Isa 49:26 the oppressors of Israel are made to eat their own flesh and drink their own blood. Clearly, 2nd Isaiah sees the nations as subservient to Israel as well as to God, but in a manner that seems incompatible with the notion that foreigners and Israelites should benefit equally from YHWH's saving acts (a notion that reflects contemporary concerns for equity in all matters).

There is in fact an extensive scholarly literature that has been generated in trying to make sense of these tensions.[11] Until very recently, almost all of the many arguments employed to explain the textual inconsistencies in Deutero-Isaiah fit into two rubrics.[12] One position maintains that 2nd Isaiah is ultimately a universalist who called for Israel to bring God's word to the heathen nations of the world. In such a reading the more particularistic and nationalist elements that recur throughout 2nd Isaiah are either ignored[13] or played down in one of the following ways. They are understood as remnants of his early ministry,[14] viewed as interpolations from a later, more regressive nationalist writer,[15] or used to prove how difficult it is to transcend one's cultural framework.[16] A second group of scholars argue that 2nd Isaiah is for all intents and purposes a nationalist, not a universalist. In this reading, many universalistic passages are challenged as misinterpretations or qualified by placing them into a larger contextual framework that is heavily nationalistic in tenor.[17] In such a reading, the passages that speak of the nations hearing about or witnessing God's actions are interpreted not as calling for Israel to convert the Gentiles, but as the Gentiles being awed by what God will do for his people Israel.

The same ambiguity occurs in other images throughout 2nd and 3rd Isaiah. When one hears of God's calling to the far parts of the earth, is he calling those nations to him or only indicating that those nations will acknowledge Israel's God and even assist in bringing the exiled Israelites back home (49:1; 51:5; 60:9; 66:19)? When God speaks of his justice or Torah going out to the world (41:1; 42:1, 4; 51:4), is this a positive thing for the nations or a proclamation of divine judgment upon them?[18] Unfortunately, it is difficult to escape the circularity of all such argumentation. Generally, if one assumes the thrust of 2nd Isaiah is universalistic, then such passages seem to vindicate this position. On the other hand, those beginning from a more nationalistic perspective scrutinize these verses, reading them in their larger textual units in which they appear far less universalistic.[19]

The recognition that neither of the two classical arguments about the true nature of 2nd Isaiah's prophecies is likely to achieve a consensus has led to the recent emergence of a third line of argumentation seeking to move beyond the current impasse by qualifying the notion of universalism. Thus, A. Gelston argues that there are three strands in this concept.

> The first is an affirmation that YHWH is the only true God, sovereign over all creation, and therefore over all mankind. The second is that this truth will be recognized by the Gentile nations no less than by Israel, with the corollary that they will submit to him and acknowledge his universal rule. . . . [and the] third strand, consisting of the universal offer of the experience of salvation.[20]

In such a view one may be able to give full due to the more nationalistic and universalistic images, as does D. W. Van Winkle.

> The tension between universalism and nationalism may be resolved by recognizing that for Deutero-Isaiah the salvation of the nations does not preclude their submission to Israel. The prophet does not envisage the co-equality of Jews and gentiles. He expects that Israel will be exalted, and that she will become YHWH's agent who will rule the nations in such a way that justice is established and mercy shown. This rule is both that for which the nations wait expectantly and that to which they must submit.[21]

However, even such views commonly endorse an evolutionary model that rates texts like 2nd Isaiah against a standard that it is assumed all agree upon. Thus, even in his more recent work on the topic Gelston approvingly cites his article from 1965 and proclaims that 2nd Isaiah "discerned in moments of high vision that glorious fact that YHWH's salvation was for all the world, while at others times he sank back to a more traditional and superior attitude towards the Gentiles."[22] It seems relatively clear that regardless of the particular line of argument taken by a given scholar, almost all modern scholarship on 2nd Isaiah assumes that being nationalistic is bad and being universalistic is good.[23] One simply needs to figure out where 2nd Isaiah falls on this scale. Few have stopped to ask whether the use of the term "universalism" might be problematic.

The attempt to fit ancient Israelite texts into the modern conceptual categories of universalism and particularism may impede one's ability to understand these texts in their own historical context.[24] For example, such discussions often assume that universalism is good because it is inclusive and therefore more tolerant of others. Alternatively, nationalism is conceived as bad because it is exclusive and thus by definition intolerant. However, one needs to be aware that a religious tendency toward universalism and inclusion is not necessarily a tolerant attitude. It can lead to a missionary zeal to make all outsiders insiders. Conversely, not every particularistic and exclusivistic image is inherently bad or simply a primitive holdover from the archaic past. One suspects that exclusivistic images so out of favor today may yet be redeemed and put to use more widely again at some future point, or may even be of use today in contexts where groups using the Bible as sacred scripture may be more marginalized or oppressed (mirroring the social situation of the Judean exiles who produced 2nd Isaiah).

More important, as texts from 2nd and 3rd Isaiah demonstrate, ancient Israelites often thought in ways that blur the distinctions between universalism and inclusivism over against particularism and exclusivism. When texts like Isa 56 speak for including foreigners and eunuchs, they are really merging inclusivism with nationalism and particularism. This text is not endorsing a multicultural approach to worship, but rather permitting a select few outsiders who wish to worship with the community to do so; yet doing so requires that they give up their former practices.

The difficulty in using the categories of universalism and particularism in analyzing the biblical text is twofold. First, because ancient Israelites never operated within these intellectual categories, their use is often less than helpful in reaching a clear understanding of various biblical passages. Second, even while many scholars are constantly measuring Israel's success on how far its universalism reached, it remains unclear that universalism so conceived is either a widespread belief today or even a belief that is more defensible than all expressions of particularism. Harry Orlinsky noted more than thirty years ago: "Apart from the fact that it is not the concern of scholarship to deal in judgment value and to mete out awards for backward- or forward- looking views, we tend to overlook all too readily that our own outlook in this area is still virtually identical with that of the Bible."[25] Orlinsky astutely observed that although many moderns believe we live in a world that has surpassed the Bible's moral and political framework, a close look at the world situation actually suggests that we may be more indebted to the Bible than is often acknowledged. Now three decades after Orlinsky wrote, there is a growing sense that national particularisms are something to be cherished, not forcibly overcome by some utopian universalist scheme. Furthermore, while some might disagree with Orlinsky's view that scholarship should never make value judgments, his words are a good caution against the tendency simply to measure the biblical text against our current values. The text must be read in its context, and its value system must be allowed to challenge our values even as we allow our values to challenge the biblical text.

The problematic nature of the dichotomous categories of universalism/particularism has begun to inspire a few scholars to analyze the biblical text on its own terms and to allow its conceptual framework to challenge contemporary values. Levenson's seminal essay, "The Universal Horizon of Biblical Particularism," explores the ambiguous manner in which the term "universalism" is used in the field of religious studies.

> Although some religious traditions may on occasion conceive of themselves as representing or answering to a universal human condition, as a matter of historical fact all religious traditions are particular, since none includes everyone. . . . To be sure, while no religion is universal, some aspire to be. In this sense, a "universal religion" may mean simply one that accepts proselytes, that is, one that is willing or eager to extend its particularity indefinitely. Or it may signify one that is found in a large number of different cultures. In this case, the term "universal" is misleading, since it has not transformed a highly diverse humanity into one universal body. Instead, it has formed symbiotic relationships with various enduring particularisms.[26]

Levenson goes on to argue that "the universalistic thrust of modern democratic, capitalistic societies undermines all particularisms, especially those based on the claim of historical revelation."[27] In other words, the idea of universalism as conceived today is fundamentally incompatible with Judaism and Christianity, religions that make particularistic claims. In Levenson's approach, biblical particularism contains a universal horizon, but this universal horizon is not a new, superior stage of religious faith that supersedes the particularism from which it grew. Rather, this universal horizon is rooted in and continues to draw its nourishment from the soil of biblical particularism. A model such as this one not only explains, but gives positive theological value to the existence of expressions in texts like 2nd Isaiah that seem to be double-edged, containing a universalistic thrust but always maintaining Israel's particularistic election.

Election and the Eschaton: The Nations Inside or Alongside Israel?

Closely allied to the discussion of universalism and particularism is the place of the foreign nations in the eschaton. Certain passages from 2nd and 3rd Isaiah have been at the center of an ongoing scholarly dispute regarding the question of whether the Hebrew Bible ever envisioned a mission to bring God's word to the Gentiles. There has been a propensity by a number of Christian thinkers to read back the Christian notion of mission into the Hebrew Bible and most particularly into various passages from 2nd Isaiah. Walter Kaiser, for example, claims that the idea of an active mission to the Gentiles is widespread in the Hebrew Bible: "The Bible actually begins with the theme of missions in the Book of Genesis and maintains that driving passion throughout the entire Old Testament and on into the New Testament."[28] Others are much more circumspect about mission within the Hebrew Bible at large, with many following the path of thinkers like Rowley who asserts that it is no surprise that 2nd Isaiah "the prophet who most stresses monotheism and its corollary universalism . . . also most stresses the thought of Israel's election and the corollary of that election . . . her world mission."[29] In this view, the Hebrew Bible is not, generally speaking, a missionary document, but certain later texts are fully missionary in their orientation. On the other hand, scholars such as Orlinsky and de Boer remain highly skeptical of the notion that even late biblical texts like 2nd Isaiah endorsed an Israelite mission.

These various assessments grow out of the enigmatic and ambiguous nature of certain verses such as Isa 42:6: "I am the LORD, I have called you in righteousness, I have taken you by the hand and kept you; I have given you as a covenant to the people, a light to the nations." There is no real agreement on the exact meaning of phrases such as לאור גוים, usually rendered as "a light to the nations" (also found in Isa 49:6; 51:4 containing a close analogue לאור עמים, "a light to the peoples"), and לברית עם, sometimes translated as "a covenant to the people" (also found in 49:8). Several layers of problems are inherent in any attempt to discern the exact meaning of these expressions. First, one must determine the actual meaning of certain words. For example, the word ברית in לברית עם is usually translated as "covenant." But Delbert Hillers argues that this word has been mispointed and is actually related to the Hebrew word for soap, בֹּרִית. He demonstrates that a variety of ancient Near Eastern texts contain words that mean "clear, pure, or bright" but function in legal contexts to mean "free or emancipated." On this basis he suggests that the expression לברית עם be translated as "emancipation of the people."[30]

Even when one knows the meaning of a specific word, such as the word עם (nation/people), questions still arise about its meaning in context. Does the singular form עם imply the plural or not? The close proximity to the plural גוים (nations) in Isa 42:6, as well as the fact that in Isa 25:3 the singular עם takes a plural verb, supports those who argue that the singular עם in 42:6 refers to other nations or all humankind. Furthermore, 42:5 has the word עם with the definite article attached and clearly refers to all humans. Nevertheless, the precise meaning of לברית עם in 42:6 remains uncertain. Not surprisingly, translation is often influenced by one's theological stance. The New Jewish Publication Service renders the expression לברית עם "a covenant people," assuming the passage is addressed to the exiled community, whereas the Protestant REB reads "a light for peoples," implying the notion of mission.

Apart from translation issues, these expressions are obscure enough to raise a host of secondary interpretive issues. Do these phrases indicate Israel's mission to the Gentile nations, or are they describing God's relationship with Israel? Given that the larger thrust of 2nd Isaiah focuses on the return of the exiled Judeans to Zion, it is possible that the expression לאור גוים may be conjuring up the image of a beacon sent out to the far corners of the earth signaling to the Israelite exiles that it is time to return to Zion. If so, then the addressee in this passage may be the faithful remnant, the elect of the elect who help reanimate the Israelite nation. Even if these expressions were taken as being addressed to the nations of the world, it is far from certain that they should be read in a missionary way. Perhaps God is doing something with all or part of Israel that is supposed to be witnessed by the now dazzled nations.[31]

While the immense secondary literature suggests that these expressions are ambiguous enough to sustain a variety of interpretations, those who read them in a missionary and universalistic fashion sometimes fail to place these verses within their larger Hebrew biblical context. To gain perspective on this issue, one must contextualize these expressions not only within 2nd Isaiah and the book of Isaiah as a whole, but within the theological universe of the Hebrew canon, rather than importing the later concerns of the New Testament back into this very different setting. Relevant passages that must be considered in such a discussion include:

Isa 2:2-4 and its close analogue Mic 4:1-5; Isa 14:1-2; 19:18-25; 24:14-16; 25:6-7; 42:1-7; 44:1-5; 45:14, 20-25; 49; 51:4-6; 56; 60; 66:18-24; Jer 3:17; 12:14-17; 16:19; Zeph 3:8-10; Zech 2:11-12; 8:20-23; 14:16-19; Mal 1:11, 14; the book of Jonah; and a number of Psalms (e.g., 2; 46; 48; 87; 96; 98; 117).

Here one finds a plethora of images, some of which are in tension or even in contradiction with one another. While texts like Isa 2 are rather irenic, others such as Isa 66 envision a violent upheaval. Some speak of the nations serving Israel (Isa 60), others of Israel or God instructing the nations during a universal pilgrimage to God's temple in Jerusalem (Isa 2; Zech 8:20-23). Certain passages employ hyperbole and thus should not be taken woodenly. Does Ps 117 really mean that all the nations will praise God, or is it the psalmist's call to awaken the congregation to praise God as loudly as possible? A number of passages that mention foreigners coming to Zion are not invoking conversion but rather explaining that the nations will witness God's redemption of Israel (Isa 52:10) or that God will use these foreigners to gather the dispersed Judean exiles and bring them home (e.g., the passage cited immediately below). While foreigners acknowledge (and may even assist in bringing about) God's saving actions on behalf of his people Israel, the Gentile nations are depicted in subservient and humiliating terms.

> Thus says the Lord GOD: I will soon lift up my hand to the nations, and raise my signal to the peoples; and they shall bring your sons in their bosom, and your daughters shall be carried on their shoulders. Kings shall be your foster fathers, and their queens your nursing mothers. With their faces to the ground they shall bow down to you, and lick the dust of your feet. Then you will know that I am the LORD; those who wait for me shall not be put to shame. (Isa 49:22-23)

Of course, there are a few exceptional texts such as Isa 19:18-25 and 66:18-24, which I will touch upon in a few moments.

What generalizations, if any, can one make about the notion of mission in the Hebrew Bible from this array of texts? First, many of these passages contain a transnational thrust, and quite a few reveal a belief in the idea that God's relationship to Israel was part of a larger salvific plan involving the whole world. The exact dimensions of God's larger plan remain enigmatic. For that matter, within the Hebrew Bible the idea of "salvation" implies a corporate restoration rather than the later notion of individuals receiving immortal life.[32] Second, although many of these texts articulate a kind of universalism in which Israel plays a central role in God's plan, it is not at all clear that they call on Israel to engage in missionary activity. Normally, the idea of mission is used in the strong sense of actively proselytizing to bring others to one's own faith.[33] Rather it seems, in the words of Robert Martin-Achard, that in these texts

> the encounter of the heathen and YHWH, effected by the agency of the Chosen People gathered together in Jerusalem, depends upon the divine initiative alone. It is grounded not in any independent intervention by Israel but in a YHWH-theophany. . . . Finally, Israel has no other mission to the heathen than to be the Chosen People.[34]

One text that might endorse human missionary activity is Isa 66:18-19, 21:

> For I know their works and their thoughts, and I am coming to gather all nations and tongues; and they shall come and shall see my glory, and I will set a sign among them. From them I will send survivors to the nations, to Tarshish, Put, and Lud—which draw the bow—to Tubal and Javan, to the coastlands far away that have not heard of my fame or seen my glory; and they shall declare my glory among the nations. . . . And I will also take some of them as priests and as Levites, says the LORD.

Here it appears that it might be Gentiles, not Israelites, who are engaged in declaring God's glory to various other nations who have not yet heard of or witnessed his deeds.[35] Yet even this passage is tempered by 66:20 (albeit a verse that some treat as a later gloss), which emphasizes the role these foreigners play in returning Israelites still in exile to their homeland. Thus, the Hebrew Bible rarely, if ever, endorses an active Israelite mission to the Gentiles.

Of course, the question of Gentiles turning to worship YHWH without human agency is slightly different, and one can find more textual evidence for this idea. Sometimes the nations or the coastlands are invoked as a way of expressing God's cosmic scope, but some passages appear to go a bit further. As noted above, many passages in 2nd Isaiah resemble Isa 45:23 in which the nations witness God's activity on behalf of Israel. In these texts the nations' recognition of Israel's God as the true God is regularly linked to their subordination to God and his people Israel, not their conversion to Israel's religion.[36]

But there are indeed prophetic texts that speak of the nations not simply submitting to, but actually worshiping Israel's God in Jerusalem. Here one thinks of texts like Isa 66:23 or Zech 14:16-19. One often overlooked fact is that while some eschatological texts within the Hebrew Bible do acknowledge the idea of foreigners worshiping Israel's God, and a few such as Isa 56:6-7 and 66:21 may encompass the possibility of certain select foreigners acting as cultic functionaries within the Jerusalem temple, even these passages continue to stress God's special election of Israel, which is paired with his love of Jerusalem, Judah, and the land of Israel (e.g., Isa 66:10-14, 20, 22; Zech 14:8, 17, 20-21). Perhaps the most radical text that speaks of other nations also worshiping Israel's God is Isa 19:18-25, especially the language invoked in verses 23-25.

> On that day there will be a highway from Egypt to Assyria, and the Assyrian will come into Egypt, and the Egyptian into Assyria, and the Egyptians will worship with the Assyrians. On that day Israel will be the third with Egypt and Assyria, a blessing in the midst of the earth, whom the LORD of hosts has blessed, saying, "Blessed be Egypt my people, and Assyria the work of my hands, and Israel my heritage."

As John Sawyer's summary of the history of scholarship on this passage makes clear: "Modern commentators on Isa 19:16-25, from Lowth (1778) and Duhm (1892) to Wildberger (1978) and Clements (1980), are agreed . . . it represents some kind of high point in the Old Testament. . . . [being] 'the most universal and missionary of all Isaiah's prophecies.'"[37] While modern scholarship has been rather enamored of this text, a number of reservations could be raised against such a positive assessment of it. To begin, why should a single isolated passage be held up as the exemplar toward which the faith of Israel was eventually progressing? In the context of the concept of election within the whole of the Hebrew Bible this passage deserves mention, but not pride of place. Historically speaking, much of this passage's appeal among modern critical commentators is due to its strong resonance with Christian missionary work, a type of work that is now implicated in imperialism. Interestingly enough, Christians viewed the spread of Christianity as a sign that this prophecy was fulfilled in spite of the fact that the larger context speaks explicitly of sacrificial worship (v. 21) as well as specifically of Assyrians and Egyptians.

Moreover, while this text shows an openness to foreigners by suggesting the possibility of a future reconciliation between Israel and some of her most ancient persecutors, it does so in ways not altogether unproblematic. Unlike Isa 2:2-4, which speaks of the nations streaming to Zion, this passage's description of others worshiping YHWH may involve an attempt to obscure Israel's movement toward ever more powerful expressions of monotheism. It seems likely that the Josianic reforms in which sacrificial worship was limited to one cult site, while motivated by a complex set of religio-political motives, had the effect of suppressing many forms of fertility and nature worship. Whereas some might see the move away from such forms of worship as a real loss, one can certainly argue that Josiah's centralization of cult worship was part of the long process that gave rise to the higher monotheistic principles that are now enshrined in Judaism, Christianity, and Islam. Since this passage loosens the reins on such centralization, it might be seen as regressive rather than progressive.

Even if one wishes to place great significance on this text, one must note a few of its features. It is not at all clear that Egypt and Assyria are a way of expressing all humanity. Rather, it is more likely that the text is focused on these two historic enemies of Israel who will be brought into peaceful relations with God and his people after they are chastised (Isa 19:16-17, 22). The mention of the highway between Egypt and Assyria may be evoking the image of Jerusalem as the cosmic center of the universe. And most important of all, Israel's particularistic relationship to God is not dissolved, but rather, Egypt and Assyria also gain unique titles affirming that they, too, have a special relationship to God. Thus, Israel's elect status is maintained, and the other two nations are elevated nearer to Israel's level. This highlights one of the most interesting features of the various prophetic texts we have just reviewed: even when they speak of Gentile inclusion, they do so not by eliminating or downplaying the idea of Israel's election, but by continuing to affirm it. In fact, many instances in 2nd and 3rd Isaiah that evoke the nations occur in those places in which Israel's election theology is most heightened. The significance of this point cannot be overstated. Rather than exhibiting the modern dichotomy in which a growing universalism must inevitably spell a waning of particularism, these prophetic texts suggest that a deepening sense of Israel's own particularistic identity as God's elect gives rise to new thoughts about the wider implications of Israel's chosen status.

The Purpose of Election: Instrumental or Intrinsic?

The purpose of Israel's election, a subject previously discussed in relation to other parts of the Hebrew Bible, is also worthy of examination in connection to the prophetic corpus. Indeed, the prophets' understanding of Israel's election has been a matter of theological divergence between Jews and Christians for centuries. Generally speaking, many contemporary scholars, likely uncomfortable with the notion that Israel's chosenness grows simply out of a divine preference for a single group of people, have strongly emphasized the instrumental purposes of election.[38] But often underlying this widespread instrumental understanding of election is also a long-standing Christian supersessionism. As discussed above, Christians regularly cite certain prophetic texts that they believe authorize the elect to spread God's word to the world. This reading is often linked to the claim that because the Jews failed to accomplish the purpose of election, God replaced the old Israel with God's new Israel, the church.

Thus, for example, Rowley proclaims that "Israel's election is for service."[39] He goes on to list three components of this service: cherishing God's revelation found in Scripture, living in a godly way as prescribed by Scripture, and spreading the word of God to all nations. Rowley argues that in each case the old people of Israel, that is, the Jews, have failed. While acknowledging that the church has not fully succeeded in all three of these tasks, he clearly sees the church as God's new Israel, but cautions that it too can lose its election, if like the old Israel, it becomes complacent. "Indeed, any such complacency betokens forfeiture of her election."[40]

Within 2nd Isaiah, the so-called Servant Songs are a particular locus of dispute.[41] The identity of the servant and the role that he is to play is an excellent place to explore questions surrounding the purpose of chosenness. These enigmatic passages have received immense attention, and thus, there have been almost as many proposals as there are scholars working on these texts.[42] Those who understand 2nd Isaiah in more nationalistic terms tend to see the servant as a representation of the people of Israel or perhaps a prophet like Jeremiah whom Israel had failed to heed. Scholars who believe these texts announce a shift in Israelite religion toward a new universalism have read the servant as an anonymous prophet who first reveals the true missionary purpose of Israel's election and is persecuted for doing so. Donald Senior and Carroll Stuhlmueller see an inherent biblical tension between the particularity required by God's election of Israel and God's plan for universal salvation. They argue that the possible resolution to this tension is first introduced within the prophecies of 2nd Isaiah. Although they do not believe this prophet ever explicitly articulated the notion of universal salvation, they view him as the first to link Israel's unique call to the fate of the other nations of the world. Commenting on Isa 49:6, "It is too light a thing that you should be my servant to raise up the tribes of Jacob and to restore the survivors of Israel; I will give you as a light to the nations, that my salvation may reach to the end of the earth," they claim the following:

> This verse not only captured and expressed the intuitions and signals of Second Isaiah's early preaching, but also enabled him to endure the suffering of being rejected by his own people. . . . It extended Israel's election to the world, and *so fulfilled the mission of Israel's being chosen in the first place.*[43]

Senior's and Stuhlmueller's understandings of the notion of election in 2nd Isaiah, while widespread, remain highly problematic. To begin with, it is quite unlikely that these eschatologically charged texts found in 2nd Isaiah ever conceived of extending Israel's elect status to the other nations of the world, as already argued above.[44] In fact, it is theologically incoherent that the very prophet who most stresses God's deep, unbreakable love for his unique people would call on them to dissolve their uniqueness by extending their elect status to everyone in the world.[45] Election by definition requires that distinctions be maintained between God's people and those not elected. The emphasis within these texts upon God's profound and unbreakable love for his people Israel highlights an element often overlooked in discussions of election: the Hebrew Bible resists reducing the meaning of Israel's special election to a matter of divine service (Deut 9:4-7; Jer 31:1-20). If one links election too strongly to service, it is impossible to understand why God restores Israel from exile. The answer, of course, is that in spite of Israel's failures she remains beloved by God:

> For your Maker is your husband, the LORD of hosts is his name; the Holy One of Israel is your Redeemer, the God of the whole earth he is called. For the LORD has called you like a wife forsaken and grieved in spirit, like the wife of a man's youth when she is cast off, says your God. For a brief moment I abandoned you, but with great compassion I will gather

> you. In overflowing wrath for a moment I hid my face from you, but with everlasting love I will have compassion on you, says the LORD, your Redeemer. (Isa 54:5-8)

This intrinsic value of Israel's election is highlighted when one relates the servant passages to a larger canonical understanding of election. A comparison with the biblical story of Joseph is especially apt, for there are striking resemblances between these two texts. In the servant passages and the Joseph narrative there are three basic categories of people: the elect of the elect who receive special attention within each text, those belonging to the larger elect group but not specially chosen, and the other nations of the world. In the Joseph story the elect of the elect is, of course, Joseph himself, while in 2nd Isaiah it is the Israelite person or group associated with the servant language. In both texts the specially elect brings about a reconciliation between the specially elected one and the larger elect group as a whole. Thus, the bulk of the Joseph story focuses on how the divided sons of Israel are reunited again in a way that overcomes many of the family troubles that led to the original rift, and gives theological meaning to Joseph's suffering (Gen 45:5-8). While the image of the servant is notoriously difficult to pin down firmly, it is fair to say that there are indeed places in 2nd Isaiah in which the servant person or group functions as the specially elect who brings about renewed national unity (Isa 42:6-7; 49:5) in a way that gives theological meaning to the suffering of the elect.[46] Certainly, the suffering of this elect person or group brings about a national rejuvenation. Finally, in the Joseph story, while the focus is more immediately on Jacob's extended family, the result is that Joseph, working under a benign Pharaoh, preserves the whole world and thus brings God's blessing to the nations of the world (Gen 41:57). Similarly in 2nd Isaiah, while the restoration of Israel as a people is the focus of the text, the specially elect working under the benign Cyrus foresee that the ultimate goal will be the recognition of God's sovereignty throughout the world, which will result in a renewed cosmos in which God's blessing will become fully manifest to the benefit of all.

It is true that service is an important feature within 2nd Isaiah and the Joseph narrative. However, such service does not imply that the elect bring about the conversion of the non-elect through mission. Rather, it describes the specially elect being a mediator of God's blessing to the more general elect group as well as to the non-elect nations of the world, who remain non-elect even while benefiting from this divine plan. And it must be stated that in the Joseph story and in the texts of 2nd Isaiah, the greater emphasis by far is on the role that the specially elect play in reuniting and reconstituting the more general elect group, that is, the family of Israel.

More to the point, while service plays an important role in the Joseph story and 2nd Isaiah, in neither text is the meaning of God's election exhausted by or reducible to the idea of divine service. Even when Joseph initially fails to recognize and fulfill his vocation in a proper manner, he remains chosen by God. Similarly, although the people of Israel failed to fulfill their obligations to God and thus were punished with exile, they eternally remain God's chosen people. While election reaches its greatest heights when the elect humbly submit to the divine service God has placed upon them, it is not reducible to service. Rather, it flows out of God's mysterious love for those chosen. Inasmuch as it is grounded in the unique relationship between God and Israel, one needs to be cautious about stating that a particular aspect of Israel's service "fulfilled the mission of Israel being chosen in the first place." Love relationships are not best conceived in instrumental terms, especially a love relationship like that between God and Israel. The prophetic recognition that Israel's election is intrinsic rather than instrumental is quite evident in the overarching shape of the prophetic corpus. Nearly every book among the fifteen canonical Latter Prophets ends on a note of hope for future restoration (Isa 40–66; Jer 52; Ezek 40–48; Hos 14; Joel 3; Amos 9:11-15; Mic 7:18-20, etc.). Clearly, Israel perceived that her special relationship with God was not primarily an instrumental one or else there would be no basis for such future hope.

None of this is to say that election is not linked closely with the notion of service or that the service rendered by the elect does not bring blessing to the wider world in its wake. But there is a difference in seeing such service and the blessing it brings as a component of election theology and proclaiming that one aspect of Israel's service explains the purpose of her election. For the latter might be taken to imply (as it has by certain Christian supersessionists through the ages) that the failure to perform said service would lead to the rejection of the chosen, an idea that finds little support within the Hebrew Bible.[47] Thus Ezekiel, a prophet who grounds election in God's transcendent power rather than his love, goes so far as to say that even though Israel may be morally incapable of fulfilling God's commandments, God maintains his bond with her. Rather than break that bond, he will do moral surgery on the recalcitrant heart of his chosen people (Ezek 36).

What is particularly odd about certain Christian attempts to speak of election in such instrumental terms is that such thinking seems to assume a type of works righteousness, which is usually strongly rebuffed by Christian thinkers influenced by Paul. Here one would be better served by recognizing that even though elements of service are integral to the notion of election, God's purposes are not totally revealed to humans. Paul uses this insight to explain how, in spite of what he sees as Israel's rebellion from God, they remain beloved by God. While to human eyes it seems that God's plan has gone awry, even these detours may be fulfilling God's purposes, purposes that remain somewhat inscrutable to the human mind (Rom 9–11). Furthermore, it is not simply a question of trying to intuit the true purposes God has in mind for Israel as if Israel was a utility tool God used for a particular purpose and then no longer needed. The God of the Hebrew Bible has an ongoing relationship with his people Israel, and thus, one needs to be cautious in employing the metaphor of service in a heavy-handed fashion that obscures the more relational elements of Israel's election theology.

Concluding Reflections

Israel's prophets loudly affirm the notion of Israel's special election. Certainly, differing prophets have differing understandings of the concept, or place more or less emphasis on aspects of election. As a whole, the prophetic literature contributed greatly to the theology of election, nuancing it in innumerable ways to the future benefit of both Jews and Christians. The above analysis has demonstrated that in a number of instances contemporary scholarship has obscured the prophetic understanding of election theology by tending to describe it in dichotomous categories, often implying a movement from a primitive nationalist mentality toward a higher universalist religion. Clearly, one can see the influences of secular Enlightenment ideas and of certain postbiblical Christian supersessionist notions in this thinking. But a careful appraisal of the relevant texts reveals that these ancient thinkers were capable of embracing and delicately balancing a variety of productive theological tensions within election theology. Rather than moving from particularism toward universalism, they move toward universalism through an ever deepening particularism. While select texts envision a growing possibility that some from the nations may come to worship Israel's God, this need not imply the dissolution of God's elect. Similarly, those passages that link the meaning of election to the idea of service continue to affirm God's mysterious and inexplicable love for his chosen people, Israel.

As will be seen in chapter 11, neither Judaism nor Christianity simply takes over the Hebrew Bible's ideas of election. Both Jews and Christians read the Hebrew Bible through the lenses of their respective later traditions and, inevitably, through the lenses of the contemporary cultures in which they live. This is as it should be. But if one believes that the Hebrew Bible may still have much to say to our world, it is urgently important to try as much as possible to understand the Hebrew Bible's theological language in its own terms. This is most especially true of election theology, which has been regularly misunderstood in both secular and religious circles.

CHAPTER TEN

ELECTION IN PSALMS AND THE WISDOM LITERATURE

Too often, the third section of the Hebrew canon, what Jews calls the *Ketuvim*, or Writings, receives little attention in scholarly surveys of major theological themes in the Bible. A number of books in the *Ketuvim*, including Chronicles, Ezra, Lamentations, and Ruth, are pervaded by election theology. Some of these have received attention above, but others have not. Although it is not possible in this brief survey to discuss every text in the Writings that has elective ideas, this chapter briefly explores two important genres found in the third section of the Hebrew Bible. One of these is the collection of ancient Israelite prayers that now constitute the book of Psalms. The other is Wisdom Literature, which scholars find in several biblical books, most especially Proverbs, Job, and Ecclesiastes. While the Psalms are replete with election imagery, scholars have generally viewed wisdom-oriented texts as much less friendly to such deeply particularistic expressions, an assumption I will challenge.

Election in Psalms

The book of Psalms is a wide-ranging collection of many types of prayers. It contains songs of praise and thanksgiving, wisdom-oriented psalms, cries of lament, and historical recitals, among others. Inasmuch as the psalms reflect a broad spectrum of Israel's prayer life, unsurprisingly, they regularly explore various aspects of Israel's election theology. This is especially true of psalms that speak from the communal rather than the individual perspective. These communal psalms generally presume and frequently articulate the notion that Israel is God's special people (Ps 148:14). Thus, the psalmist declares, "Happy is the nation whose God is the LORD, the people whom he has chosen as his heritage" (Ps 33:12). Because Israel is not just any nation, but God's own people, they deserve God's attention and help, a sentiment expressed clearly in numerous psalms that focus on communal lament: "You have sold your people for a trifle" (Ps 44:12); "You have made your people suffer hard things" (Ps 60:3); and if God answers, the psalmist reports, "Then we your people, the flock of your pasture, will give thanks to you forever" (Ps 79:13). Many psalms speak of God's restoring or giving strength to his people (Pss 14:7; 28:8-9; 29:11; 69:36; 126).

This does not mean that the nations have no place in the psalmist's worldview. Here, much is contingent on the attitude of the nations toward the people of Israel. When they come as hostiles, prayers are offered for their destruction: "Pour out your anger on the nations that do not know you, on the kingdoms that do not call your name. For they have devoured Jacob and laid waste his habitation" (Ps 79:6-7; see similarly Ps 83). But other psalms open the possibility that the nations will submit to God and benefit from God's lordship (Ps 47). Several psalms express the hope that all people will recognize God and praise him (Pss 66; 96; 100; 117; 148). While some of these are more likely employing hyperbole in an attempt to speak poetically of the fact that all creation should indeed be singing praises to its Creator, it is certainly possible to read such verses as having an eschatological vision in which the nations will all eventually proclaim Israel's God as the one true God.[1] In support of such an idea, one rather unusual psalm may go so far as to entertain the notion that other nations will wish to claim that they were born in Zion (Ps 87; cf. 47:8-9).[2]

The Psalms touch on other aspects of election theology. The chosen king and/or God's chosen place are mentioned in several psalms. This should not be surprising because the Psalms as a whole are attributed to King David, and many were likely written under royal patronage and composed or sung by temple personnel employed within the palace-temple complex. Psalm 2 speaks of the king as God's vicar on earth, and Ps 89 makes clear that through an enduring promise, God chose David and his descendants to rule his people (Ps 89:19-37; see similarly Ps 132).

In Ps 78, God's choice of David is linked to his choice of Judah and Jerusalem as well as to his specific rejection of Ephraim and the former sanctuary at Shiloh. Psalms 46 and 48 probe the deep connections between God and the Jerusalem temple.

Finally, there are psalms that contain historical recitals (Pss 78; 81; 105; 106; 136). Since these relate Israel's *Heilsgeshichte*, her holy history, they presume the notion of Israel's special election. An allied idea that is pervasive in these and many other psalms is that Israel's special relationship to God has been formalized in an enduring covenant: "He sent redemption to his people; he has commanded his covenant forever" (Ps 111:9; see similarly 25:10; 50:5; 106:45). As discussed in chapter 5 above, covenant and election are deeply interlinked with each other. Inasmuch as the psalms are the prayers of the people of Israel, it is to be expected that they regularly evoke aspects of Israel's election theology, a theology that in many ways defines Israel's identity and gives meaning to her existence.

Election in the Wisdom Literature

Many scholars engaged in writing a comprehensive biblical theology have stumbled over the fact that some parts of the Hebrew Bible are less overtly theological. In particular, one thinks of the difficulties raised by wisdom-oriented texts such as Proverbs, Job, and Ecclesiastes that contain a "natural theology." By this I mean that these texts deduce God's activity in the world through observing everyday human experience, rarely, if ever, invoking YHWH's special relationship to Israel his people as catalogued in the Pentateuch, Prophets, and Psalms.[3]

> So whether canon, saving history or covenant is taken as the central structuring concept for Old Testament theology, wisdom is forced to appear at the periphery rather than at the centre. Probably very much the same result would accrue if the idea of God were given the central role.[4]

While I have emphasized the importance of election within the Bible, I do not claim that the theology of election can be found in every biblical book, nor that it is central to each and every part of the Bible. Inasmuch as the present book is not a comprehensive unified biblical theology, but rather an attempt to trace out a single important theological theme along with some of its allied ideas, the existence of biblical books that pay little, if any, attention to the theme under discussion is neither troubling nor surprising.

However, having acknowledged that election is not a major concern of wisdom-oriented texts is not the same as saying that such literature contains no connection at all to this idea. Furthermore, even when no link at all can be found between a given wisdom book and the notion of divine chosenness, this is not proof that the scribes who produced the wisdom books rejected such a theology. Rather, they focus more on human observation of the world and how such observation reveals God's presence to anyone who takes the time to look at the world in more than a passing manner.

One needs to turn only to a text like Prov 21:31 to see that wisdom texts share certain theological presuppositions with Israel's election theology: "The horse is made ready for the day of battle, but the victory belongs to the LORD." This text implies that God may upset human expectations, especially those based on the assurance of greater military might. Such an idea is closely akin to the way in which election frequently operates by upsetting human expectations, particularly expectations that are generated by assuming the prevailing societal power arrangements are reliable indicators of God's favoritism toward those in power. Other proverbs like Prov 19:21, "The human mind may devise many plans, but it is the purpose of the LORD that will be established," speak of God's using human actions to bring about outcomes that differ from those intended by the human actors involved (cf. Prov 16:9). Such proverbs seem to spring to life in stories from Genesis like that of Jacob and Esau, or Joseph and his brothers. These proverbs and the sibling rivalry stories from Genesis share a similar view of the enigmatic relationship between divine providence and human free will. Humans may act freely, intending to bring about a particular result, but often the hidden hand of providence utilizes these very actions to reach a goal that is different from and sometimes even antithetical to the intentions that the human actors thought to achieve.

There are also certain sections of Proverbs, such as chapter 16's meditation on how wisdom can impress kings and win one favor, that strongly echo sentiments found in the Joseph story as well as in the Succession Narrative about the right and wrong use of one's natural gifts. And one wonders whether the strong condemnation of sexual infidelity in Prov 5–7 has not also influenced the shape of the Joseph narrative, particularly of the danger posed by Potiphar's wife to Joseph. In fact, some have argued that the scribes associated with wisdom circles are ultimately responsible for some, or perhaps even much, of the theological content of the Joseph story, likely the single most sustained reflection on election theology within the Bible.[5] This wisdom influence likely also explains the fact that God is in the background in both the Joseph and the Succession Narratives, stories that tell of the mysterious rise of the younger sibling to preeminence.

Interestingly enough, another narrative with God so far in the background that he is never mentioned is the scroll of Esther. This book has strong links to wisdom ideas as well as to other texts that show wisdom influence (Joseph's story and Daniel).[6] The whole narrative, which is set in the Persian king's court, involves a wise and foolish courtier and culminates in an incident in which the foolish courtier Haman is thought to be propositioning the queen (Esth 7:8). Yet the book of Esther appears to praise Jewish particularity, and as noted in chapter 7 above, its portrayal of Haman shows strong links to aspects of election theology. While wisdom theology, commonly described as universalistic in its outlook, is thought to have little concern with particularistic notions like election, the story of Esther and the Jewish people's triumph over those who sought to destroy them suggests otherwise. In this text, not only are wisdom and elective ideas not antithetical; they sit comfortably next to each other. Daniel is yet another text that contains strong wisdom influences and is unabashed in asserting Israel's special election. Daniel emphasizes the idea that certain individuals receive special gifts by which they can discern God's will (thus, the characters in the tales of Dan 1–6 share certain characteristics with the Joseph narrative), as well as the notion that the Jewish people as a whole are God's specially elect who will eventually triumph over their enemies (Dan 7–12).

Perhaps the most striking election-related trope is that suggested by the figure of Job. Job, likely a non-Israelite, is singled out by God in a manner that marks him as one who will experience great degradation and be treated harshly by others in the human community. Eventually, through divine intervention, he is justified and restored to his preeminent position. While not identical to any single story concerning election, and taking account of the fact that Job is not a story about chosenness per se, Job shares certain common features with the story of Abraham's near sacrifice of Isaac, the life of Joseph, and the servant in 2nd Isaiah. Thus, Job follows the trajectory of someone who is marked as beloved by God at the beginning of the account, but this very feature leads to his severe tribulation and, of course, his eventual restoration to a position of favor at the end of the book.[7] The fact that Job is probably not an Israelite and furthermore that the story may have been a piece of Edomite literature adopted into the Hebrew canon (note the striking similarity between the names of Job's comforters and the names of some of Esau's descendants in Gen 31) provides further support for my contention throughout this book that Israel's elective theology was quite open to the possibility that various non-Israelites, while not part of God's chosen people, could live in right relationship to God.

The Melding of Election and Wisdom Theologies in the Second Temple Period

At this point, a critic could object that although one might grant some of the points raised above, others are more speculative. Such a critic might continue by arguing that, in any case, true Wisdom Literature can have no real connection to Israel's election theology in that the latter is inherently particularistic, while wisdom texts are pervaded by a spirit of internationalism. However, such an objection fails to account for the fact that wisdom ideas and election theology are drawn into an ever closer relationship to each other beginning in rather subtle but important ways in the book of Deuteronomy (as well as in the Deuteronomistic History), flowering in fuller form in the intertestamental period as witnessed by texts like Sirach, Tobit, 4 Ezra, and the Wisdom of Solomon, finally reaching fruition in the New Testament and rabbinic corpus. Thus, in Deuteronomy one finds extensive reflections on the theme of Israel's election, but much of the discourse reflecting on the centerpiece of Israel's election, that is, her being given and having accepted the Torah, is itself framed by terms and concepts drawn from wisdom circles.[8]

> Until the seventh century Law and Wisdom existed as two separate and autonomous disciplines. Law belonged to the sacral sphere, whereas Wisdom dealt with the secular and mundane. These two disciplines were amalgamated in the book of Deuteronomy, and the laws of the Torah were now identified with wisdom: ". . . for this is your wisdom and your understanding" (Deut 4:6).[9]

This process of amalgamating the notion that God specially chose Israel to receive the Torah with the notion that Wisdom Herself is sent down by God to instruct the human community is furthered in the following passage from Sirach, a book written in the second century B.C.E.

> Wisdom praises herself, and tells of her glory in the midst of her people. In the assembly of the Most High she opens her mouth, and in the presence of his hosts she tells of her glory: "I came forth from the mouth of the Most High, and covered the earth like a mist. I dwelt in the highest heavens, and my throne was in a pillar of cloud. Alone I compassed the vault of heaven and traversed the depths of the abyss. Over waves of the sea, over all the earth, and over every people and nation I have held sway. Among all these I sought a resting place; in whose territory should I abide? Then the Creator of all things gave me a command, and my Creator chose the place for my tent. He said, 'Make your dwelling in Jacob, and in Israel receive your inheritance.' Before the ages, in the beginning, he created me, and for all the ages I shall not cease to be. In the holy tent I ministered before him, and so I was established in Zion. Thus in the beloved city he gave me a resting place, and in Jerusalem was my domain. I took root in an honored people, in the portion of the Lord, his heritage. . . . Come to me, you who desire me, and eat your fill of my fruits. For the memory of me is sweeter than honey, and the possession of me sweeter than the honeycomb. Those who eat of me will hunger for more, and those who drink of me will thirst for more. Whoever obeys me will not be put to shame, and those who work with me will not sin." All this is the book of the covenant of the Most High God, the law that Moses commanded us as an inheritance for the congregations of Jacob. (Sir 24:1-12, 19-23)

Sirach 24 builds upon Prov 8:22-31 as well as on the idea already raised by Deuteronomy that Torah is itself a marker of Israel's wisdom. While Wisdom may have started out in Proverbs as something equally accessible to all humans, Sirach affirms and expands upon the notion first adumbrated in texts like Deut 4:6 that Israel's election includes the idea that Wisdom is located in Israel in a way that is not true of other nations. Furthermore, obeying Wisdom is now made equivalent to obeying God's covenant, the Torah given to Moses. Now it is true Sirach does not emphasize the Pentateuch's highly particularistic commandments, and thus, it is more the case that he has universalized Torah than particularized Wisdom.[10] But his association of Wisdom and Israel's Torah opened a very productive avenue of speculation. This trope is further filled out in a number of ways within the Wisdom of Solomon, a Jewish book perhaps from the early first century C.E. While Wis 7:22–8:1 appears to borrow neo-platonic imagery in describing Wisdom, this text goes on to speak of Wisdom becoming manifest among humans as "in every generation she passes into holy souls and makes them friends of God and prophets" (Wis 7:27). In chapters 10–11, Wisdom is tied to a number of stories that describe God's unfolding plan of Israel's election and how God's wisdom overcame human resistance to it. The triumph of God's providence is attributed to the operation of Wisdom possessed by certain elect individuals and the people of Israel as a whole. Here Israel's particularistic holy history (her *Heilsgeschichte*) is incorporated into a Wisdom-oriented theological framework.[11]

As many scholars have recognized, a line can be drawn from the personification of Wisdom as God's consort first mentioned in Prov 8:22-31 to texts like Sir 24 and Wis 7:22–8:1 and ultimately to John 1:1-4.

> In the beginning was the Word, and the Word was with God, and the Word was God. He was in the beginning with God. All things came into being through him, and without him not one thing came into being. What has come into being in him was life, and the life was the light of all people.

This text from John amplifies the notion that Wisdom was God's companion who assisted God in creating the world. This image hearkens back to texts like Prov 8, merging this idea with Deuteronomy's and Sirach's notion that such wisdom is not universally available at all times to all peoples but rather specially available to one people. Here Christ is Wisdom incarnate who is now located specifically in the Christian community.

Not surprisingly, the opening paragraph in *Midrash Rabbah*, commenting upon Gen 1:1, makes a similar claim for Judaism. This midrash begins with a series of reflections on Prov 8:30 and is focused specifically on the unusual word **אמון**, frequently translated as "nursemaid" or "craftsman/architect." The last interpretation is the relevant one for this discussion.

> Another interpretation: **אמון** is a workman *(uman)*. The Torah declares: "I was the working tool of the Holy One, blessed be He." In human practice, when a mortal king builds a palace, he builds it not with his own skill but with the skill of an architect. The architect moreover does not build it out of his head, but employs plans and diagrams to know how to arrange the chambers and the wicket doors. Thus God

> consulted the Torah and created the world, while the Torah declares, *In the beginning God created,* beginning referring to the Torah, as in the verse, *The Lord made me the beginning of his way* (Prov 8:22).[12]

To grasp this midrash, one needs to be aware that the rabbis assume that God's partner in Prov 8:22-31 is in fact the Torah, inasmuch as in the rabbinic mind Torah and Wisdom are utterly interchangeable. By drawing an association between the similar wording used in both Gen 1:1 and Prov 8:22 (בראשית in Gen 1:1 and ראשית in Prov 8:22), they claim that God first looked into the Torah and then created the world. Such a reading, while recognizing that all creation contains God's wisdom that is available to any human who opens his or her eyes, also claims that it is most fully found in the Torah, which is the special possession of God's chosen people Israel (cf. Ps 19).

Thus by the time rabbinic Judaism and early Christianity begin to flower, both religions had managed to bring biblical currents of thought associated with Israel's particularistic election into an integrated theology with what are usually described as more universalistic and internationalist ideas flowing from wisdom circles. When one traces the trajectories of wisdom and election thinking over time, it becomes clear that some of the cross-pollination between these two major streams of biblical thought was rather ancient. This suggests that even though wisdom thinkers and those engaged in producing the Bible's election theology employ very different discourses, these variant discourses need not be viewed as antagonistic or antithetical to each other.

CHAPTER ELEVEN

NEW TESTAMENT AND RABBINIC VIEWS OF ELECTION

The previous chapters of this book have focused on various aspects of the concept of election in the Hebrew Bible, occasionally making references to later Christian or Jewish interpretations. Thus, this chapter is dedicated to exploring the ways in which rabbinic Judaism and early Christianity adopted and adapted the Hebrew Bible's elective ideas.[1] Though conducting a comprehensive study of election within these two complex, multifaceted traditions is well beyond the reach of a single chapter, one can sketch out in more systematic form some of the distinctive ways that each tradition uniquely highlighted or downplayed various aspects of this rich biblical concept. To articulate the meaning of election for Jews and Christians, it is necessary to examine how this idea fits into the theological grammar of each religion.

Before proceeding with this comparison, it may be worth stressing that election is a central idea not only within Judaism but also for Christianity. This point needs emphasis because some modern and contemporary thinkers assume that election and the particularism and exclusivism it entails are Old Testament/Jewish ideas that were transcended by the New Testament and Christianity.[2] A brief example from Arnold Toynbee, a very widely read author, exhibits this propensity to deride election as a mistaken Jewish idea: "They [the Jews] persuaded themselves that Israel's discovery of the One True God had revealed Israel itself to be God's Chosen People."[3] An explicitly Christian attempt to disown the idea of election can be found in the following excerpt from a 1937 *Christian*

Century editorial, which blames the Jews for inventing and sustaining Nazi anti-Semitism: "It is just this obsession with the doctrine of a covenant race that now menaces the whole world. . . . [The Jewish] idea of an . . . exclusive culture, hallowed and kept unified by a racial religion, is itself the prototype of Nazism."[4] This viewpoint is still in vogue today, albeit in more covert forms. E. P. Sanders states that "Christian scholars habitually discuss the question [of Jewish pride in separatism] under the implied heading 'What was wrong with Judaism that Christianity corrected?' "[5]

While major streams of New Testament thinking broadened the elect group to include those Gentiles who came to believe in Jesus as the Christ, this does not mean that Christianity rejected the biblical concept of election and its implied exclusivism.[6] The following passage from Rom 4 illustrates that early Christians did not see themselves as universalists who accepted everyone because they shared common descent from Adam, but rather as particularists who found a new way to link believing Gentiles to Abraham and through him to God's elect people.

> For this reason it depends on faith, in order that the promise may rest on grace and be guaranteed to all his descendants, not only to the adherents of the law but also to those who share the faith of Abraham (for he is the father of all of us, as it is written, "I have made you the father of many nations")—in the presence of the God in whom he believed, who gives life to the dead and calls into existence the things that do not exist. Hoping against hope, he believed that he would become "the father of many nations," according to what was said, "So numerous shall your descendants be." . . . Therefore his faith "was reckoned to him as righteousness." Now the words, "it was reckoned to him," were written not for his sake alone, but for ours also. (Rom 4:16-18, 22-24)

The effect of this is that Christians, like their Jewish counterparts, believed that those belonging to the people of God had relinquished their fallen Adamic state.

> Yet death exercised dominion from Adam to Moses, even over those whose sins were not like the transgression of Adam, who is a type of the one who was to come. But the free gift is not like the trespass. For if the many died through the one man's trespass, much more surely have the grace of God and the free gift in the grace of the one man, Jesus Christ, abounded for the many. And the free gift is not like the effect of the one

> man's sin. For the judgment following one trespass brought condemnation, but the free gift following many trespasses brings justification. If, because of the one man's trespass, death exercised dominion through that one, much more surely will those who receive the abundance of grace and the free gift of righteousness exercise dominion in life through the one man, Jesus Christ. (Rom 5:14-17)

Here Paul portrays Adam's sin as creating a state of alienation between God and humans that leads to death. This rift is overcome through belief in Jesus as the Christ who gives believers access to eternal life.

The argument between Judaism and Christianity is over who held the proper key to repair the fractured relationship between humans and God. Was this accomplished through the giving of the Torah to the Jews at Sinai (and the dynamics of repentance and reconciliation inherent in Torah observance), or through the death and resurrection of Christ at Golgotha (with its alternative schema of divine-human reconciliation)?[7] While various New Testament authors may have changed the particular way one joined the people of God, on the whole New Testament Christianity clearly appropriated the concept of chosenness.

> But you are a chosen race, a royal priesthood, a holy nation, God's own people, in order that you may proclaim the mighty acts of him who called you out of darkness into his marvelous light. Once you were not a people, but now you are God's people; once you had not received mercy, but now you have received mercy. (1 Pet 2:9-10)

Here, 1 Peter reapplies to the early church language found in Exod 19:6, a passage that is central to ancient Israel's understanding of her own election. Thus, the nascent Christian community not only took over the concept of election, but at times it even utilized the Hebrew Bible's terminology for election.

Clearly, the New Testament authors maintained the fundamentals of the Hebrew Bible's particularistic notion of election. This should not be surprising because the master narrative of the New Testament—the passion, death, and resurrection of Jesus—is itself a re-presention of the central motif of the sibling rivalry stories from Genesis: the death and resurrection of the beloved son.[8] Thus, the church saw Jesus, and by association those who believed in him, as the chosen son who was persecuted but ultimately exalted. That the New Testament, like rabbinic Judaism, affirms the Hebrew Bible's election theology should not obscure the fact that the two traditions diverge on a number of central theological issues including these: missionary outreach, the fate of those not elected, the role played by God's actions and human actions respectively, and the acceptability of God's arbitrariness.

Of course, any attempt to draw hard and fast distinctions between two traditions as vast and ancient as Judaism and Christianity is difficult. After all, the two traditions grew out of a common matrix and share much in common. More important, even when most texts in one tradition diverge in substantial ways from the dominant strain of thinking in the other faith, there are subcurrents in each tradition, which sometimes seem more at home in the sister religion than in the textual corpus in which they occur. Thus, none of the arguments below should be taken as evidence for the univocality of each of these two traditions. Rather, they are useful observations about the ideas to which each tradition gives greatest weight and emphasis.

The Question of Mission and the Fate of Those Not Elected

A basic difference between Judaism and Christianity centers on how each faith addresses the following two interrelated issues: (1) the manner and extent that one absorbs or accepts outsiders into the community of believers; (2) the way in which those who are not part of the elect are viewed. Each religion's stance on the place of those not elected informs its stance on questions of integrating outsiders or missionizing them. It is important to recognize this fact to avoid labeling Judaism as close-minded and intolerant while portraying Christianity as tolerant and universalistic in its stance toward others. The truth is that there is an inverse relationship between these two issues. Judaism is more tolerant of the non-elect in that its general propensity is to assume that one can remain non-elect and still be in right relationship to God. This fact makes it less necessary to seek to convert non-Jews. On the other hand, although Christianity has historically been committed to evangelize outsiders, this is not necessarily a sign of its great tolerance for "the other" as "other." Rather, Christianity's strong impulse to convert those outside the faith seems at least partially driven by the realization that without faith in Christ, these individuals are damned. In other words, dominant streams of Christian tradition[9] have reduced the three biblical categories of the elect, the anti-elect (that is, those few groups like the Canaanites of the Hebrew Bible doomed for destruction), and the non-elect (that is, all other non-Israelites) down to the two categories of the saved and those lost to God. Such binary categorization led Christians to missionize those who without conversion would have been lost to God. This is far from what a modern liberal society would consider tolerance. As noted above in chapter 9, "Prophecy and Election," in reference to certain biblical materials, modern dichotomies such as universalism/particularism or tolerance/intolerance are of equally limited utility when speaking about rabbinic Judaism and early Christianity. Bearing in mind that the issues of mission and the fate of outsiders are intertwined, and furthermore that modern scholarly biases have frequently distorted each religion's stance on these issues, let us briefly discuss each topic independently.

Mission

One of the central pillars of early Christianity is that Christians are charged with the task of actively spreading the faith (Matt 28:19). It may be true that Jesus originally intended his message only to reach other Jews (Matt 10:5-15), but by the time of Paul's death broad swaths of Christianity accepted that the gospel was to be preached to the whole world.

While some scholars have argued that Judaism during the Second Temple period was also a missionary religion for a time, the general consensus is that this was not the case. Even a scholar such as Scot McKnight, who finds wide evidence of Jewish acceptance of Gentile converts in antiquity, draws the following conclusions:

> [A] positive attitude toward, and an acceptance of, proselytes is to be methodologically distinguished from aggressive missionary activity among the Gentiles. In other words, although Jews clearly admitted proselytes, and although they clearly encouraged Gentiles to convert, and although they anticipated that Day when hordes of Gentiles would convert, there is almost no evidence that Jews were involved in evangelizing Gentiles aggressively and drawing them into their religion.[10]

A notable change in the rabbinic era was the development of a conversion procedure that normalized the path for joining the chosen people. Although some rabbinic texts praise converts, Robert Goldenberg makes clear, "There is no evidence whatever from late antiquity that rabbinic leaders in any Jewish community anywhere ever set up an organized program to attract gentiles to Judaism."[11] And truth be told, not only do the rabbis have a rule that one should discourage converts at first in order to test their sincerity, but there are also a number of negative rabbinic statements concerning converts.[12] As touched upon above and explored in greater depth below, while the rabbis made the community's boundary more porous, they did not presume, as major streams of Christianity did, that only the elect could be saved or could be righteous in God's eyes. It may well be that this belief in the existence of the righteous non-elect contributed to the lack of full-blown missionary activity within late antique and early rabbinic Judaism.[13]

Interestingly enough, Judaism's resistance to missionizing and Christianity's forceful call to engage in it have been used by not a few Christians to justify a supersessionist displacement theology in which the church as the new Israel has replaced those obstinate Jews who refused to share the word of God with others. Thus, H. H. Rowley sees election as ultimately requiring Israel "to mediate to all men the law of her God, and to spread the heritage of her faith through all the world."[14] Inasmuch as the historic people of Israel failed to actively missionize, Rowley strongly implies that they thereby forfeited their elect status to the church who engaged in such active missionizing.

> Through the Church Gentiles from every corner under heaven . . . have learned the law of God. The Jewish Bible has been translated into innumerable languages and has become the cherished Scripture of multitudes who would never have heard of it through Jews alone. These are objective facts. It is not merely that the church believed she was commissioned to take over the task of Israel. She did in fact take over from an Israel that was less willing to undertake it; and she has indisputably fulfilled that task in a great, though still insufficient, measure.[15]

It needs to be stressed that Rowley is not alone in his view and that similar assertions occur regularly in more recent scholarship. The contemporary and widely read New Testament scholar N. T. Wright endorses this same idea: "Paul argues that ethnic Israel has failed in the purpose for which she was called into being. . . . Israel rejected the call of Jesus and now rejects the apostolic message *about* Jesus because it challenges . . . her relentless pursuit of national, ethnic and territorial identity."[16]

Of course, this type of claim grows out of the assumption that the Hebrew Bible endorsed the notion of an active mission to the Gentiles. As discussed in chapter 9 above, the evidence that the Hebrew Bible endorsed the idea of an active mission to convert the Gentile nations is very tenuous. Thus, it appears that the stance of Second Temple and later rabbinic Judaism is in fact more consonant with most, if not all, streams of the Hebrew Bible's theological speculation on this topic. If this is true, it may be time for contemporary Christians to stop claiming that Israel lost its elect status by refusing to actively missionize others as its prophets called it to do.

On the other hand, Jewish critics of Christian missionary activity must realize that the notion of Christian mission has a basis in the Hebrew Bible. Later biblical texts contain growing speculation about the possibility of Gentile conversion through non-human agency, and at least one text mentions something resembling the idea of Christian mission. Furthermore, certain postexilic eschatological texts within the Hebrew Bible like Isa 65 begin to move toward a more dualistic idea of the saved and the damned, a move that would eventuate in the loss of the more neutral category of the non-elect. Once Christians came to believe that Gentiles could be linked to Israel's God through Abraham, thereby attaining salvation, a number of enigmatic texts within late prophetic collections were now understood as prophecies foretelling this shift in theological understanding.

The Fate of Those Not Elected

As indicated in the brief summary above as well as in my much lengthier treatment of the non-elect and anti-elect earlier in this book, the Hebrew Bible generally conceived of three categories of people: the elect, who are called the People of Israel; the anti-elect, who are beyond divine mercy and thus doomed for destruction; and the non-elect, who are the vast majority of those not chosen. This latter group is seen as playing an important part in the divine economy, and Israel works out her destiny in relation to these other peoples, even while remaining separate from them. Within the vast bulk of eschatological oracles the nations continue to persist alongside Israel. Generally, such nations come to recognize God, or become subservient to God and his people Israel, yet they continue to exist as separate, non-elect peoples. Now it is true that in certain late proto-apocalyptic texts one begins to see a breakdown of these three groups into two, the righteous chosen against the wicked who are doomed for total destruction (Isa 65–66). While these apocalyptic images eventually gave rise to the full-blown Christian categories of the saved and the damned, it is worth noting that these dualistic texts from the Hebrew Bible never fully dissolve the distinction between Israel and the survivors from among the nations who submit to God's dominion and make pilgrimage to Jerusalem (Zech 14:16-19; Dan 7:27). This is different from early Christianity in which the saved are coextensive with the new Israel (i.e., the nascent church), God's chosen people. More important, even where such apocalyptic images begin the process of collapsing the Hebrew Bible's categories of the non-elect and anti-elect into each other, within the context of the Hebrew Bible as a whole the vast bulk of texts preserve a place in the divine economy for the non-elect peoples of the world.

The dominant streams of rabbinic Judaism continued to maintain the idea of the non-elect and affirmed that righteous non-Jews could attain salvation. One can indeed find isolated statements such as that by Rabbi Eliezer who in *t. Sanh.* 13:2 declares that "none of the gentiles has a portion in the world to come" on the basis of Ps 9:18 [Eng. 9:17]. But his statement is decisively challenged by Rabbi Joshua, who shows that the wording of this psalm, which says, "All the gentiles (lit. nations) who forget," "indicates that there are also righteous people among the nations of the world, who do have a portion in the world to come."[17] Rabbinic Judaism developed the idea that Gentiles could indeed attain salvation through observing the seven Noahide commandments, and contemporary Judaism continues to affirm that Gentiles can be righteous before God and thus they need not convert to Judaism.[18] While some rabbis, in ways analogous to their Christian counterparts, speculated that in the messianic era everyone would eventually acknowledge the God of Israel and the truth of Torah, many rabbinic texts leave room for righteous Gentiles to attain salvation during the premessianic era through observance of the Noahide commandments alone.[19]

On the other hand, New Testament and early Christian thinkers make clear that there is no salvation outside faith in Jesus as the risen Christ (John 14:6; Acts 4:12; Gal 2:15-16). This creates not only an openness to converts but also a drive to convert as many people as possible, and this missionary impulse is not a sign of respect for those not chosen. Thus, missionary activity assumes the inadequacy of the religion of those being missionized, and it has frequently been driven by intolerance and/or imperialism.[20]

Furthermore, as explained in chapter 8, Christians are strongly cautioned about the dangers of associating with nonbelievers as well as tolerating sinners within the community (1 Cor 5; 2 Cor 6:14–7:1). The point is that Christians are indeed more open to converts, but they are less open to "the other" as other. Clearly, many Christians believe they are called to actively missionize non-believers in order to bring about their conversion to Christ because it is not possible to attain salvation or be in right relationship with God unless one becomes a believing Christian.

Judaism is less interested in mission because the non-elect nations of the world are accorded greater respect, requiring only that they maintain the Noahide laws. In this particular case, rabbinic Judaism is more in tune with the dominant streams of the Hebrew Bible's election theology, which portray the non-elect in neutral or positive terms. Within the Hebrew Bible the elect play a key role in God's salvific plan, but rarely if ever does this involve actively missionizing the non-elect.[21] This is not to say that the Christian stance is not grounded in the Hebrew Scriptures, for surely it is. But the tendency to conceive of election as a binary opposition between the saved and the damned, as well as the allied tendency to missionize to those who are not yet saved, are ideas at home in late apocalyptic literature rather than in broad swaths of the Hebrew canon.

Grace and Works in Judaism and Christianity

Another important area of divergence between Judaism and Christianity centers on the emphasis that each tradition places on the roles played by divine and human initiative in the redemptive process. This distinction is often spoken of by employing the Protestant dichotomy of grace versus works, and unfortunately, such discussions often reach simplistic conclusions that are derogatory to Judaism. Typically, Judaism is characterized as a religion that focuses on works, and Christianity is portrayed as a higher religion centered on faith. But this is a generalization; a closer look at the larger range of texts in each tradition soon complicates this portrait. While one finds the following statement in Paul's Letter to the Romans, one need only look at the second passage listed below from James to gather that the radical emphasis on faith alone was not a view held by all early Christians.[22] In fact, the parable of the sheep and goats (Matt 25:31-46) appears to endorse the position of James, not that of Paul.

> Is this blessedness, then, pronounced only on the circumcised, or also on the uncircumcised? We say, "Faith was reckoned to Abraham as righteousness." How then was it reckoned to him? Was it before or after he had been circumcised? It was not after, but before he was circumcised. He received the sign of circumcision as a seal of the righteousness that he had by faith while he was still uncircumcised. The purpose was to make him the ancestor of all who believe without being circumcised and who thus have righteousness reckoned to them, and likewise the ancestor of the circumcised who are not only circumcised but who also follow the example of the faith that our ancestor Abraham had before he was circumcised. For the promise that he would inherit the world did not come to Abraham or to his descendants through the law but through the righteousness of faith. If it is the adherents of the law who are to be the heirs, faith is null and the promise is void. (Rom 4:9-14)

> What good is it, my brothers and sisters, if you say you have faith but do not have works? Can faith save you? If a brother or sister is naked and lacks daily food, and one of you says to them, "Go in peace; keep warm and eat your fill," and yet you do not supply their bodily needs, what is the good of that? So faith by itself, if it has no works, is dead. But someone will say, "You have faith and I have works." Show me your faith apart from your works, and I by my works will show you my faith. You believe that God is one; you do well. Even the demons believe—and shudder. Do you want to be shown, you senseless person, that faith apart from works is barren? Was not our ancestor Abraham justified by works when he offered his son Isaac on the altar? You see that faith was active along with his works, and faith was brought to completion by the works. Thus the scripture was fulfilled that says, "Abraham believed God, and it was reckoned to him as righteousness," and he was called the friend of God. You see that a person is justified by works and not by faith alone. (Jas 2:14-24)

Similarly, while much of rabbinic literature, continuing a movement already begun within the Pentateuch itself, places ever greater emphasis on the revelation of the *mitzvot* (the commandments) given at Sinai, one can still find rabbinic passages that emphasize the salvific power of faith over works. Take, for example, the following comment from a second-century Tannaitic collection of halakic (legal) midrashim, *The Mekilta de*

Rabbi Ishmael, which sounds strikingly Pauline in its conclusion that salvation and redemption were gained by faith alone.

> And so you also find that our father Abraham inherited both this world and the world beyond only as a reward for the faith with which he believed, as it is said: *And he believed in the Lord*, etc. (Gen 15:6). And so you also find that Israel was redeemed from Egypt only as a reward for the faith with which they believed, as it is said, *And the people believed* (Exod 4:31).[23]

Clearly, it is wrong to label Judaism as a religion that never mentions the importance of faith in God's gracious actions or Christianity as religion that is never concerned with the importance of human actions. Furthermore, the dichotomy between grace (or faith) and works (or law) is itself part of a Christian paradigm that inherently does an injustice to any attempt to understand Judaism in its own terms. While rabbinic Judaism affirms that the human/divine relationship reaches its highest consummation when the people of Israel fulfill the obligations of the Sinai covenant, Israel's failure to live up to these obligations does not nullify God's gracious actions toward his people. In the Jewish paradigm, the giving of the commandments is itself the greatest manifestation of God's grace toward the human community. The commandments are not opposed to grace; they are grace, in that they contain the road map to heal the rift between humans and the divine.

Bearing in mind the nuances that I have brought to the fore, it still seems fair to say that Christianity, especially the forms that draw heavily on Paul, places greater weight on the notion of faith, correspondingly deemphasizing human works.[24] Much of the Pauline corpus is occupied with arguing this position at length (but note Rom 2:5-10 for an exceptional argument to the contrary), and it seems reasonable to assert that Paul has occupied a much larger place in the Christian imagination than has James. Similarly, while occasional rabbinic texts stress the virtue of faith apart from any observance of the commandments, one would be overwhelmed if one attempted to collect every rabbinic text that praised the commandments or noted their salvific power.

One can gain a greater appreciation of how each tradition grapples with this theological tension by seeing that the ancient rabbis and Paul are forced to deal with the opposite sides of the same problem. Paul, who wished to make faith central and demote the place of Sinai, has to face two interpretive issues: (1) How does one explain Abraham's act of circumcision, which appears to imply that Abraham engaged in works as well as had faith? (2) Why did God give the law to Israel if ultimately it could not be obeyed and thus, in Paul's view, failed as a vehicle for Israel's salvation? Paul addresses each of these problems several times. In Galatians he asserts that the law that came four hundred and thirty years later cannot annul the unconditional Abrahamic covenant (Gal 3:17), while in Rom 4 (cited above), he argues that even if Abraham himself was circumcised in Gen 17, it occurred after he had received the unconditional divine promise back in Gen 15. In terms of demoting Sinai, in Gal 3:19-20 he claims the law was delivered not by God but by the angels, while in Romans he attempts to shift the inadequacy of the law to human sinfulness (Rom 7:7-24).

The rabbis who wish to emphasize the place of the law do not have to explain why it has been displaced, as Paul does, but they do have to explain why, if it is so important, God failed to reveal it to the patriarchs. These figures appear to be in right relationship to God with knowledge of only a few named commandments like circumcision and an assumed knowledge of other more general prohibitions such as those against murder and theft, resembling a type of natural law.[25] Through various midrashim like the two cited below, the rabbis claim that the patriarchs knew the whole of the law before it was revealed to Israel at Sinai.

> We thus find that Our Father Abraham had practiced the whole Torah in its entirety before it had been given, as it is said, *inasmuch as Abraham obeyed me and kept my charge: my commandments, my laws, and my teachings* (Gen 26:5).[26]

> How did our father Jacob come in this world to merit a life with no distress, with no evil inclination—a life something like the life that God bestows upon the righteous only in the time to come? Because from his youth to his old age he frequented the house of study, familiarizing himself with Scripture, Mishnah, and Midrash of Halakhot as well as Aggadot, as is said, *Jacob was an ideal man—he sat in tents* [of study] (Gen 25:27).[27]

Before leaving this discussion on grace and works in Judaism and Christianity, it may be useful to highlight a couple of points. To begin with, both Judaism and Christianity are choosing to emphasize differing parts of a partially shared, although not identical, biblical heritage.[28] Both traditions are faced with the fact that the Hebrew Bible itself contains internal tensions on the question of how much of a role God and humans each play in the divine economy. These biblical tensions can be seen in a variety of loci. Perhaps they are most clearly in view when one examines the variety of covenants. As discussed in chapter 5, not only does one find tensions between more and less conditional covenants, but one also discovers that a single covenant—we see this particularly with the Abrahamic and Davidic covenants—can be alternatively framed as conditional or unconditional. The existence of differing covenantal theologies and tensions between these variant theologies make it difficult to determine how precisely divine grant and human responsibility relate to each other. Even more interesting is that similar issues also occur in other major streams of biblical thought, such as in questions surrounding how election occurs. Is election by divine fiat, due to human action, or is it finally some mysterious interaction that includes both a divine and a human component? Because these tensions are already embedded in the biblical text, each tradition's theological trajectory will inevitably show signs of struggle with certain parts of the biblical heritage. Thus, the distinct theological currents that ultimately grew into Judaism and Christianity were present within the Hebrew Bible itself. Once the two traditions blossomed it was almost inevitable that they would become vociferous rivals over who was the true heir and proper interpreter of the biblical tradition. But in this recent era of rapprochement between these two rival traditions, it is important to see that each tradition has much to learn from the other about those pieces of the biblical heritage it chose to de-emphasize.

Divine Inscrutability

One of the starkest contrasts between the two traditions surrounds the character of God's elective actions. On the whole, Christianity has chosen to elevate the motif of God's mysterious and inscrutable choice. On the other hand, Judaism has tended to soften the Deity's seeming arbitrariness by midrashically filling in the biblical story in ways that explain why those chosen by God deserved this status, or how those not chosen had forfeited their election. On the Christian side, one can look to the following Pauline text as a classical example of the movement to further emphasize God's mysterious, free, and inscrutable actions.

> For I could wish that I myself were accursed and cut off from Christ for the sake of my own people, my kindred according to the flesh. They are Israelites, and to them belong the adoption, the glory, the covenants, the giving of the law, the worship, and the promises; to them belong the patriarchs, and from them, according to the flesh, comes the Messiah, who is over all, God blessed forever. Amen. It is not as though the word of God had failed. For not all Israelites truly belong to Israel, and not all of Abraham's children are his true descendants; but "It is through Isaac that descendants shall be named for you." This means that it is not the children of the flesh who are the children of God, but the children of the promise are counted as descendants. For this is what the promise said, "About this time I will return and Sarah shall have a son." Nor is that all; something similar happened to Rebecca when she had conceived children by one husband, our ancestor Isaac. Even before they had been born or had done anything good or bad (so that God's purpose of election might continue, not by works but by his call) she was told, "The elder shall serve the younger." As it is written, "I have loved Jacob, but I have hated Esau." What then are we to say? Is there injustice on God's part? By no means! For he says to Moses, "I will have mercy on whom I have mercy, and I will have compassion on whom I have compassion." So it depends not on human will or exertion, but on God who shows mercy. (Rom 9:3-16)

In this text Paul, paying close attention to the text of Genesis, sees election as unearned by any human action. One might object that this text only reflects Pauline concerns but does not apply to other parts of the New Testament. However, it seems quite likely that the New Testament's central story, which tells a tale of human failures that are only remedied by God's resurrecting of Jesus, lead one to suspect that God's unconditioned actions would indeed receive strong emphasis throughout this textual corpus.[29] Further evidence might be found in the dualistic language employed by the Fourth Gospel. While some might argue that the Gospel of John is just using persuasive rhetoric when it speaks in dualistic terms of light and darkness, those who belong to God as opposed to coming from Satan, such language shares certain affinities with gnostic notions that one's fate has been fully determined before one's birth, thereby leaving little room for human initiative (John 3:17-21; 8:47).

On the other hand, the rabbis, while not eliminating the notion of God's free and mysterious action, clearly are troubled by the idea that God acts in arbitrary ways. In such texts the ancient rabbis demonstrate that God's actions may at times seem utterly mysterious in the cryptic language of the Bible, yet on a deeper midrashic level, once the gaps in our knowledge are filled in, God's behavior becomes morally and rationally understandable. In these rabbinic midrashim God elects certain individuals because they were, in fact, deserving human beings. An obvious example is the series of midrashic tales that describe Abraham as someone who reasons his way to monotheism through a variety of personal circumstances and is only then chosen by God as the founder of Judaism.

> Terah was a manufacturer of idols. He once went away somewhere and left Abraham to sell them in his place. . . . [Once] a woman came with a plateful of flour and requested of him, "Take this and offer it to them." So he took a stick, broke them, and put the stick in the hand of the largest. When his father returned he demanded, "What have you done to them?" "I cannot conceal it from you," he rejoined. "A woman came with a plateful of fine meal and requested me to offer it to them. One claimed, 'I must eat first,' while another claimed, 'I must eat first.' Thereupon the largest arose, took the stick, and broke them." "Why do you make sport of me," he [Terah] cried out; "have they then any knowledge!" "Should not your ears listen to what your mouth is saying," he [Abraham] retorted.[30]

Whereas it is important not to overstate things by implying that midrashic texts speak with a unified voice that always diminishes God's arbitrariness while enhancing the human role in warranting election,[31] major streams of rabbinic thinking rationalize God's election of Israel by enhancing Israel's deservedness. One can see this quite clearly in the following midrash that claims that other nations were offered the Torah and found undeserving, while Israel unreservedly accepted it.

> And it was for the following reason that the nations of the world were asked to accept the Torah: In order that they should have no excuse for saying: Had we been asked we would have accepted it. For, behold, they were asked and refused to accept it, for it is said: *And he said: The Lord came from Sinai,* etc. (Deut 33:2). He appeared to the children of Esau the wicked and said to them: Will you accept the Torah? They said to Him: What is written in it? He said to them: *Thou shalt not murder* (Deut 5:17). They then said to Him: The very heritage which you left us was: *And by thy sword shalt thou live* (Gen 27:40). He then appeared to the children of Amon (*sic*) and Moab. He said to them: Will you accept the Torah? They said to Him: What is written in it? He said to them: *Thou shalt not commit adultery* (Deut 5:18). They, however, said to Him that

> they were all of them children of adulterers, as it is said: *Thus were both daughters of Lot with child by their father* (Gen 19:36). Then he appeared to the children of Ishmael. He said to them: Will you accept the Torah? They said to Him: What is written in it? He said to them: *Thou shalt not steal* (Deut 5:19). They then said to Him: The very blessing that has been pronounced upon our father was: *And he shall be as a wild ass of a man: his hand shall be upon everything* (Gen 16:12). . . . But when He came to the Israelites and: *At His right hand was a fiery law unto them* (Deut 33:2), they all opened their mouths and said: *All that the Lord hath spoken we will do and obey* (Exod 24:7).[32]

While at first glance these midrashim appear far removed from the portrayal of the God of the Bible, it is quite likely that the rabbinic tendency to rationalize God's actions is something that began to occur in the biblical text itself. Thus, one finds biblical texts like Gen 22:15-18 in which Abraham's election is finally fully secured by his positive response to God.[33] Similarly, passages in Exodus that portray Moses as someone who early on exhibited a deep sense of righteous indignation when other weaker parties were maltreated (Exod 2:11-22) may indicate why God selected Moses to lead the Israelites, thereby implying he was deservedly chosen. Of course, the rabbis deepen the evidence of Moses' earlier righteous behavior beyond what one finds in the biblical text just as they do with Abraham (see *Exod Rab* 2:2). But the process of linking the special status of Abraham and Moses to their previous actions, rather than attributing their selection solely to God's inscrutable preferences, was already under way in the biblical period itself. Although in this instance Pauline Christianity's emphasis on God's mysterious and inscrutable actions may be more attuned to the characterization of God as he is found in most narratives in the Hebrew Bible, the rabbinic drive to explain that God did not act arbitrarily is built upon earlier biblical rationalizations.

It is an open question whether the rabbinic attempts to rationalize Israel's election by portraying Israel and her progenitors as having warranted God's favor is part of a natural unfolding of earlier theological ideas, or is primarily driven by a need to defend the Jewish notion of election from Christian attacks to the contrary.[34] Ascertaining the background behind these midrashic innovations is difficult. Not only do the editorial practices employed in rabbinic literature obscure the original social location of each pericope, but also the fragmentary nature of the historical evidence makes it difficult to determine the extent of interreligious interchange at this time. On occasion, as I will argue below about a particular set of midrashim, a strong case can be made that a certain exegetical move was generated by an interreligious polemic. However, some scholars have reached beyond the meager evidence and claimed that a vast array of exegesis is attributable to interreligious polemic.[35] Such arguments often fail to consider that many of these exegetical developments might be better explained by looking at internal Jewish considerations.[36] It is also quite possible that these midrashic developments are due to a complex interaction between a variety of internal theological factors and certain external social and religious pressures and that any attempt to posit a single causal explanation may obscure the truth of the matter. In the case of the two longer midrashim considered above, interreligious polemic might be driving such ideas; however, they may be better attributed to internal Jewish reflection on Abraham's election as well as on the meaning of Israel's subsequent reception of the Torah.

Rabbinic and New Testament Uses of the Rivalry Stories

As the above arguments have made clear, there are indeed many differences in how Judaism and Christianity uniquely appropriated the Hebrew Bible's notion of election. However, sometimes the very split between the two traditions grows out of moments in which they most closely mirror each other. Oddly enough, as explored at length in Jon Levenson's masterful study on the biblical trope of the death and resurrection of the beloved son, Christianity is perhaps most Jewish when it rereads the various stories of brotherly struggle in Genesis in order to substantiate its supersessionist theology.[37] Although these biblical tales from Genesis often present election in much more nuanced and ambiguous terms,[38] both rabbinic Judaism and New Testament Christianity reinterpret and deploy these stories in an attempt to secure their own legitimacy as the true people of God and delegitimize other rival claimants.

A paradigmatic Christian example of this maneuver can be found in the following text from Paul's Letter to the Galatians:

> For it is written that Abraham had two sons, one by a slave woman and the other by a free woman. One, the child of the slave, was born according to the flesh; the other, the child of the free woman, was born through the promise. Now this is an allegory: these women are two

> covenants. One woman, in fact, is Hagar, from Mount Sinai, bearing children for slavery. Now Hagar is Mount Sinai in Arabia and corresponds to the present Jerusalem, for she is in slavery with her children. But the other woman corresponds to the Jerusalem above; she is free, and she is our mother. For it is written, "Rejoice, you childless one, you who bear no children, burst into song and shout, you who endure no birth pangs; for the children of the desolate woman are more numerous than the children of the one who is married." Now you, my friends, are children of the promise, like Isaac. But just as at that time the child who was born according to the flesh persecuted the child who was born according to the Spirit, so it is now also. But what does the scripture say? "Drive out the slave and her child; for the child of the slave will not share the inheritance with the child of the free woman." So then, friends, we are children, not of the slave but of the free woman. For freedom Christ has set us free. Stand firm, therefore, and do not submit again to a yoke of slavery. (Gal 4:22–5:1)

In this text, Paul uses an early biblical tale that originally legitimated ancient Israel's claim to be God's chosen people and reinterprets it in a rather radical fashion so that this very story now bolsters the claim that the emerging church, rather than the Jewish people, is the true people of God.[39] He does this by associating the newer religion (what will eventually come to be called Christianity) with the younger sibling in the story, Isaac, and by associating Judaism, the older religion, with the older and ultimately non-chosen sibling, Ishmael. A number of unusual details help Paul in his attempt to read this story counterintuitively. For example, the fact that Hagar came from Egypt and that later she and Ishmael are placed in the wilderness of Paran (Gen 21:21), generally understood as a place in the Sinai Peninsula, allows him to read the story in Genesis as a negative allegory against law-observant Jews who linked their practice to the Israelites who came out of Egypt and received the law at Sinai. Paul also manages to explain the Jewish reaction against the church at his time by midrashically exegeting the cryptic ending of Gen 21:9. The Masoretic Text reads, "When Sarah saw the son that Hagar the Egyptian had borne for Abraham playing."[40] In this reading, either Ishmael is simply playing in a frivolous manner, or perhaps "Ishmael was acting like Isaac, claiming Isaac's spot."[41] However, the Septuagint adds the words "with Isaac her son" *(meta Isaak tou huiou autēs)*, helping clarify the text, although still leaving it ambiguous enough to sustain a variety of interpretations. The easiest option would be to assume that Ishmael was playing with Isaac, but the text can support more sinister readings such as mocking, persecuting, or even molesting Isaac.[42] Paul, likely working from some form of the Septuagint, reads the text as describing Ishmael's persecuting Isaac, perhaps suggesting that the persecution was over the attempt to claim Isaac's elect status for himself.[43] This would then support Paul's construal of his contemporary situation as one in which the elder displaced sibling, that is, the historic Jewish community, is persecuting the younger chosen sibling, that is, the church.

Interestingly enough, in the biblical text itself Ishmael appears much less nefarious, and he may be a young child at this time, as indicated by the description of him possibly being placed on Hagar's shoulders (Gen 21:14), as well as the fact that he appears to be a crying infant or small boy when Hagar abandons him under the bush (Gen 21:15). Furthermore, as noted in our lengthier analysis earlier in this book, the real rivalry in this story is between Sarah and Hagar, not between Isaac and Ishmael, who are rarely interacting. Finally, Ishmael—ultimately excluded from the covenant God made with Abraham and his chosen seed—inherited many of the promised blessings. As discussed in chapter 2, he becomes the father of twelve tribes, receives a divine blessing of great fertility, and is even circumcised. But while the text of Genesis is both more subtle and less excluding of the non-chosen brother in the various sibling rivalry stories in Genesis, Paul's reading removes much of this ambiguity in order to heighten the election of the elect as well as the full rejection of the non-elect.

However, such thinking is far from unique to Paul. Rabbinic interpretations at times move along lines strikingly similar to Paul's reading of Gen 21. Thus, one finds midrashim like the following one, in which the rabbis remove much of the ambiguity surrounding the various non-chosen siblings in order to marginalize and delegitimize them completely. This is surely done to secure Jewish claims to God's election against rival claimants who might argue that they are God's elect in that they are related to Abraham. As a quick glance at the following text makes clear, the rabbis link election to Jacob in order to void any claims by others, likely including Christian others, who wish to make counterclaims on the basis of their relationship to Abraham.

> *For the portion of the Lord is His people* (Deut 32:9): A parable; A king had a field which he leased to tenants. When the tenants began to steal from it, He took it away from them and leased it to their children. When the children began to act worse than their fathers, he took it away from them and gave it to (the original tenants') grandchildren.

> When these too became worse than their predecessors, a son was born to him. He said to the grandchildren, "Leave my property. You may not remain therein. Give me back my portion, so that I may repossess it." Thus also, when our father Abraham came into the world, unworthy (descendants) issued from him, Ishmael and all of Keturah's children. When Isaac came into the world, unworthy (descendants) issued from him, Esau and all the princes of Edom, and they became worse than their predecessors. When Jacob came into the world, he did not produce unworthy (descendants), rather all his children were worthy, as it said, *And Jacob was a perfect man dwelling in tents* (Gen 25:27). When did God repossess His portion? Beginning with Jacob as it said, *For the portion of the Lord is His people, Jacob the lot of His inheritance* (Deut 32:9), and, *For the Lord hath chosen Jacob for Himself* (Ps 135:4).[44]

Although it can never be known for certain if this midrash is directed against the early church in the same way that many commentators have seen Paul's midrash on Hagar and Sarah as an attempt to delegitimize Judaism, at least one scholar has made a strong argument that certain nuances of this midrash indicate that it is a point-by-point refutation of various common Christian arguments.[45] Additional evidence might be drawn from the fact that this midrash has an uncanny resemblance to the parable of the wicked tenants (Matt 21:33-46; Luke 20:9-19), another text that in its current form appears to be used as a Christian polemic against the Jewish claim of God's permanent and irrevocable election of the Jewish people.

That both Jews and Christians read themselves back into the sibling stories in Genesis certainly makes clear how central these stories and the notion of election are to both traditions. It is only natural and even expected that the rabbinic Jewish and early Christian communities, religious groups that imbibed their theological worldviews from the Hebrew Bible, would identify themselves with God's chosen people. The very act of claiming the Hebrew Bible as one's sacred text would have led each group to envision themselves as the people of God. However, the historical rivalry that arose between the leaders of the nascent church and their rabbinic counterparts may explain why both traditions mirror each other in their propensity to read the biblical rivalry tales against the grain, emphasizing the rejectedness of the non-chosen sibling or group. Although Paul portrays Judaism as the older sibling, implying that Christianity grew out of some form of pre-existing Judaism, such a portrait ignores the reality that rabbinic Judaism, the religion we know today as Judaism, and Christianity "were born at the same time and nurtured in the same environment."[46] In the Hebrew Bible the non-chosen characters are presented in a more nuanced fashion that allows them a greater and frequently positive place in the divine economy. In fact, the destiny of the chosen group is worked out in relation to the non-chosen others, who themselves benefit from the blessings that flow from God through the elect and, in turn, to the world at large.

While both traditions could benefit by emphasizing those elements in their shared scriptural heritage that create greater theological space for the other community, the truth is that Christianity is disproportionately more in need of such a scriptural corrective. There are indeed rabbinic midrashim, like the *Sifre* passage discussed above, in which the non-elect are depicted in unfairly harsh terms. Additionally, while the ancient rabbis erect a theoretical framework that affirms Gentiles can attain salvation through observing the seven Noahide laws, at times they characterize the Gentile nations of the world as utterly depraved and thus beyond redemption (*b. 'Avod. Zar.* 2-3). Clearly, the heat of such passages can be tempered by the Hebrew Bible's message that the righteous non-elect are not only not damned, but are also recipients of God's blessing. But one should not lose sight of the fact that vast swaths of rabbinic Judaism remained quite in tune with the Hebrew Bible's understanding that the non-elect can indeed stand in right relationship to God.

Furthermore, within the Hebrew Bible and within classical Jewish sources there is recognition that certain Gentiles may actually occupy a middle ground between the elect and the non-elect by drawing near to the Israelite community and her God. Thus, some eschatological texts have members of the Gentile nations worshiping Israel's God while still remaining distinct from the people of Israel, God's elect (Isa 56; Zech 8:20-23). And we know from New Testament (Acts 13:15, 43; 16:14; 17:4; et al.) and rabbinic sources that some Gentiles observed aspects of Jewish religious life but never fully converted.[47] Thus, while Judaism generally treats Christians under the rubric of the non-elect, there may be theological space to view Christians (and Muslims as well) as non-elect peoples who are more closely bound to Israel and her God.[48]

For Christians, the situation is somewhat more complicated. To begin with, in Christianity the status of Jewish non-believers is distinct from the status of Gentile non-believers as clearly recognized by Paul in Rom 9–11. This means that any discussion of providing correctives to the Christian treatment of non-Christians must proceed along two differing tracks. In terms of Gentile non-believers, I see little hope of ameliorating the classical Christian distinction between the saved and the damned except possibly through an idea like that developed by Karl Rahner of the anonymous Christian (i.e., that an adherent of another faith may be practicing a Christian lifestyle while never acknowledging Jesus as savior).[49] The difficulty here flows from the way that Christians understand God's promise to Abraham that the Gentiles would be blessed through him. Within New Testament and classical Christian tradition Gentiles receive this Abrahamic blessing by being joined to the elect people through belief in Jesus as the Christ. While tremendously inclusive toward believing Gentiles, it leaves little, if any, positive theological space for those Gentiles who fail to acknowledge Jesus as the Christ.

When one turns to the Christian theological understanding of Jews who reject the idea that Jesus is the Messiah, let alone God incarnate, there is a bit more flexibility. Many recent commentators, beginning with Krister Stendahl, have argued that Paul conceived of two ways to join God's people, Torah observance for Jews, Christ for Gentiles.[50] Although this theory is highly appealing to anyone interested in furthering Jewish/Christian tolerance (including myself), the Pauline evidence, such as the metaphor of some of the native olive branches being ripped out (Rom 11:17-24), speaks against it. Nevertheless, Paul's language toward the end of Rom 11 is quite cautious, leaving the matter in God's hands. This might at least suggest that Christians need not missionize Jews.[51]

In addition, one wonders whether the Christian theological conceptualization of Judaism might be able to draw upon the Hebrew Bible, the church's earliest scripture, to provide a hermeneutical corrective to the New Testament, the part of the canon given greatest authority within later Christian tradition. Here one gets into issues of the theological relationship between the two testaments. Christian thinkers may ultimately decide that the New Testament, even when it interprets texts from the Hebrew Bible in ways at odds or in direct contradiction with a passage's contextual meaning, is the final authority in the church's attempt to understand its sacred scriptures. But one can imagine certain instances, especially places in which the New Testament's language is highly polemical, in which the church might accord greater weight to the Hebrew Bible's theological vision. In particular, Paul's propensity to assimilate non-believing Jews to the non-chosen sibling in the Genesis stories (Rom 9:6-18; Gal 4:21–5:1) and then to read such stories as endorsing the notion that the non-chosen sibling has been utterly rejected by God might be canonically tempered. Such a reading of the sibling stories distorts the Hebrew Bible's view of the non-chosen sibling, most especially in the case of Ishmael who clearly receives many of the fruits of the Abrahamic promises. It is possible that this type of divisive reading of the sibling tales may have been overemphasized in early Christian thinking when the apocalyptic fervor was at its highest and the nascent church felt most threatened by rival Jewish groups. Aside from a scriptural warrant, Christian culpability for Jewish persecutions over millennia may provide a moral incentive for Christians to rethink some aspects of their theology of election.

The possibility that contemporary Jewish or Christian theologians might consider recalibrating their visions of each other by giving renewed attention to the Hebrew Bible's construal of election theology should not be mistaken for a move to eliminate election's exclusivism. Whether one is speaking of the Hebrew Bible's idea of election or of later Jewish and Christian appropriations of it, election remains a stubbornly particularistic notion. The purpose of any such theological realignment would be to reattune one's tradition to the deepest wellsprings of the Bible's election theology, a theology in which any universal horizon is only glimpsed through God's particularistic interaction with God's chosen people, but a theology that leaves a great deal of space for the non-chosen sibling.

Jews and Christians, while sharing much, will continue to disagree with each other theologically. Judaism and Christianity each emphasize certain aspects of the Hebrew Bible's election theology while deemphasizing others. Recognition of this fact should lead both communities toward a greater clarity of their own tradition's theological development as well as toward a deeper understanding of the sister tradition. This is not to imply that the two traditions now can be reconciled theologically. While Judaism and Christianity grew in analogous ways out of a common theological and social matrix, the fact remains that each tradition developed an elaborate and distinctive theological system that poses a real critique of the other. However, this does not mean that Jewish/Christian dialogue is ultimately an exercise in futility. Jews and Christians can learn a great deal about their respective traditions by understanding the unique ways each tradition has appropriated the Hebrew Bible. Sometimes an insight from the other tradition may lead to a rethinking of one's own theology or to a recovery of an idea that was present but muted. In any case, such honest and critical dialogue helps each tradition's adherents clarify their own distinctive theological claims while at the same time leading to greater understanding of the other tradition's unique but somewhat analogous claims.

Whether such understanding ultimately yields greater respect for the sister tradition remains an open question. After all, reaching a deeper understanding of each tradition's theological development may lead to a heightening of the differences between them and possibly a sharpening of each tradition's critique of the other tradition.[52] Nevertheless, both traditions have the resources to create a bit more theological space for the other community, even while continuing to assert their elective claims. More important, there is a very strong biblical basis for such generosity. The Hebrew Bible hints that the special blessing reserved for the elect can be fully enjoyed only if one is reconciled with one's non-elect brethren. Thus, the chosen brother, Jacob, tells Esau, "For truly to see your face is like seeing the face of God" (Gen 33:10), as he voluntarily shares the fruits of the blessing he stole from Esau and seeks reconciliation with his non-chosen brother.

Concluding Reflections

In this book I hope to have demonstrated the centrality, pervasiveness, and complexity of election theology within the Hebrew Bible as well as its continuing importance to both classical Jewish and Christian thought. Of course, a demonstration of the major role that election plays in the Hebrew Bible as well as in the later Jewish and Christian traditions that grew from this ancient corpus does not compel the conclusion that election is a good theological idea. As noted many times above, election theology is often attacked for being nothing more than a form of raw ethnocentrism. Thus, before concluding this book, it might be useful to review some of the different theological explanations for this most unusual idea proposed within the Hebrew Bible.

Some texts view election as instrumental and connect Israel's chosenness to a larger divine plan or purpose. Thus, election is frequently associated with some type of service. One set of texts sees the fulfillment of Israel's election in her covenantal obedience (e.g., Exod 19:4-6). In other passages, God elects Israel to fulfill a greater teleological purpose in the world as a whole. In such a schema, the elect mediate a blessing to the non-elect (e.g., Gen 12:2-3), or Israel serves as a witness to God's unity and purpose (e.g., Isa 43:10), or the chosen become an exemplar that will attract the non-elect to God (Isa 14:1-2; Zech 8:20-23). In many of these texts, Israel plays a pivotal and salutary role in relation to the other nations of the world. Yet one should not ignore the fact that other texts offer yet other explanations for Israel's election. Deuteronomy 9:4-9, for example, grounds Israel's election in promissory and oddly negative terms: God bestows gracious treatment on an undeserving Israel because of a debt owed to the patriarchs, and also because the Israelites are less evil than the Canaanites. Perhaps the most unusual rationale for Israel's favored status is that proposed in Deut 7:7-8. While the promissory dimension is touched upon, here one finds that ultimately election is grounded in God's mysterious love for Israel. Moreover, this is the rationale that propels much of the action in Genesis, a text in which God repeatedly mysteriously chooses to elevate some over others. Although such election might serve a purpose, it is no longer grounded in that purpose, but in an inexplicable divine love. This distinction is important because it indicates that Israel's failure to own up to her responsibilities does not dissolve that relationship. This is the strange paradox that prophets like Hosea and Ezekiel explore at length.

The Hebrew Bible's assertion of God's special love for Israel suggests that God relates to humans in a much more profound and intimate way than does the widespread contemporary notion that God should have a generic and equal love for all humans. If God's love is like human love in any way whatsoever, then it is unlikely that God has an identical love for all nations and all individuals. While this theological idea may seem arbitrary and unfair, it may also be taken as a sign of God's close and merciful relationship toward humanity as a whole, and of his profoundly *personal* character. Will Herberg has perceptively grasped the deep connection between election and the biblical God's characterization:

> [T]o be scandalized by the universal God acting in and through particularities of time, place, and history, is to conceive the divine in essentially impersonal intellectual terms. . . . The insistence on historical particularity contained in the notion of "chosenness" is . . . part of the Biblical-rabbinic affirmation of the "*living*" God, who meets man in personal encounter in the context of life and history.[1]

The notion of God's mysterious love for Israel, far from being simply a blunt assertion of unbridled ethnocentrism, is intimately bound to Israel's conception of how God lovingly interacts with the world.

While Judaism and Christianity each appropriate the Hebrew Bible's election theology in unique ways, both continue to affirm the Bible's particularistic elective ideas, ideas that are themselves bound up with the biblical understanding of God's personal character. As Jon Levenson has written, "Each community claims to be Israel and to give its members a unique and otherwise unavailable opportunity for participation in divine sonship."[2] Thus both Jews and Christians, "to the extent that they are true to their foundational literatures, must continue to affirm the essential dichotomy between insiders and outsiders."[3] This places a limit on either tradition's ability to fit into the modern pluralistic context, which looks askance at exclusivistic theological claims.

As noted in the introduction to this book, Enlightenment thinkers attempted to split off the Bible's election theology from the idea of monotheism in order to argue that their philosophical agenda was consistent with the Bible's central claims concerning God. While the attempt to reject election theology and preserve biblical monotheism was widely accepted, a number of recent scholars have attacked Israelite monotheism itself. Though, as I have argued, these attacks are misguided, they are correct in recognizing that one cannot isolate Israel's elective ideas from its claims about God and his character.[4] Thus, the Enlightenment attempt to merge biblical and modern philosophic claims has ultimately proved to be unsuccessful. This is not to say that one must reject all Enlightenment values. But it is to say that adherents of both traditions should be aware that the Bible's theological worldview poses a challenge to some of the underlying presuppositions of modernity.

Jewish and Christian believers need to continue to wrestle with the idea of election in all its fullness rather than surrender to the temptation to empty it of its theological power by downplaying its particularistic dimensions or, worse yet, attempting to banish it from the larger theological landscape (the latter being an exercise in futility in my opinion).[5] One must measure the loss that would be sustained by discarding such a central idea—central to both Judaism and Christianity—against the gain to be had by embracing it. It is difficult to see how either Judaism or Christianity could continue to assert its unique theological claims while jettisoning election theology, especially since this theology is so closely tied to biblical claims concerning God's nature and character. It is indisputable that one of the major sources of sustenance for both theological traditions has been the perception at the root of each community's identity that they are God's specially beloved people. This is not to say that the biblical or later Jewish and Christian election theologies pose no problems or deserve no critique. However, it is essential to critique such ideas in a thoughtful and judicious fashion so as to avoid carelessly and needlessly harming or completely destroying some of the most treasured parts of the human religious imagination. My own suspicion is that this ancient idea can speak to us anew today as it has for countless generations of Jews and Christians in the past. Finding a way to accomplish this goal should be the concern of every Jew and Christian. For it is difficult to see how Judaism and Christianity can flourish if they are utterly cut off from the Bible's election theology, a seminal idea that gave rise to and nourished these two traditions for millennia.

NOTES

Introduction to the Topic

1. H. H. Rowley, *The Biblical Doctrine of Election* (London: Lutterworth, 1950), 15.

2. Will Herberg, "The 'Chosenness' of Israel and the Jew of Today," in *Arguments and Doctrines: A Reader of Jewish Thinking in the Aftermath of the Holocaust* (ed. Arthur Cohen; New York: Harper & Row, 1970), 270–83, at 280.

3. Benedict de Spinoza, *A Theologico-Political Treatise* (trans. R. Elwes; New York: Dover, 1951 [originally published anonymously in Latin in 1670]), 55.

4. Ibid., 49.

5. Immanuel Kant, *Religion Within the Boundaries of Mere Reason* (trans. Allen Wood and George Di Giovanni; Cambridge: Cambridge University Press, 1998), 130.

6. Rowley, *Election*, 162.

7. Ibid., 164.

8. Joseph Blenkinsopp, "YHWH and Other Deities: Conflict and Accommodation in the Religion of Israel," *Int* 40.4 (October 1986): 354–66, at 360.

9. I say "most" because one still finds statements such as the following from a work published in 1983 and still in print today: "This task of uniting 'election' with 'universal salvation' required the entire length of the Old Testament as a preparatory stage, the struggles of Jesus and the New Testament writers as a firm base for theological expression, and the missionary endeavors of the church for these last two millennia as only partial fulfillment." Donald Senior and Carroll Stuhlmueller, *The Biblical Foundations for Mission* (Maryknoll, N.Y.: Orbis Books, 1983), 94.

10. Rolf P. Knierim, *The Task of Old Testament Theology: Substance, Method, and Cases* (Grand Rapids: Eerdmans, 1995), 135.

11. For a fuller summary and critique of Knierim's work, see Joel Kaminsky, "Wrestling with Israel's Election: A Jewish Reaction to Rolf Knierim's Biblical Theology," in *Reading the Hebrew Bible for a New Millennium: Form, Concept, and Theological Perspective*, vol. 1 (ed. W. Kim, D. Ellens, M. Floyd, and M. Sweeney; Harrisburg, Pa.: Trinity Press International, 2000), 252–62.

12. Jorge V. Pixley, "History and Particularity in Reading the Hebrew Bible: A Response to Jon D. Levenson," in *Jews, Christians, and the Theology of the Hebrew Scriptures* (ed. A. Bellis and J. Kaminsky; SBL Symposium Series 8; Atlanta: SBL, 2000), 231–37, at 235–36.

13. Jon D. Levenson, "The Perils of Engaged Scholarship: A Rejoinder to Jorge Pixley," in *Jews, Christians, and the Theology of the Hebrew Scriptures*, 239–46, at 243.

14. Thus, even scholars who disagree on their understandings of Paul's view of ethnicity agree that he is not interested in preserving various ethnic identities. Most recently, see Denise K. Buell and Caroline Johnson Hodge, "The Politics of Interpretation: The Rhetoric of Race and Ethnicity in Paul," *JBL* 123.2 (Summer 2004): 235–51, and Charles Cosgrove, "Did Paul Value Ethnicity?" *CBQ* 68.2 (April 2006): 268–90.

15. While the Conservative movement certainly has not rejected election theology, I have heard a number of Conservative rabbis and many Conservative laypeople express their hope that this will eventually occur. As will be seen below, the early Reform movement rejected the particularism of the Bible's election theology. Although not discussed here, later Reform figures did leave a bit more space for the notion of election by seeing the Jews as endowed with a mission to bring biblical monotheism to the larger world. See, for example, K. Kohler, *Jewish Theology: Systematically and Historically Considered* (New York: Ktav, 1918), 323–491.

16. From W. Guenther Plaut, ed., *The Rise of Reform Judaism: A Sourcebook of Its European Origins* (New York: World Union for Progressive Judaism, 1963), 59, cited in Arnold Eisen, *The Chosen People in America* (Bloomington: Indiana University Press, 1983), 19.

17. See Eisen, *The Chosen People*, for fuller elaboration of the manifold approaches that were put forward in the American context.

18. Mordecai Kaplan, *Judaism as a Civilization* (New York: Macmillan, 1934), 253–63.

19. Ibid., 263 (emphasis his).

20. Judith Plaskow, *Standing Again at Sinai: Judaism from a Feminist Perspective* (San Francisco: Harper, 1990), 75–107. Plaskow links election theology to the subordination of Jewish women.

21. Eisen, *Chosen People*, 95–98. I am speaking of the situation in America, but these comments could possibly be applied to Judaism in Canada and other Western European countries. Contemporary Judaism in Israel is a bit unique in that the more liberal Jewish movements have not had much success there.

22. For two clear-headed appraisals, see Paul J. Griffiths, *Problems of Religious Diversity* (Malden, Mass.: Blackwell Publishers, 2001), and Jon D. Levenson, "How Not to Conduct Jewish-Christian Dialogue," *Commentary* 112.5 (December 2001): 31–37, now published in fuller form as "Judaism Addresses Christianity," in *Religious Foundations of Western Civilization: Judaism, Christianity, and Islam* (ed. Jacob Neusner; Nashville: Abingdon Press, 2006), 581–608.

23. On the Jewish theological side of things, see David Novak, *The Election of Israel: The Idea of the Chosen People* (Cambridge: Cambridge University Press, 1995) and Michael Wyschogrod, *The Body of Faith: Judaism as Corporeal Election* (New York: Seabury, 1983). On the Christian side, one finds strong assertions of Christian particularity in the writings of Karl Barth and those theologians who have followed in his path. An example of a compelling Christian theology that takes election quite seriously is R. Kendall Soulen's *The God of Israel and Christian Theology* (Minneapolis: Fortress Press, 1996).

24. In many ways this project is an extension of Jon Levenson's penetrating study titled *The Death and Resurrection of the Beloved Son* (New Haven: Yale University Press, 1993), as well as being strongly influenced by Michael Wyschogrod's work cited in the previous note.

25. This connection was made clear to me from an oral presentation by W. Moberly, "Are Election and Monotheism Bad for You?" (paper presented at SBL, Philadelphia, Pa., 2005).

Moberly has produced a more in-depth article, "Is Monotheism Bad for You? Some Reflections on God, the Bible, and Life in the Light of Regina Schwartz's *The Curse of Cain*" (forthcoming in *The God of Israel*, ed. R. P. Gordon, 2007). He cites as examples not only Schwartz's book but also comments from prize-winning novelist Philip Pullman.

26. See, for example, Seock-Tae Sohn, *The Divine Election of Israel* (Grand Rapids: Eerdmans, 1991); the comprehensive two-volume biblical theology organized around the theme of Israel's election: Horst D. Preuss, *Old Testament Theology* (Louisville: Westminster/John Knox, 1995–1996 [German original 1992]); or Michiel D. Joubert, "The Election of Israel from Old Testament to Rabbinical Times (a Terminological Study)" (PhD diss., Univ. of South Africa, 1986).

Introduction to Chapters 1–4

1. Regina Schwartz, *The Curse of Cain: The Violent Legacy of Monotheism* (Chicago: University of Chicago Press, 1997).

2. This line of argument is invoked several times in Burton Visotzky's *Genesis of Ethics: How the Tormented Family of Genesis Leads Us to Moral Development* (New York: Crown, 1996). For example, on pp. 131–40 note how Visotzky treats Rebekah's tendency to favor Jacob as leading to the fracturing of her family without taking full account of the fact that God himself also favored Jacob, and that perhaps the story saw the fracturing of the family as inevitable. While somewhat more accepting of divine favoritism, Cohen's book, too, seems to imply that authors of Genesis subscribe to the same assumptions found in contemporary magazines on good parenting techniques. See Norman J. Cohen, *Self, Struggle and Change: Family Conflict Stories in Genesis and Their Healing Insights for Our Lives* (Woodstock, Vt.: Jewish Lights, 1995).

3. Mark G. Brett, *Genesis: Procreation and the Politics of Identity* (London/New York: Routledge, 2000). Also see R. Christopher Heard, *Dynamics of Diselection: Ambiguity in Genesis 12–36 and Ethnic Boundaries in Post-Exilic Judah* (Semeia Studies 39; Atlanta: SBL, 2001). Heard, like Brett, dates the final redaction of the stories in Gen 12–36 to the Persian era, but unlike Brett he argues these materials ultimately endorse the group of returnees and the Persian governmental apparatus that supports them in excluding other groups. A similarly reductive historical/ideological approach to these stories can be found in S. David Sperling, *The Original Torah: The Political Intent of the Bible's Writers* (New York: New York University Press, 1998), although Sperling places most of these materials in the monarchic period.

4. Yiu-Wing Fung, *Victim and Victimizer: Joseph's Interpretation of His Destiny* (JSOTSup 308; Sheffield: Sheffield Academic Press, 2000).

5. Wyschogrod, *The Body of Faith*.

1. Cain and Abel

1. A number of these explanations are already generated in ancient Jewish and Christian exegesis of this passage, as discussed in Jack P. Lewis, "The Offering of Abel (Gen 4:4): A History of Interpretation," *JETS* 37.4 (December 1994): 481–96.

2. As argued by Herschel Hobbs, "Was Cain's Offering Rejected by God Because It Was Not a Blood Sacrifice?" in *The Genesis Debate: Persistent Questions About Creation and the Flood* (ed. Ronald Youngblood; Nashville: Thomas Nelson, 1986), 130–47.

3. As argued by Frank Spina, "The Ground for Cain's Rejection (Gen 4): *'ădāmāh* in the Context of Gen 1–11," *ZAW* 104.3 (1992): 319–32.

4. James G. Williams, *The Bible, Violence, and the Sacred: Liberation from the Myth of Sanctioned Violence* (San Francisco: HarperSanFrancisco, 1991), 27.

5. Exactly this argument is made by Frederick E. Greenspahn, *When Brothers Dwell Together: The Preeminence of Younger Siblings in the Hebrew Bible* (New York: Oxford University Press, 1994), 91–92.

6. James Kugel, *The Bible as It Was* (Cambridge: Harvard University Press, 1997), 88–91, citing *Gen. Rab.* 22:5, *Midrash Tanhuma* 9, and Ephraem's *Commentary on Genesis* 3:2. This idea is taken further in some sources where Cain and Abel are seen as each having a long history of bad and good deeds, respectively. See Kugel, 91–92, citing 1 John 3:12 and Heb 11:4, Augustine, *City of God* 15.7, and many other texts. Joel Lohr, "Resisting Temptation: Genesis 4:1-16 and the Urge to Rationalize," unpublished essay, argues very persuasively that the LXX tends to rationalize this story by removing a number of ambiguities preserved in the MT. He goes on to argue that the LXX, in turn, has influenced New Testament readings of this story in ways that do an injustice to the narrative as presented in the Hebrew text.

7. Levenson, *Death and Resurrection*, 72. Levenson also observes that if the text wanted to emphasize the importance of bringing firstfruits, why does it fail to include an etiology of this based on Cain's and Abel's proper or improper offerings?

8. Claus Westermann, *Genesis 1–11: A Commentary* (Minneapolis: Augsburg Press, 1984 [German 1974]), 297.

9. While some have argued that the biblical stress on younger sons preserves a remembrance of a time in which ultimogeniture was the custom, this seems quite unlikely from the biblical evidence, which presents the preeminence of the younger sibling as a surprising turn in the expected outcome of events, as well as from the comparative material from the ancient Near East. For an in-depth study of this particular issue, see Greenspahn, *When Brothers Dwell Together*, 9–29. It should be noted that I dissent from Greenspahn's later arguments (pp. 30–83) that the many biblical stories about younger siblings triumphing over elder ones have nothing to do with the concept of primogeniture, and that the term בכר is utterly unrelated to being an elder child.

10. Although Gruber might be correct that Cain's initial state is one of depression, this doesn't preclude the possibility that such depression is driven by jealousy. Mayer Gruber, "The Tragedy of Cain and Abel: A Case of Depression," *JQR* 69 (October 1978): 89–97.

11. The Hebrew word עון can represent all these concepts at once. It can be translated as "my sin is too great to bear" or possibly "my sin is too great to forgive" inasmuch as the root נשא can carry this latter connotation as well. Thus, the rabbis understood it as Cain confessing his sin, while most interpreters see it as a reference to his punishment being too much to bear. See Kugel, *The Bible as It Was*, 96, citing *Pesiqta de Rav Kahana, Shuvah, piska* 24:11.

12. Kugel, *The Bible as It Was*, 86–87, citing 1 John 3:10-12 and *PRE* 21, among other texts.

13. Professor Patrick Miller drew my attention to this distinction in an oral conversation.

2. *Ishmael and Isaac (and Hagar and Sarah)*

1. Whenever it can be done without creating confusion, I use the names Abram and Sarai when speaking about narratives that occur before their names are changed to Abraham and Sarah in Gen 17.

2. Borrowing Heard's term (from *Dynamics of Diselection*).

3. While many scholars believe that the patriarchal narratives may have originated apart from the framework of the patriarchal promises and that certain of the promises are from an earlier or later redaction, this literary theological treatment of the text is reading the text in its current form. For an example of the fruitfulness of a holistic approach to the function of the promises within their narrative settings, see Martin Hauge, "The Struggles of the Blessed in Estrangement I," *Studia Theologica* 29 (1975): 1–30. The importance of these promises to the larger notion of election will be explored in more depth in chapter 5.

4. For an insightful article on exactly this point in relation to the three wife-sister stories in Genesis, see Mark E. Biddle, "The 'Endangered Ancestress' and Blessing for the Nations," *JBL* 109.4 (Winter 1990): 599–611.

5. Of course, another purpose of this narrative is to foreshadow (or using Jon Levenson's term, have Abraham "pre-enact") the exodus movement that later all Israel will experience. Thus Abraham, like Jacob's whole family, is driven to Egypt by a famine; both are endangered and then rescued through plagues sent by God, and both leave Egypt with great wealth.

6. A point explored at length in Larry Heyler, "The Separation of Abram and Lot: Its Significance in the Patriarchal Narratives," *JSOT* 26 (1983): 77–88.

7. The concept of covenant and its connections to election will receive further attention in chapter 5 so as not to interrupt this extended narrative analysis of the sibling stories.

8. Gerhard von Rad, *Genesis: A Commentary* (OTL; Philadelphia: Westminster, 1972), 191.

9. Joel Rosenberg, *King and Kin: Political Allegory in the Hebrew Bible* (Bloomington: Indiana University Press, 1986), 94.

10. Michael David Goldberg, "God, Action, and Narrative: *Which* Narrative? *Which* Action? *Which* God?" *JR* 68 (January 1988): 39–56.

11. Levenson, *Death and Resurrection*, 92.

12. While I recognize that according to classical source criticism chapter 16 belongs to J and 21 to E, this does not preclude one from reading these materials as a literary whole.

13. Cynthia Gordon, "Hagar: A Throw-Away Character Among the Matriarchs," in *SBL 1985 Seminar Papers* (ed. Kent Richards; Atlanta: Scholars Press, 1985), 273.

14. These and other interesting facets of her character are explored at length in Phyllis Trible, "Hagar: The Desolation of Rejection," in her *Texts of Terror* (Philadelphia: Fortress Press, 1984), 9–35.

15. This point is made with great depth and sensitivity in S. Nakaido's "Hagar and Ishmael as Literary Figures: An Intertextual Study," *VT* 51.2 (2001): 219–42.

16. Levenson, *Death and Resurrection*, 61–169.

17. Larry Lyke, "Where Does 'The Boy' Belong? Compositional Strategy in Genesis 21:14," *CBQ* 56.4 (October 1994): 637–48.

18. Hauge, "The Struggles of the Blessed," 6–10.

19. Thus, Hugh White ("The Initiation Legend of Isaac," *ZAW* 91 [1979]: 1–30; "The Initiation Legend of Ishmael: Gen 16 and 21:8-21," *ZAW* 87 [1975]: 267–306) argues that Isaac's and Ishmael's ordeals function as initiation rituals. It is likely that Israel's survival of the ten plagues visited upon the Egyptians, particularly the final one resulting in the deaths of all the firstborn children and animals, contributed to Israel's sense that she was God's supernatural people (Exod 4:23; 12:27; Deut 14:1-2).

20. Exactly what Ishmael did in Gen 21:9 is a matter of some controversy. The Masoretic Text of this verse ends abruptly with the word "playing," which is a pun on the name Isaac: "When Sarah saw the son that Hagar the Egyptian had borne for Abraham playing." This version of the text may imply that Ishmael was doing nothing more than playing frivolously. However George Coats ("Strife Without Reconciliation: A Narrative Theme in the Jacob Traditions," in *Werden and Werken des Alten Testaments* [ed. Albertz, Muller, Wolff, and Zimmerli; FS Claus Westermann; Gottingen: Vandenhoeck and Ruprecht, 1980], 82–106, at 97), likely attempting to account for Sarah's harsh reaction, suggests the possibility that "Ishmael was acting like Isaac, claiming Isaac's spot." This passage's Pauline interpretation, that Ishmael was persecuting Isaac (Gal 4:29), is discussed in chapter 11.

21. Rosenberg, *King and Kin*, 90. In n. 69 on p. 237 Rosenberg draws attention to the fact that the alternate tradition that Joseph was taken down by Midianites would square the debt that Abraham might owe to the descendants of Keturah who were also sent away without full inheritance rights, in that Midian is one of Keturah's children (Gen 25:1-6). Yair Zakovitch also sees a close causal link between Israel's Egyptian sojourn and Abraham's and Sarah's treatment of Hagar: "The striking resemblance between Hagar's story and the history of Israel in Egypt is not accidental. The message is clear: the oppression of the Israelites is a 'measure for measure' punishment for Hagar's treatment in Abraham's house." Yair Zakovitch, *"And You Shall Tell Your Son . . .": The Concept of the Exodus in the Bible* (Jerusalem: Magnes Press, 1991), 28.

22. For example, see *Gen. Rab.* 38:13, a text that will receive treatment in the final chapter of this book, which examines election in rabbinic Judaism and early Christianity. The seminal importance of Gen 22:15-19 is discussed in R. W. L. Moberly, "The Earliest Commentary on the *Akedah*," *VT* 38 (1988): 302–23.

23. For a more in-depth treatment of this narrative, see the following: Joseph Blenkinsopp, "Abraham and the Righteous of Sodom," *JJS* 33 (Spring 1982): 119–32; Joel S. Kaminsky, "The Sins of the Fathers," *Judaism* 46.3 (Summer 1997): 323–29; Mordecai Roshwald, "A Dialogue Between Man and God," *SJT* 42 (1989): 145–65.

24. This point will be argued more fully in chapter 5.

25. Claus Westermann, *Genesis 12–36: A Commentary* (Minneapolis: Augsburg Press, 1985 [German edition 1981]), 288.

26. Some of these observations are drawn from Mary Donovan Turner, "Rebekah: Ancestor of Faith," *Lexington Theological Quarterly* 20.2 (April 1985): 42–49.

3. *Jacob and Esau*

1. Richard E. Friedman, *The Disappearance of God: A Reverent Investigation of Three Divine Mysteries* (Boston: Little, Brown, 1995), 112.

2. The Hebrew word שׂדה is frequently translated as "field," which does not work well in this instance. I prefer Speiser's translation in that here it refers to the unsown areas like the forest rather than to a plowed field. Another possible translation might be "steppe." Ephraim Speiser, *Genesis* (AB; New York: Doubleday, 1964), 193.

3. The verse could be rendered in rather literal style as "Isaac loved Esau because food was in his mouth" (כי־ציד בפיו). The antecedent of "his" is probably Isaac and thus the NJPS translation, "because he had a taste for game."

4. There is some evidence that the expression in Deuteronomy פִּי שְׁנַיִם means two-thirds. See R. Gordis, "A Note on 1 Sam 13:21," *JBL* 61 (1942): 209–11.

5. I believe the first modern interpreter to suggest this idea is David Daube, *Studies in Biblical Law* (Cambridge: Cambridge University Press, 1947), 190–200. It is also mentioned by K. Luke, "Isaac's Blessing: Genesis 27," *Scripture* 20 (April 1968): 37, n. 13 [33–41], and by James G. Williams, *The Bible, Violence, and the Sacred*, 41.

6. Further evidence supporting the possibility that this may have involved a ruse intended to convince Esau he was consuming blood soup may be found early on in the Joseph story. Here Jacob receives a deed-for-deed punishment for his earlier actions when his ten sons present him with Joseph's garment dipped in goat's blood. It seems likely that a goat is used in this deception to call to mind the goatskin garment that Jacob wore to fool Isaac in order to obtain Esau's blessing. But it is possible that the blood hearkens back to Jacob's other misdeed, that is, his obtaining Esau's primogeniture through offering him a red-colored soup that Esau took to be goat's blood.

7. Whether Esau himself lives out such a curse or Jacob himself lives out Isaac's blessing is discussed below.

8. Although these variations in the story line may be due to variant sources (Gen 27:41-45=J, 27:46–28:9=P), it is clear that in this instance the way in which they are ordered is literarily significant.

9. As one can see from David Marcus's "Traditional Jewish Responses to the Question of Deceit in Genesis 27," in *Jews, Christians, and the Theology of the Hebrew Scriptures* (ed. A. Bellis and J. Kaminsky; Atlanta: SBL, 2000), 293–305.

10. Speiser, *Genesis*, 193, 205.

11. Laurence A. Turner, *Announcements of Plot in Genesis*, (JSOTSup 96; Sheffield: Sheffield Academic Press, 1990), 179–80.

12. Terence Fretheim, "Which Blessing Does Isaac Give Jacob?" in *Jews, Christians, and the Theology of the Hebrew Scriptures* (ed. Bellis and Kaminsky; Atlanta: SBL, 2000), 279–91.

13. Fretheim, "Which Blessing?" 287, citing Hugh White, *Narration and Discourse in the Book of Genesis* (Cambridge: Cambridge University Press, 1991), 225.

14. Goldberg, "God, Action, and Narrative," as well as Fretheim, "Which Blessing?"

15. Anthony Thiselton, "The Supposed Power of Words in the Biblical Writings," *JTS* (1974): 283–99.

16. Rowley, *Election*, 34–35.

17. Susan Niditch, *Underdogs and Tricksters* (San Francisco: Harper & Row, 1987), 99–101. Kevin Walton, *Thou Traveller Unknown: The Presence and Absence of God in the Jacob Narrative* (Paternoster: Carlisle, Cumbria, 2003), 108–10, astutely notes that while Rebekah and Jacob may be ambiguous characters, so too is God within this narrative.

18. For evidence that Rebekah is often portrayed negatively as well as a much more sympathetic treatment of her character, see Christine Garside Allen, "On Me Be the Curse, My Son!" in *Encounter with the Text: Form and History in the Hebrew* Bible (ed. Martin Buss; Philadelphia: Fortress Press, 1979), 159–72.

19. Edward L. Greenstein, "The Formation of the Biblical Narrative Corpus," *AJSR* 15 (Fall 1990): 151–78, and Sperling, *The Original Torah*.

20. Levenson, *Death and Resurrection*, 118.

21. K. Luke, "Isaac's Blessing: Genesis 27," 39–40, notes the phrasing "your brothers"

and "sons of your mother" found in Gen 27:29 is a set word pair that also occurs in Ps 50:20; Deut 13:7; and Judg 8:19. The plural forms here might come from the previous plural mention of "peoples" and "nations," also a set word pair.

22. George W. Coats, *From Canaan to Egypt: Structural and Theological Context for the Joseph Story* (CBQMS 4; Washington, D.C.: Catholic Biblical Association, 1976), 80–92.

23. Coats, "Strife Without Reconciliation," 106.

24. Levenson, *Death and Resurrection*, 67–68.

25. Coats, "Strife Without Reconciliation," 103.

26. Westermann, *Genesis 12–36*, 527.

4. Joseph and His Brothers

1. Some might wonder how one can speak of Joseph as the elect one when all of Jacob's sons are part of God's chosen people. However, it is clear that even among those chosen, some are specially elevated over the general elect. This can be seen in numerous places in the Hebrew Bible, including God's selection of David's household to be Israel's royal house as well as by the language surrounding God's priestly choice, especially in the covenant he makes with Phineas in Num 25:10-13. The election of the nation does not lead to a cessation of all further acts of divine favoring.

2. While some of the arguments made here concerning Reuben's and Judah's motivations may seem a bit forced, they are bolstered once one takes account of the close literary and theological similarities between Gen 37–50 and the Succession Narrative in 2 Sam 9–1 Kgs 2 that are discussed more fully further below. In the narratives describing David's household turmoil, many of the characters act in ways that may be viewed positively on the surface level, but upon deeper inspection their actions become much more ambiguous and can be read as being motivated by raw self-interest. Thus, Absalom's murder of Amnon appears to be revenge for Amnon's rape of Absalom's full sister Tamar. But the truth is that Absalom needs his older firstborn brother (see 2 Sam 3:2) out of the way if he is to become the next king, which the later narrative implies is his hidden agenda all along. Similar ambiguities can be found in many other characters' actions in 2 Samuel (Ziba and Joab, to mention the two most obvious). I believe the same holds true for many characters in the Joseph story, which, as I explore at greater length toward the end of this chapter, shares a host of literary affinities with the Succession Narrative.

3. James L. Kugel, *In Potiphar's House* (Cambridge: Harvard University Press, 1990), 73–84, 94–98.

4. Ibid., 77–79; *Gen. Rab.* 87:3.

5. Thus Claus Westermann (*Genesis 37–50: A Commentary* [Minneapolis: Augsburg Press, 1986 (German edition 1982)], 49) states that "the narrative of Judah and Tamar has not been inserted into the Joseph story; it has nothing to do with it but rather is an insertion into the Jacob story, into its conclusion." See similarly Bruce Vawter's proclamation (*On Genesis: A New Reading* [Garden City, N.Y.: Doubleday, 1977], 398) that "this chapter did, as a matter of fact, originally have no connection with the Story of Joseph and that it is therefore, in some sense an intrusion here."

6. Robert Alter, *The Art of Biblical Narrative* (New York: Basic Books, 1981), 5–11.

7. Levenson, *Death and Resurrection*, 157–64. Levenson makes clear that many of the connections he notes were already found in early rabbinic midrash.

8. Ibid., 166, citing an oral communication with James Nohrnberg.

9. Alter, *Biblical Narrative*, 163–64.

10. See n.2 in "Introduction to Chapters 1–4."

11. Further proof of this is that even after the reconciliation occurs, Benjamin continues to receive preferential treatment. Joseph gives him three hundred pieces of silver and five sets of garments while giving only a single set of garments to each of the other brothers (Gen 45:22).

12. Wyschogrod, *The Body of Faith*, 64–65.

13. Coats, *From Canaan*, 81–85.

14. This insight comes from Walter Moberly in oral communication.

15. Charles T. Fritsch, "God Was with Him: A Theological Study of the Joseph Narrative," *Int* 9 (1955): 21–34.

16. Coats, *From Canaan*, 85–86.

17. Ibid., 84–92.

18. John Rogerson, "Can a Doctrine of Providence Be Based on the Old Testament?" in *Ascribe to the Lord: Biblical and Other Studies in Memory of Peter C. Craigie* (ed. L. Eslinger and G. Taylor; JSOTSup 67; Sheffield: JSOT Press, 1988), 529–43. It is important to keep in mind that not every eschatological oracle sees history coming to a final consummation. Many announce a time of coming judgment or good fortune.

19. For some interesting observations on the importance of the motif of sight/blindness in the Abraham stories, see Devora Steinmetz, *From Father to Son: Kinship, Conflict, and Continuity in Genesis* (Louisville: Westminster/John Knox, 1991), 76–85.

20. See Greenstein, "Formation of the Biblical Narrative," 165–67, and Joseph Blenkinsopp, "Theme and Motif in the Succession History (2 Sam. xi 2ff) and the Yahwist Corpus," in *Volume du Congrès. Genève 1965* (VTSup 15; Leiden: Brill, 1965), 44–57. Blenkinsopp notes on p. 53 that the two stories have a very similar sounding character, e.g., Bath Shua in Gen 38 and Bath Sheba in 2 Sam; in 1 Chr 3:5 Solomon's mother is called Bath Shua.

21. For an example of how this last idea might operate, see Larry Lyke's book, *King David with the Wise Woman of Tekoa* (JSOTSup 255; Sheffield: Sheffield Academic Press, 1997), an insightful analysis of the relationship between 2 Sam 14 and the Genesis stories of sibling rivalry.

22. Reuben Ahroni, "Why Did Esau Spurn the Birthright? A Study in Biblical Interpretation," *Judaism* 29 (1980): 323–31, at 325–26.

23. For further theological reflections on such subversions, see my "Humor and the Theology of Hope in Genesis: Isaac as a Humorous Figure," *Int* 54 (October 2000): 363–75.

5. Promise and Covenant

1. For a full review of the development of the history of scholarship on this issue, see Claus Westermann, *The Promises to the Fathers: Studies on the Patriarchal Narratives* (Philadelphia: Fortress Press, 1980 [German original 1976]). Westermann actually speaks of six distinct forms of promise texts as well as numerous combined forms. He sees the promise of a son and its separate but close ally, the promise of numerous progeny, as being the earliest form of this motif. He argues that the promise of land in its current form is a

later development that might have had an ancient analogue that became irrelevant once the patriarchal cycle included the notion that Abraham arrived in Canaan.

2. The ancient rabbis developed the idea that Israel was bound by 613 commandments and the rest of humanity by only a few. The exact number varies in different texts, but one commonly finds references to seven commandments Gentiles must observe, including such basic ideas as setting up proper courts, not murdering, stealing, committing idolatry, committing adultery, and so on.

3. For an extended syntactic analysis of Gen 12:1-3, see William Yarchin, "Imperative and Promise in Genesis 12:1-3," *Studia Biblica et Theologica* 10 (1980): 164–78. For a sensitive theological reading of the placement of these verses and their relationship to the larger structure of the patriarchal narratives in Genesis, see Hans Walter Wolff, "The Kerygma of the Yahwist," in *The Vitality of Old Testament Tradition* (ed. Walter Brueggemann and Hans W. Wolff; Atlanta: John Knox, 1975), 41–66. For a close analysis of these verses in relation to larger canonical themes, see R. W. L. Moberly, *The Bible, Theology, and Faith: A Study of Abraham and Jesus* (Cambridge: Cambridge University Press, 2000), 120–27, and Jo Bailey Wells, "Blessing to All the Families of the Earth: Abram as Prototype of Israel," chap. 6 in idem, *God's Holy People: A Theme in Biblical Theology* (JSOTSup 305; Sheffield: Sheffield Academic Press, 2000), 185–207.

4. For a full discussion of all the possible options, see Paul R. Williamson, *Abraham, Israel and the Nations: The Patriarchal Promise and Its Covenantal Development in Genesis* (JSOTSup 315; Sheffield: Sheffield Academic Press, 2000), 220–34, or more recent yet, Keith Nigel Grüneberg, *Abraham, Blessing and the Nations: A Philological and Exegetical Study of Genesis 12:3 in its Narrative Context* (BZAW 332; New York; Berlin: Walter de Gruyter, 2003).

5. As Williamson and Grüneberg note, it is possible that the authors of the text wished to communicate two distinct but related ideas through the use of these two different verbal forms. If so, then the *niphal* and the *hithpael* should be translated in differing ways rather than assimilated to each other.

6. A point made with great persuasiveness by Moberly in *The Bible, Theology, and Faith*, 123–24.

7. The intercessory role played by Abraham/Israel on behalf of the nations of the world is emphasized in Wolff, "Kerygma," 56.

8. For a wide-ranging theological meditation on this passage, see John A. Davies, *A Royal Priesthood: Literary and Intertextual Perspectives on an Image of Israel in Exodus 19:6* (JSOTSup 395; London: T&T Clark, 2004).

9. Rowley, *Election*, 161.

10. Cited in n. 3 above.

11. The literature on covenant is extensive. What follow are some of the most important works: Delbert Hillers, *Covenant: The History of a Biblical Idea* (Baltimore: Johns Hopkins, 1969); Jon D. Levenson, *Sinai and Zion: An Entry into the Jewish Bible* (Minneapolis: Winston Press, 1985); Dennis J. McCarthy, *Treaty and Covenant* (AnBib 21A; Rome: Pontifical Biblical Institute, 1978); George Mendenhall, "Covenant Forms in Ancient Israel," *BA* 17 (1954): 50–76; Ernest W. Nicholson, *God and His People: Covenant and Theology in the Old Testament* (Oxford: Clarendon Press, 1986).

12. Contemporary Christian interpreters with a strong Calvinist streak have argued that it is a mistake to call the covenant with Abraham unconditional. See Ronald Youngblood, "The Abrahamic Covenant: Conditional or Unconditional?" in *The Living*

and Active Word of God (ed. Morris Inch and Ronald Youngblood; FS Samuel Schultz; Winona Lake, Ind.: Eisenbrauns, 1983), 31–46.

13. Moberly, "Earliest Commentary."

14. Moshe Weinfeld, "The Covenant of Grant in the Old Testament and in the Ancient Near East," *JAOS* 90 (1970): 184–203. While the text of 2 Sam 7 never employs the word ברית, it is found in Ps 89, a text that closely parallels 2 Sam 7 in many ways.

15. There is an ongoing debate about whether the passages in Kings that conditionalize the promise of eternal dynasty to David are the work of Dtr 2, or whether these texts are the work of Dtr 1, who conceived of two different promises: one of conditional eternal dynasty over all Israel, and one of unconditional eternal dynasty over Judah. See Richard E. Friedman, *The Exile and Biblical Narrative* (HSM 22; Chico: Scholars Press, 1981), 10–13; Baruch Halpern, *The First Historians* (San Francisco: Harper & Row, 1988), 144–80; Jon D. Levenson, "From Temple to Synagogue: 1 Kings 8," in *Traditions in Transformation* (ed. Halpern and Levenson; Winona Lake, Ind.: Eisenbrauns, 1981), 143–66, and idem, "The Last Four Verses in Kings," *JBL* 103 (September 1984): 353–61, at 354–56. While there are good arguments on both sides, my suspicions are that these passages are exilic additions from Dtr 2. Even if these specific passages come from the hand of Dtr 1, they still may demonstrate a conditionalizing of the Davidic covenant found in 2 Sam 7. In any case, texts like Jer 7 challenge the Zion theology, a theology that was closely related to Davidic claims of eternal dynasty over Jerusalem, by noting that God reserved the right to abandon Jerusalem if her inhabitants failed to abide by his laws. Of course, Jer 7 itself relies on a very ancient idea, already found in 1 Sam 3–4, that the Deity's unconditioned promises carried implicit demands, which, if ignored, nullified the promises.

16. The terminology used of the two types of covenants is somewhat problematic. The Sinaitic covenant, which is compared to ancient Near Eastern suzerainty-vassal treaties, is described as conditional. The Davidic covenant, which is compared to a type of covenantal grant, is described as unconditional, at least in its earliest form. But as noted by Levenson, "This terminology is regrettable, since it can encourage the notion that the covenant with David is without stipulations, a covenant of grace rather than of law. In fact, however, the Davidid is still obligated and hence subject to punishment." Jon D. Levenson, "Who Inserted the Book of the Torah?" *HTR* 68 (July 1975): 203–33, at 225. Levenson suggests the term "ancestral" (Davidic) versus "contemporary" (Sinaitic) as well as mentioning Weinfeld's preference for "obligatory and treaty" (Sinaitic) versus "promissory and grant" (Davidic). It seems that no single pair of terms can do full justice to the nuances of each type of covenant, and thus, I have employed the more common terms, "conditional" and "unconditional," but with qualification.

17. Levenson, *Sinai and Zion*, 211. Also see his article "The Davidic Covenant and Its Modern Interpreters," *CBQ* 41 (1979): 205–19.

18. Brooks Schramm, "Exodus 19 and Its Christian Appropriation," in *Jews, Christians, and the Theology of the Hebrew Scriptures* (ed. A. Bellis and J. Kaminsky; Symposium Series 8; Atlanta: SBL, 2000), 327–52, at 342 (emphasis mine).

19. A similar point is made by Rolf Rendtorff, *The Covenant Formula: An Exegetical and Theological Examination* (OTS; Edinburgh: T&T Clark, 1998 [German original 1995]), 1–4. He also notes here that while scholars separate covenant and election, they are unified from the perspective of Neh 9.

20. This is not to say that human behavior is irrelevant to Paul. While human behavior plays no role in the elective process, immoral human behavior can indeed alienate one from God (Rom 10:21-23; 1 Cor 5:9-13).

21. In Rom 11:13-24 Paul allows for a bit more human participation in these matters. In some sense the radical idea that God accomplishes his ends with little to no human help is first opened by thinkers like Ezekiel, whose view of the human ability to act morally becomes dimmer over the course of his ministry, as noted by Jacqueline Lapsley, *Can These Bones Live? The Problem of the Moral Self in the Book of Ezekiel* (BZAW 301; Berlin: Walter de Gruyter, 2000).

6. *Election in Leviticus and Deuteronomy*

1. P is generally considered to have authored substantial parts of the first four biblical books. Much, if not all, of the legislation found in Leviticus and Numbers belongs to P. Furthermore, this source is responsible for parts of the narrative material in Genesis and Exodus. Some scholars believe that the P school actually redacted the Pentateuch. While Wellhausen saw P as the latest of the four written sources of the Pentateuch, many scholars today think that much of P is older than D and thus likely pre-exilic or at least it contains many elements that are pre-exilic. For full discussion and bibliography, see Jacob Milgrom's monumental three-volume Anchor Bible Commentary on Leviticus (New York: Doubleday, 1–16=1991, 17–22=2000, 23–27=2001). Although I recognize that there is a distinction between most of the P materials and what scholars call H, the Holiness Code (Lev 17–26), for the purposes of this book I will be treating all the Priestly material as a unity and contrasting it to Deuteronomy. For more on the distinctive innovations of the Holiness Code, see Israel Knohl, *The Sanctuary of Silence: The Priestly Torah and the Holiness School* (Minneapolis: Fortress Press, 1995).

2. On the concept of holiness in the Hebrew Bible see John G. Gammie, *Holiness in Israel* (OBT; Philadelphia: Fortress Press, 1989). For a survey of the ways in which the concept of holiness changed between the biblical and rabbinic periods see Jacob Neusner, *The Idea of Purity in Ancient Judaism* (SJLA 1; Leiden: Brill, 1973), and more recently Howard Eilberg Schwartz, *The Savage in Judaism* (Bloomington: Indiana University Press, 1990). For an overview of holiness in general see Rudolf Otto, *The Idea of the Holy* (trans. John W. Harvey; London: Oxford University Press, 1958).

3. Jacob Milgrom, *Studies in Cultic Theology and Terminology* (SJLA 36; Leiden: Brill, 1983), 75–84.

4. A similar claim seems to be made about David's plans for the temple in 1 Chr 28:11-19.

5. According to P, it appears that in certain instances even a non-Israelite could affect God's environment in a negative way if he ate impure things within the land of Israel (Lev 17:15).

6. I have relied on Jacob Milgrom's ideas about the nature of sin and its relationship to the cult in ancient Israel. One of Milgrom's central ideas is that the failure to guard against sin and to neutralize sins by ritual action causes God to abandon his sanctuary, thus wreaking havoc on Israel. Interestingly enough, Milgrom claims that the חטאת sacrifices are not really for the atonement of the sinner, but for the cleansing of the sanctuary where the sin has come to roost. The sinner is already forgiven as soon as he acknowledges his misdeed. It is the pollution of the sanctuary, which happens whenever any Israelite sins, that requires the sacrifice.

7. Baruch A. Levine, *In the Presence of the Lord* (SJLA 5; Leiden: Brill, 1974), 75.

8. Ibid., 78.

9. I reject the notion advocated by some scholars that negative human behavior in Genesis 1–11 shatters the image of God, which afterward is only located among Israel. See for example, John T. Strong, "Israel as a Testimony to YHWH's Power: The Priests' Definition of Israel," in *Constituting the Community* (FS S. Dean McBride; ed. John Strong and Steven Tuell; Winona Lake, Ind.: Eisenbrauns, 2005), 89–106.

10. An excellent comparison of the differences between P and D can be found in *Encyclopedia Judaica*, vol. 13, cols. 232–63, s.v. "Pentateuch," by Moshe Weinfeld. See esp. cols. 243–57.

11. Of course, it is difficult to know whether Deuteronomy assumes the validity of most P legislation even though it isn't explicitly mentioned by Deuteronomy, or whether Deuteronomy's silence on a topic indicates a rejection of that piece of Levitical legislation.

12. This has been the consensus, but it has recently been challenged by Sandra Richter, *The Deuteronomistic History and the Name Theology* (BZAW 318; Berlin: Walter de Gruyter, 2002).

13. Davies, *Royal Priesthood*, 45 (emphasis his).

14. Moshe Weinfeld, *Deuteronomy and the Deuteronomic School* (Oxford: Oxford University Press, 1972), 191–243.

15. For example, see Eyal Regev, "Priestly Dynamic Holiness and Deuteronomic Static Holiness," *VT* 51.2 (2001): 243–61.

16. This is generally deduced from two facts, one linguistic, the other socio-historical. Often in Deuteronomy, the alien is paired with the orphan and widow (Deut 10:18; 24:19; 27:19), all seen as generally dispossessed parties. It may be that D was concerned about such marginalized parties in the wake of two events that would have occurred during the time the first edition of D was being composed: the fall of the northern kingdom in 722 B.C.E., and Sennacherib's siege of Jerusalem in 701. Both events would have created many dispossessed persons who would have ended up within the orbit of Jerusalem, as argued by José Ramírez Kidd, *Alterity and Identity in Israel* (BZAW 283; Berlin: Walter de Gruyter, 1999), 35–47. However, in other instances, such as that found in the cultic legislation in Deut 14:21, the alien certainly refers to a non-Israelite resident alien. The various terms surrounding foreigners and aliens are discussed in chapter 8 below.

17. Patrick Miller, "God's Other Stories: On the Margins of Deuteronomic Theology," in *Realia Dei* (ed. Theodore Hiebert and Prescott Williams; FS Edward Campbell; Atlanta: Scholars Press, 1999), 185–94; idem, "The Wilderness Journey in Deuteronomy: Style, Structure, and Theology in Deuteronomy 1–3," *Covenant Quarterly* 55 (1997): 50–68.

Introduction to Chapters 7–8

1. Jeremy Cott, "The Biblical Problem of Election," *JES* 21.2 (Spring 1984): 199–228, at 204.

2. Ibid., 224.

3. Schwartz, *Curse of Cain*, 18–19.

4. Ibid., 20.

5. Gerd Lüdemann, *The Unholy in Holy Scripture: The Dark Side of the Bible* (trans. John Bowden; Louisville: Westminster/John Knox, 1997), 71.

6. Cott, "The Biblical Problem," 207.

7. See, for example, Steven McKenzie, *All God's Children: A Biblical Critique of Racism* (Louisville: John Knox, 1997) and Daniel Smith-Christopher, "Between Ezra and Isaiah: Exclusion, Transformation, and Inclusion of the 'Foreigner' in Post-Exilic Biblical Theology," in *Ethnicity and the Bible* (ed. Mark Brett; Leiden: Brill, 1996), 117–42.

8. See my argument in "The Concept of Election and Second Isaiah: Recent Literature," *BTB* 31.44 (Winter 2001): 135–44, as well as chapter 9 below.

7. *The Anti-elect in the Hebrew Bible*

1. Here I have benefited from D. W. Van Winkle's "Genocide and the God of Love" (Winifred E. Weter Faculty Award Lecture, Seattle Pacific University, 1989) as well as from C. S. Cowles, Eugene Merrill, Daniel Gard, and Tremper Longman, *Show Them No Mercy: 4 Views on God and Canaanite Genocide* (Grand Rapids: Zondervan, 2003).

2. Lawson Stone, "Ethical and Apologetic Tendencies in the Redaction of the Book of Joshua," *CBQ* 53 (1991): 25–36.

3. Lori Rowlett, *Joshua and the Rhetoric of Violence: A New Historicist Analysis* (JSOTSup 226; Sheffield: Sheffield Academic Press, 1996). As noted below, Rowlett places these texts in the late monarchic era and sees them primarily as an attempt to prevent internal dissent.

4. Several scholars have argued that the Genesis texts offer an alternative view on how one should deal with the natives of the land or perhaps a subtle critique of texts like Joshua. See Mark Brett, "Reading the Bible in the Context of Methodological Pluralism: The Undermining of Ethnic Exclusivism in Genesis," in *Rethinking Contexts, Rereading Texts: Contributions from the Social Sciences to Biblical Interpretation* (ed. M. Daniel Carroll R.; JSOTSup 299; Sheffield: Sheffield Academic Press, 2000), 48–75; idem, *Genesis*; Robert L. Cohn, "Before Israel: The Canaanites as Other in Biblical Tradition," in *The Other in Jewish Thought and History: Constructions of Jewish Culture and Identity* (ed. Laurence Silberstein and Robert Cohn; New York: New York University Press, 1994), 74–90; idem, "Negotiating (with) the Natives: Ancestors and Identity in Genesis," *HTR* 96 (2003): 147–66; and Ellen F. Davis, "Critical Traditionalism: Seeking an Inner-Biblical Hermeneutic," in *The Art of Reading Scripture* (ed. Ellen Davis and Richard Hays; Grand Rapids: Eerdmans, 2003), 163–80. Of course, one could argue that although the Genesis texts are more open to living with the Canaanites, from a canonical perspective, the patriarchs in Genesis often act in ways that the later tradition found unacceptable in the post-Mosaic period.

5. In Gen 38, it is clear that Judah's wife is a Canaanite, and the fact that Tamar's lineage is not supplied may indicate that she too has Canaanite roots.

6. For a well-reasoned assessment of the historical accuracy of the relevant biblical texts as well as of various scholarly models of the emergence of Israel in the land of Canaan, see J. Maxwell Miller, "The Israelite Occupation of Canaan," in *Israelite and Judean History* (ed. J. H. Hayes and J. M. Miller; OTL; Philadelphia: Westminster, 1977), 213–84.

7. Henry Bullinger, *The Decades of Henry Bullinger* (ed. Thomas Hardy; Cambridge: Cambridge University Press, 1849), 376. Cited in James Turner Johnson, *Ideology, Reason, and the Limitation of War: Religious and Secular Concepts 1200–1740* (Princeton: Princeton University Press, 1975), 111.

8. William Gouge, *Gods Three Arrowes: Plague, Famine, Sword, in Three Treatises* (London: George Miller for Edward Brewster, 1631), 188. Cited in Johnson, *Ideology*, 124.

9. Cited in Roland Bainton, *Christian Attitudes Toward War and Peace: A Historical Survey and Critical Re-evaluation* (New York: Abingdon Press, 1960), 168. Bainton catalogs many other instances of the equation of Native Americans with the biblical anti-elect on pp. 165–72.

10. See Rowlett, *Joshua*. Recently, Nathan MacDonald, *Deuteronomy and the Meaning of "Monotheism"* (Tübingen: Mohr Siebeck, 2003), 108–22, has put forward a theological explanation for the call to put the Canaanites to the ban. He argues that in Deuteronomy such language is a metaphorical expression of devoting oneself totally to YHWH alone.

11. A number of recent scholars who assume a minimalist view of the historicity of the biblical text advocate this position in some form. See Brett, *Genesis*, as well as Heard, *Dynamics of Diselection*.

12. For a balanced assessment see Jon D. Levenson, "Is There a Counterpart in the Hebrew Bible to New Testament Antisemitism?" *JES* 22 (1985): 242–60, esp. 248–50.

13. Translation taken from *The Schocken Passover Haggadah* (ed. Nahum Glatzer; 1953; repr., New York: Schocken, 1996), 39.

14. Moses Maimonides, *Laws Concerning Kings and Wars* 6.4, cited in Avi Sagi, "The Punishment of Amalek in Jewish Tradition: Coping with the Moral Problem," *HTR* 87.3 (1994): 323–46, at 342.

15. Thus, *Sifre* on Deut 20:18 argues that this verse implies that if they do repent, the Canaanites are not to be slain. For the text, see Louis Finkelstein, ed., *Sifre on Deuteronomy* (New York: Jewish Theological Seminary, 1993), 238 (פיסקא ר"ב). The standard English translation is *Sifre: A Tannaitic Commentary on the Book of Deuteronomy* (trans. Reuven Hammer; Yale Judaica Series 24; New Haven: Yale University Press, 1986), §202, p. 218. A similar but more elaborate tradition is found in *b. Sot.* 35b, which informs us that the Canaanite nations were indeed given full notice because they could read the stones that Joshua erected in the Jordan and be moved to repent. And a similar midrashic idea about Amalek is expressed in *b. Sanh.* 96b, which reports that the descendants of Haman studied Torah in the academies of Bnei Braq.

16. Sagi, "The Punishment of Amalek in Jewish Tradition," 331–36.

17. Stone, "Ethical and Apologetic Tendencies" and Davis, "Critical Traditionalism." For an argument that the anti-Amalek text in Deut 25 is actually an attempt to spiritualize the commandment and direct it at unethical Israelite behaviors, see Diana Lipton, "Remembering Amalek: A Positive Biblical Model for Dealing with Negative Scriptural Types," in *Reading Texts, Seeking Wisdom: Scripture and Theology* (ed. D. F. Ford and G. N. Stanton; London: SCM, 2003), 139–53.

18. Even in those texts like Deuteronomy, in which the anti-Canaanite polemic is quite important, it is likely (as discussed earlier) that the call to annihilate the Canaanites is primarily an inner-directed attempt to call Israel to be fully devoted to YHWH alone.

8. *The Non-elect in the Hebrew Bible*

1. Frequently, the schools that produced Leviticus and Numbers, Ezek 40–48, and Ezra and Nehemiah are lumped together and viewed as the regressive Priestly forces opposed

valiantly, but unsuccessfully, by the parties behind texts like Isa 56–66. This view is adumbrated in Paul Hanson's seminal book, *The Dawn of Apocalyptic: The Historical and Sociological Roots of Jewish Apocalyptic Eschatology* (Philadelphia: Fortress Press, 1975). Hanson explicitly links Ezek 40–48 to Ezra and Nehemiah and sees these as coming from a Priestly or, in his language, "hierocratic" group. He views Isa 56–66 as the product of a prophetic or "visionary" group. While Hanson does not link the Priestly group to the authors of Leviticus, it seems likely that he would see Leviticus as a text that was, if not authored by the postexilic hierocracy, at least used by that group to oppress the visionary group and exclude it from power. For a thoughtful and balanced critique of Hanson's proposal, see Brooks Schramm, *The Opponents of Third Isaiah: Reconstructing the Cultic History of the Restoration* (JSOTSup 193; Sheffield: Sheffield Academic Press, 1995), 81–182. That the Priestly authors of Leviticus and Numbers are indeed frequently viewed as exponents of intolerance can be deduced from the fact that Leviticus and Numbers have traditionally received scant attention in most Protestant biblical scholarship, as well as from the novelty of Mary Douglas's arguments to the contrary. See Mary Douglas, "The Stranger in the Bible," *Archives européennes de sociologie* 35 (1994): 283–98; and idem, *In the Wilderness: The Doctrine of Defilement in the Book of Numbers* (JSOTSup 158; Sheffield: Sheffield Academic Press, 1993).

2. Smith-Christopher, "Between Ezra and Isaiah," 117–42.

3. Actually, this word has quite a number of meanings, not all of which are relevant to the points argued here. For a full study, see L. A. Snijders, "The Meaning of זר in the Old Testament: An Exegetical Study," *OtSt* 10 (1954): 1–154.

4. There is a growing body of literature on both the alien in Israel and the question of how ancient Israel as well as rabbinic Judaism dealt with those wishing to attach themselves to the people of Israel. On the alien in the biblical period, see the following works: Douglas, "The Stranger in the Bible"; Christiana van Houten, *The Alien in Israelite Law* (JSOTSup 107; Sheffield: Sheffield Academic Press, 1991); D. Kellermann, גור, *TDOT* 2:439–49; Jacob Milgrom, "Religious Conversion and the Revolt Model for the Foundation of Israel," *JBL* 101 (1982): 169–76; Saul Olyan, "Generating 'Self' and 'Other': The Polarity of Israelite/Alien," chap. 3 in idem, *Rites and Rank: Hierarchy in Biblical Representations of Cult* (Princeton: Princeton University Press, 2000); Kidd, *Alterity and Identity in Israel*; Rolf Rendtorff, "The *gēr* in the Priestly Laws of the Pentateuch," in *Ethnicity and the Bible* (ed. Mark Brett; Leiden: Brill, 1996), 77–87; and Frank Spina, "Israelites as *gērîm*, 'Sojourners' in Social and Historical Context," in *The Word of the Lord Shall Go Forth: Essays in Honor of David Noel Freedman in Celebration of His Sixtieth Birthday* (ed. Carol Myers and M. O'Connor; ASOR Special Volume Series 1; Winona Lake, Ind.: Eisenbrauns, 1983), 321–35. On the shift that took place between the biblical and rabbinic periods, see Shaye J. D. Cohen, *The Beginnings of Jewishness: Boundaries, Varieties, Uncertainties* (Berkeley: University of California Press, 1999); Robert Goldenberg, *The Nations That Know Thee Not: Ancient Jewish Attitudes Towards Other Religions* (New York: New York University Press, 1998); David Novak, *The Image of the Non-Jew in Judaism: An Historical and Constructive Study of the Noahide Laws* (TST 14; New York: Edwin Mellen, 1983).

5. Van Houten, *The Alien*, 175.

6. A passage such as Esth 8:17 may suggest otherwise, but even this account may be describing an alliance rather than full-blown conversion, insofar as the Persians are motivated by fear of the Judeans and not reverence for their Deity! Of course, there are some

exceptional texts. One thinks of Ruth in particular in which one could argue that 1:16-17 might be the equivalent of an ancient conversion formula (cf. Ps 87). But Ruth is still called the Moabitess even after this (Ruth 4:5). Some would want to include the sailors in Jonah as well, although the evidence is even less clear-cut. The sailors might be offering a one-time sacrifice to YHWH, not making a permanent practice of it. In any case, many scholars would argue that Ruth, Jonah, and Esther are all late texts, and thus, it is unsurprising that something like conversion appears in such texts.

7. Cohen, *Beginnings of Jewishness*, and Milgrom, "Religious Conversion."

8. Thus, the Hebrew Bible tends to use the root לוה, meaning something like "to attach oneself to" or "to ally oneself with" Israel, in the passages that describe the closest thing to conversion in the biblical period (Isa 14:1; 56:3, 6; Zech 2:15; Esth 9:27). Greenberg draws attention to a possible distinction between a text such as Isa 14:1, in which aliens attach themselves to the people of Israel, and Isa 56:3, in which non-Israelites attach themselves to the God of Israel. He sees the former as an instance of social convenience for those living among Israelites while the latter he describes as signaling "a conversion." Moshe Greenberg, "A House of Prayer for All People," in *Jerusalem: House of Prayer for All Peoples in the Three Monotheistic Religions* (ed. Alviero Niccacci; Jerusalem: Franciscan Printing Press, 2001), 31–37, at 32–34. Although even in Isa 56, as Greenberg notes, the sacrifices of such "joiners to the Lord" are acceptable not because they are reckoned as Israelites, but because God's temple is a house of prayer open to all peoples (Isa 56:8).

9. It is also possible that war brides are a special class of people in that their identities are erased by a ritual, a point suggested in oral communication by Walter Moberly.

10. Jeffrey Tigay, *Deuteronomy: The JPS Torah Commentary* (Philadelphia: JPS, 1996), 480, citing *Sifrei* 249.

11. Another possible solution is offered by Shaye Cohen ("From the Bible to the Talmud: The Prohibition of Intermarriage," *HAR* 7 [1983]: 23–39, at 31–34), who argues that Deut 23 is not about intermarriage per se, but about entry into the temple precincts. He cites similar language found in Lam 1:10, which describes Gentiles invading the sanctuary. While this may be possible, other intertextual evidence renders it improbable. First, the passage immediately preceding Deut 23 deals with questions of marriage. Second, it seems likely from 1 Kgs 11 that the Deuteronomistic Historian understood the laws in Deut 23 to be about intermarriage.

12. Gary Knoppers ("Sex, Religion, and Politics: The Deuteronomist on Intermarriage," *HAR* 14 [1994]: 121–41) has argued that 1 Kgs 11 and the text of Josh 23, which he sees as a major influence on 1 Kgs 11, indicate that a more general polemic against intermarriage with non-Canaanite Gentiles was already in existence in the pre-exilic period.

13. On the relation between the image of the "strange/foreign woman" in Prov 1–9 and the attempts by Ezra and Nehemiah to redefine the boundaries of communal identity for political, social, and economic reasons, see Harold C. Washington, "The Strange Woman (אשה זרה/נכריה) of Proverbs 1–9 and Post-Exilic Judean Society," in *Second Temple Studies* (vol. 2, *Temple and Community in the Persian Period*; ed. Tamara Eshkenazi and Kent Richards; JSOTSup 175; Sheffield: Sheffield Academic Press, 1994), 217–42; and Joseph Blenkinsopp, "The Social Context of the 'Outsider Woman' in Proverbs 1–9," *Biblica* 72 (1991): 457–73. On the social situation behind the conflict over intermarriage in the books of Ezra and Nehemiah, see Daniel L. Smith-Christopher, "The Mixed Marriage

Crisis in Ezra 9–10 and Nehemiah 13: A Study of the Sociology of the Post-Exilic Judean Community," in *Second Temple Studies*, 2:243–65; and Tamara Eshkenazi and Eleanore Judd, "Marriage to a Stranger in Ezra 9–10," in *Second Temple Studies*, 2:266–85.

14. Schwartz, *Curse of Cain*, 88.

15. H. G. M. Williamson, "The Concept of Israel in Transition," in *The World of Ancient Israel: Sociological, Anthropological and Political Perspectives* (ed. R. E. Clements; Cambridge: Cambridge University Press, 1989), 141–61, at 144.

16. D. J. A. Clines, *Ezra, Nehemiah and Esther* (NCB; Grand Rapids: Eerdmans, 1984), 116. One senses a similar harshness in the assessments of Eshkenazi and Judd, "Marriage to a Stranger in Ezra 9–10."

17. Lüdemann, *The Unholy*, 75. For a similarly negative assessment, see Lester Grabbe, "Triumph of the Pious or Failure of the Xenophobes? The Ezra-Nehemiah Reforms and Their *Nachgeschichte*," in *Jewish Local Patriotism and Self-Identification in the Graeco-Roman Period* (ed. Sian Jones and Sarah Pearce; JSPSup 31; Sheffield: Sheffield Academic Press, 1998), 50–65.

18. I say "more likely," for even here it is possible that Tobiah is an Israelite who is being smeared as an Ammonite because his family had holdings in the former Ammonite territories, as argued by Gabriele Boccaccini in *Roots of Rabbinic Judaism: An Intellectual History, from Ezekiel to Daniel* (Grand Rapids: Eerdmans, 2002), 86.

19. For an exhaustive appraisal of the specific texts employed by Ezra and Nehemiah in their attempts to apply the law to the circumstances they faced, see Michael Fishbane, *Biblical Interpretation in Ancient Israel* (Oxford: Oxford University Press, 1985), 114–29. One error in Fishbane's otherwise penetrating analysis that must be pointed out is his claim that the Ammonites "*and* the Moabites *and* the Egyptians are population groups explicitly prohibited from entering the 'congregation of YHWH' in Deut 23:4-9" (p. 116, emphasis his). In fact, vv. 8-9 (Eng. 7-8) make clear that Egyptians are *not* to be treated in the negative fashion prescribed for Ammonites and Moabites.

20. Eshkenazi and Judd, "Marriage to a Stranger in Ezra 9–10," 268.

21. As in the case of Tobiah, one could argue that when Ezra refers to the brides as "foreign women" in chapter 10, he is using a smear tactic against women who really were of Israelite extraction but had not been among those who returned from exile.

22. The ambiguity in this verse may be seen by comparing the translations of the NRSV and the NJPS. Also compare the position of Joseph Blenkinsopp (*Ezra-Nehemiah: A Commentary* [OTL; Philadelphia: Westminster, 1988], 200–201), who interprets this ambiguous verse as signaling the failure of Ezra's policy, to the position of Jacob Myers (*Ezra, Nehemiah* [AB; Garden City, N.Y.: Doubleday, 1965], 82), who emends the text (on the basis of 1 Esdras 9:36) to prove that Ezra was indeed successful in dissolving these marriages.

23. Boccaccini, *Roots of Rabbinic Judaism*, 49.

24. Blenkinsopp, *Ezra-Nehemiah*, 176.

25. Ibid., 363 (emphasis his).

26. H. G. M. Williamson, *Ezra-Nehemiah* (WBC; Waco: Word Books, 1985), 160.

27. Daniel L. Smith-Christopher, "The Politics of Ezra: Sociological Indicators of Postexilic Judean Society," in *Second Temple Studies* (vol. 1, *The Persian Period;* ed. Philip Davies; JSOTSup 117; Sheffield: Sheffield Academic Press, 1991), 73–97, at 97.

28. Williamson, *Ezra-Nehemiah*, 132, 161.

29. See the conclusions reached by Smith-Christopher, "Between Ezra and Isaiah," 140–42.

30. In fact, the development of the notion that only some of Israel are truly Israel is rather widespread in the postexilic period and its root causes are quite complicated. For an insightful critique of many reductionistic scholarly explanations of this phenomenon and an outline of a more sophisticated model, see Ehud Ben Zvi, "Inclusion and Exclusion from Israel as Conveyed by the Term 'Israel' in Post-Monarchic Biblical Texts," in *The Pitcher Is Broken: Memorial Essays for Gösta Ahlström* (ed. Steven Holloway and Lowell Handy; JSOTSup 190; Sheffield: Sheffield Academic Press, 1995), 95–149.

31. While the notion of a surviving remnant probably reaches all the way back to the story of Noah's ark in Gen 6–9, it was picked up by prophets such as Elijah (1 Kgs 19:18) and given a strong eschatological twist in Isa 6:13. For a full analysis of this idea in biblical and ancient Near Eastern culture, see Gerhard Hasel, *The Remnant: The History and Theology of the Remnant Idea from Genesis to Isaiah* (Berrien Springs, Mich.: Andrews University Press, 1972).

32. Interestingly enough, there appear to be examples of a group taking a more tolerant stance on one of these questions but a less tolerant stance on the other. A close reading of 3rd Isaiah suggests that the party responsible for the text was open to including certain foreign individuals (Isa 56:3-7), but at the same time this author was convinced that many native Judeans had fallen away into sin (Isa 65:11-16).

33. This issue will receive further attention in chapters 9 and 11 below.

34. Jerome, *Dialogue with Jovinianus* 1:10, cited in Christine Hayes, *Gentile Impurities and Jewish Identities: Intermarriage and Conversion from the Bible to the Talmud* (New York: Oxford University Press, 2002), 101. This passage from 2 Corinthians may actually be a more general prohibition against social intercourse with non-believers rather than specifically an intermarriage prohibition.

35. Cyprian, *Heads and Testimonies*, Heads 62–63, cited in Hayes, *Gentile Impurities*, 99.

36. Hayes, *Gentile Impurities*, 102.

37. This tendency continues unabated even among more liberal-minded scholars such as those advocating "New Perspective" readings of Paul. Thus Dunn, a scholar who usually makes careful arguments, proclaims the following about the law-observant Jews Paul criticizes: "We have been reminded of just how serious such an attitude can be in the horrors of the Holocaust. . . . The seriousness of an exclusivist attitude to the law is that it leads inexorably to exclusivist conduct. . . . [and that it] was that sort of 'attitude to the law' which Paul came to abhor." Dunn here makes two highly dubious claims: (1) exclusivism inevitably results in violence; (2) Pauline Christianity was less exclusivistic than were other more law-emphasizing Judaisms of the Second Temple period. James Dunn, "*Noch einmal* 'Works of the Law': The Dialogue Continues," in his *New Perspective on Paul* (WUNT 185; Tübingen: Mohr Siebeck, 2005), 407–22, at 411.

38. Blenkinsopp, *Ezra-Nehemiah*, 201.

39. In fairness, other trends within Christianity push in more generous directions, at least with unbelievers who lived before Jesus' advent. Thus, the patristic logos theology was often invoked to find a way to recognize that the great thinkers of Greco-Roman culture may have had insights that were attuned to revelation.

9. *Prophecy and Election*

1. It should be noted that the term ברית does appear in Amos 1:9 to describe a breach of international standards.

2. Herbert B. Huffmon, "The Treaty Background of Hebrew *Yada'*," *BASOR* 181 (1966): 31–37; and Herbert B. Huffmon and Simon B. Parker, "A Further Note on the Treaty Background of Hebrew *Yada'*," *BASOR* 184 (1966): 36–38.

3. George Mendenhall, "Covenant Forms in Israelite Tradition," in *The Biblical Archaeologist Reader*, vol. 3 (ed. E. Campbell and D. N. Freedman; Garden City, N.Y.: Doubleday, 1970), 25–53.

4. Thus, some scholars suggest that this passage must be a late editorial addition. Of course, one could just as easily argue that Amos simply influenced the Levitical passage or that both passages draw on a common idea.

5. Herbert Huffmon, "The Covenant Lawsuit in the Prophets," *JBL* 78 (1959): 285–95.

6. This list is drawn from Sohn, *Divine Election*, 159–77.

7. I do not believe that Jonah is *primarily* written to critique Jewish exclusivist claims (as argued by certain scholars). Rather, it is focused more squarely on questions of divine and human repentance as well as on the role of the prophet as an intermediary. Still, the book probes a number of issues connected to Israel's election theology, including God's relationship with non-Israelites.

8. Walter Brueggemann, *Theology of the Old Testament: Testimony, Dispute, Advocacy* (Minneapolis: Augsburg/Fortress Press, 1997), 178. For a fuller critique of Brueggemann's theological approach, see my review of this book in *RBL* 1 (Fall 1999): 1–6.

9. John J. Collins, "The Exodus and Biblical Theology," in *Jews, Christians, and the Theology of the Hebrew Scriptures* (ed. A. Bellis and J. Kaminsky; SBL Symposium Series 8; Atlanta: SBL, 2000), 247–61, at 257–58.

10. Jon D. Levenson, "The Exodus and Biblical Theology: A Rejoinder to John J. Collins," in *Jews, Christians, and the Theology of the Hebrew Scriptures*, 263–75, at 272–73.

11. I will list several important works from the immense secondary literature. P. A. H. de Boer, *Second Isaiah's Message* (OTS; Leiden: Brill, 1956); R. Davidson, "Universalism in Second Isaiah," *SJT* 16 (1963): 166–85; A. Gelston, "The Missionary Message of Second Isaiah," *SJT* 18 (1965): 308–18; idem, "Universalism in Second Isaiah," *JTS* 43 (1992): 377–98; R. Halas, "The Universalism of Isaias," *CBQ* 17 (1950): 162–70; D. E. Hollenberg, "Nationalism and 'the Nations' in Isaiah xl–lv," *VT* 19 (1969): 23–36; Harry Orlinsky, "The So-called 'Servant of the Lord' and 'Suffering Servant' in Second Isaiah," and Norman Snaith, "Isaiah 40–66: A Study of the Teaching of the Second Isaiah and Its Consequences," published together as *Studies on the Second Part of the Book of Isaiah* (VTSup XIV; Leiden: Brill, 1977); Moshe Weinfeld, "Universalism and Particularism in the Period of Exile and Restoration," *Tarbiz* 33 (1964): 228–42; Andrew Wilson, *The Nations in Deutero-Isaiah: A Study on Composition and Structure* (Lewiston: Edwin Mellen, 1986); D. W. Van Winkle, "The Relationship of the Nations to YHWH and to Israel in Isaiah XL–LV," *VT* 35.5 (1985): 446–58.

12. A concise and reasonably up-to-date survey of this issue can be found in Wilson, *The Nations in Deutero-Isaiah*, 1–10.

13. Sheldon H. Blank (*Prophetic Faith in Isaiah* [New York: Harper & Row, 1958], 148–58) is rather apologetic and tends to overlook the nationalist and particularist elements in these texts.

14. J. Lindblom, *Prophecy in Ancient Israel* (Philadelphia: Fortress Press, 1962), 400–403, 428 and Carroll Stuhlmueller, "Deutero-Isaiah (chaps. 40–55): Major Transitions in the Prophet's Theology and in Contemporary Scholarship," *CBQ* 42 (January 1980): 1–29.

15. A good example of this argument is Claus Westermann's treatment of 45:14, which he argues must be a later misplaced fragment from Isa 60. Claus Westermann, *Isaiah 40–66: A Commentary* (OTL; Philadelphia: Fortress Press, 1969), 169–70.

16. Gelston, "Missionary Message," 316.

17. Here one thinks particularly of Orlinsky's and Snaith's essays in *Studies on the Second Part of the Book of Isaiah*, esp. pp. 36–51, 97–117, 154–65, and de Boer's *Second Isaiah's Message*, 80–101.

18. Thus, Whybray notes that "the majority of references in the book to the nations are either contemptuous or hostile" and goes on to show that texts like Isa 42:1-4 are likely invoking God's coming judgment upon the nations rather than their salvation. R. N. Whybray, *The Second Isaiah* (Sheffield: Sheffield Academic Press, 1997 [1983 1st ed.]), 62–65, here at 63.

19. For a balanced attempt to understand these passages in their larger contexts, see Joel S. Kaminsky and Anne W. Stewart, "God of All the World: Universalism and Developing Monotheism in Isaiah 40–66," *HTR* 99.2 (April 2006): 139–63.

20. Gelston, "Universalism," 396.

21. Van Winkle, "Relationship of the Nations," 457. Similarly, but from a more judgmental viewpoint, see Roy Melugin, "Israel and the Nations in Isaiah 40–55," in *Problems in Biblical Theology* (ed. H. T. C. Sun and K. Eades; FS R. Knierim; Grand Rapids: Eerdmans, 1997), 249–64.

22. Gelston, "Universalism," 397, citing Gelston, "Missionary Message," 316.

23. Here Urbach ("Self-Isolation or Self-Affirmation in Judaism in the First Three Centuries: Theory and Practice," in *Jewish and Christian Self-Definition*, vol. 2 [ed. E. P. Sanders et al; Philadelphia: Fortress Press, 1981], 269–98, at 269) seems on the mark: "In studies of Jewish history and religion terms such as 'particularism and universalism,' 'limitation and delimitation' are frequently used. This terminology also serves ideological purposes, and accordingly acquires a different weighting, depending on whether it is used by the opponents of Judaism or its defenders, while both fervently uphold the ideal of universalism."

24. A thoughtful treatment of this problem can be found in Mark G. Brett, "Nationalism and the Hebrew Bible," in *The Bible and Ethics: The Second Sheffield Colloquium* (ed. J. W. Rogerson, M. Davies, et al.; JSOTSup 207; Sheffield: Sheffield Academic Press; 1995), 136–63. For a critique of the ideas of universalism versus particularism in New Testament scholarship, see Anders Runesson, "Particularistic Judaism and Universalistic Christianity? Some Critical Remarks on Terminology and Theology," *JGRChJ* 1 (2000): 120–44.

25. Harry Orlinsky, "Nationalism-Universalism and Internationalism in Ancient Israel," in *Translating and Understanding the Old Testament* (ed. Harry Frank and William Reed; Nashville: Abingdon Press, 1970), 206–36, at 236.

26. Jon D. Levenson, "The Universal Horizon of Biblical Particularism," in *Ethnicity and the Bible* (ed. Mark Brett; Leiden: Brill, 1996), 143–69, at 144–45. One finds a similar point made by Blenkinsopp, "YHWH and Other Deities," 361.

27. Levenson, "Universal Horizon," 160.

28. Walter C. Kaiser, *Mission in the Old Testament: Israel as a Light to the Nations* (Grand Rapids: Baker, 2000), 7. Another recent book following much the same logic is Arthur Glasser, *Announcing the Kingdom: The Story of God's Mission in the Bible* (Grand Rapids: Baker, 2003). The opening subheading of this latter volume is "The Whole Bible Is a Missionary Book."

29. Rowley, *Election*, 62.

30. Delbert Hillers, "*Bĕrît ʿām*: Emancipation of the People," *JBL* 97.2 (1978): 175–82. This argument is similar to a proposal by H. Torczyner, "Presidential Address," *JPOS* 16 (1936): 1–8, that has come under criticism because the Akkadian cognates are suspect.

31. Orlinsky, "So-called 'Servant of the Lord,'" 117.

32. On salvation in the Hebrew Bible, see James Barr, "An Aspect of Salvation in the Old Testament," in *Man and His Salvation: Studies in Memory of S. G. F. Brandon* (ed. E. J. Sharpe and J. R. Hinnells; Manchester: Manchester University Press, 1973), 39–52. On this concept in Judaism more generally, see R. J. Zwi Werblowsky, "Salvation in Judaism," *Tantur Yearbook* (1976–1977): 51–58.

33. I realize that I am using the term more loosely than certain evangelicals who might distinguish between the activity of mission, which might include doing good works among the poor, and evangelization proper, that is, attempting to preach the gospel.

34. Robert Martin-Achard, *A Light to the Nations: A Study of the Old Testament Conception of Israel's Mission to the World* (Edinburgh: Oliver and Boyd, 1962 [French original 1959]), 75.

35. Joseph Blenkinsopp, *Isaiah 56–66* (AB; New York: Doubleday, 2003), 314.

36. On the other hand, individual Gentiles like Naaman or the foreigners in Isa 56 who join themselves to the cult of YHWH do so in a way that involves their subordination to God rather than to Israel.

37. John F. A. Sawyer, "'Blessed Be My People Egypt' (Isaiah 19:25): The Context and Meaning of a Remarkable Passage," in *A Word in Season: Essays in Honor of William McKane* (ed. James Martin and Philip Davies; JSOTSup 42; Sheffield: Sheffield Academic Press, 1986), 57–71, at 57. Similar sentiments are expressed by Christopher Begg, "The Peoples and the Worship of Yahweh in the Book of Isaiah," in *Worship and the Hebrew Bible: Essays in Honour of John T. Willis* (ed. M. Patrick Graham et al.; JSOTSup 284; Sheffield: Sheffield Academic Press, 1999), 35–55. Perhaps even more radically, Brueggemann (*Theology of the Old Testament*, 522) proclaims: "In this daring utterance we witness the process by which other peoples are redesignated to be YHWH's chosen peoples so that, taken paradigmatically, all peoples become YHWH's chosen peoples."

38. This is true of Jewish as well as of Christian commentators, as noted in Moberly's discussion of Gen 12:3 in *The Bible, Theology, and Faith*, 125 (citing passages from Cassuto, Sarna, and Jacob as evidence).

39. Rowley, *Election*, 161.

40. Ibid., 165.

41. Classically, scholars have spoken of four Servant Songs, which were viewed as distinct compositions that were inserted, at certain key junctures, into 2nd Isaiah: Isa 42:1-4; 49:1-6; 50:4-11; 52:13–53:12. A few contemporary scholars (e.g., Tryggve Mettinger, *A Farewell to the Servant Songs* [Lund: CWK Gleerup, 1983]) have made a compelling case that the tendency to separate these materials from 2nd Isaiah as a whole is wrongheaded. In any case, one will need to make sense of the imagery and message of these passages within the whole of 2nd Isaiah.

42. The literature on this subject is enormous, and one can see any of the standard commentaries for a fuller bibliography.

43. Senior and Stuhlmueller, *The Biblical Foundations for Mission*, 105 (emphasis mine).

44. For fuller argumentation, see Kaminsky and Stewart, "God of All the World."

45. This point is substantiated by Brevard Childs' observation on Isaiah 49:6 (*Isaiah* [OTL; Louisville: WJK, 2001], 385): "Commentators have usually argued that, lest the task of restoring Israel seem too small a task for the servant, God expands his mission to include the nations. However, nowhere in Second Isaiah is the restoration of Israel set in competition with the salvation of the nations."

46. While I think Hollenberg ("Nationalism and 'the Nations'") has overstated the matter by arguing that in all of 2nd Isaiah the servant is one part of Israel who is addressing the larger people who have fallen away, there are passages in 2nd Isaiah in which this explanation is highly probable.

47. I discuss this problem at greater length in chapter 11, in which I quote Rowley, who moves in a supersessionist direction. I should say that such Christian supersessionism likely grows partially out of those texts in which the prophets proclaim that because Israel has rejected God, he is rejecting them (Jer 6:18, 30; Hos 4:6). But the fact is that within the vast majority of prophetic texts and certainly in the larger shaping of the canon, these judgment texts are mitigated by the notion that following Israel's repentance (either before or after God has executed judgment), God holds out a promise of hope and renewal to Israel.

10. *Election in Psalms and the Wisdom Literature*

1. The poetic nature of these psalms is sometimes glossed over by those who wish to find in them a missionary intent. Note Martin-Achard's caution (*Light to the Nations*, 58) in reference to those psalms that call for all the nations to praise God: "The Gentiles are summoned in their capacity as creatures. No conversion is actually expected of the forest and water; and by the same token, the Psalmist is not proclaiming that the nations will be radically transformed." Similarly, Artur Weiser (*The Psalms* [OTL; Philadelphia: Westminster, 1962 (German original 1959)], 629) argues that Ps 96 may refer to representatives of the nations present at a festival, but "there can hardly be any question here of missionary activity in the strict sense."

2. Alternatively, this psalm may be addressing a few select proselytes, or those Israelites who reside in the Diaspora and speak of themselves as ultimately belonging to Zion. For full critical and theological discussion of this psalm and its relationship to the larger Psalter, see Norbert Lohfink and Erich Zenger, "Zion as the Mother of the Nations in Psalm 87," chap. 5 in idem, *The God of Israel and the Nations: Studies in Isaiah and the Psalms* (trans. Everett Kalin; Collegeville: Liturgical Press, 2000), 123–60.

3. John J. Collins, "The Biblical Precedent for Natural Theology," *JAAR* 45/1 Supp. B (1977): 35–67.

4. R. E. Clements, "Wisdom and Old Testament Theology," in *Wisdom in Ancient Israel* (ed. John Day, Robert Gordon, and H. G. M. Williamson; FS J. A. Emerton; Cambridge: Cambridge University Press, 1995), 269–86, at 270.

5. Gerhard von Rad, "The Joseph Narrative and Ancient Wisdom," in idem, *The Problem of the Hexateuch and Other Essays* (New York: McGraw-Hill, 1966), 292–300.

6. Shemaryahu Talmon, "'Wisdom' in the Book of Esther," *VT* 13 (1963): 419–55; Jon D. Levenson, *Esther: A Commentary* (OTL; Louisville: Westminster/John Knox, 1997). For a much more skeptical view of wisdom influences on these narrative materials, see James Crenshaw, "Method in Determining Wisdom Influence upon 'Historical Literature,'" *JBL* 88 (1969): 129–42.

7. Levenson (*Death and Resurrection*, 176–78) notes a number of close linguistic and thematic connections, some picked up in rabbinic literature and Jubilees, between Abraham's test in Gen 22 and Job's in Job 1–2. Moberly (*The Bible, Theology, and Faith*, 84–88) also probes various theological connections between Job 1–2 and Gen 22.

8. Weinfeld, *Deuteronomy and the Deuteronomic School*, 158–78, 244–319.

9. Ibid., 255–56.

10. For a more extensive set of reflections on Sirach's views of the relationship between wisdom and law, see John J. Collins, *Jewish Wisdom in a Hellenistic Age* (OTL; Louisville: Westminster/John Knox, 1997), 42–61.

11. For a thoughtful analysis of the various theological currents present in this interesting book, see Shannon Burkes, "Wisdom and Apocalypticism in the Wisdom of Solomon," *HTR* 95.1 (January 2002): 21–44.

12. *Midrash Rabbah: Genesis*, vol. 1 (trans. H. Freedman; 3rd ed.; London: Soncino, 1983), 1.

11. New Testament and Rabbinic Views of Election

1. I recognize that comparing New Testament to rabbinic texts involves a theological rather than a historical comparison in that these materials were likely composed in different historical contexts. Furthermore, I am aware that I have not mapped out the many ways in which various para-biblical texts from the Second Temple period contributed to the development of elective ideas. While a more sustained reflection on elective themes in the Apocrypha, Pseudepigrapha, Dead Sea Scrolls, Philo, Josephus, and so forth, would be immensely informative as background to the following chapter, such a study would require a book of its own and would be of much less interest to most Jews and Christians who wish to know how their canonical traditions appropriated Israel's election theology.

2. There are indeed Christians, particularly those with strong Lutheran and Calvinist roots or others influenced by Karl Barth, who recognize the important role election plays in the Christian tradition. But the fact remains, on the popular level, many contemporary Western Christians see election as an exclusivistic Jewish idea that a universal Christianity transcended.

3. Arnold Toynbee, A *Study of History*, abridged vols. 1–6 (New York: Oxford University Press, 1947), 310.

4. From an editorial "Jewry and Democracy," *Christian Century* (June 9, 1937): 734–36, at 736.

5. E. P. Sanders, "Jewish Association with Gentiles and Galatians 2:11-14," in *The Conversation Continues: Studies in Paul & John* (ed. Robert Fortna and Beverly Gaventa; FS J. Louis Martyn; Nashville: Abingdon Press, 1990), 170–88, at 181.

6. Thus, Sanders in "Jewish Association," 181, goes on to state that Christians would "follow the same range of behavior as Jews. They would hesitate to marry pagans, Jews, and even Christians who belonged to the wrong party."

7. For those who would object to the notion that Judaism has any sense of a fall, or for deeper discussion of the parallels between how Judaism and Christianity each heal the rift caused by human disobedience to God, see Joel Kaminsky, "Paradise Regained: Rabbinic Reflections on Israel at Sinai," in *Jews, Christians, and the Theology of the Hebrew Scriptures* (ed. A. Bellis and J. Kaminsky; SBL Symposium Series 8; Atlanta: SBL, 2000), 15–43.

8. For a fuller discussion, see Levenson's book titled after this motif. For a detailed comparison between the Joseph and the New Testament Passion stories, see Gary Anderson, "Joseph and the Passion of Our Lord," in *The Art of Reading Scripture* (ed. Ellen Davis and Richard Hays; Grand Rapids: Eerdmans, 2003), 198–215.

9. Some significant Christian thinkers over the centuries (Origen and Barth among them) have argued, on the basis of texts such as Rom 5:18-19, for the idea that all souls will ultimately be saved. Nevertheless, major streams of the New Testament and later Christian tradition make salvation contingent on one's confession of belief in Christ as Lord and Savior (Rom 10:9-13; John 3:16). For a recent endorsement of universal salvation, see Richard John Neuhaus, *Death on a Friday Afternoon* (New York: Basic, 2000), 35–70. Neuhaus acknowledges that this position has been marginalized for much of Christian history, and even though he thinks it deserves renewed attention, he is aware that Origen's teachings on this and other subjects were condemned by the Council of Constantinople in 553. Whether such universalism reaches back to Paul himself is a matter of debate. Scholars like E. P. Sanders think that Paul had two strains in his work that were never fully reconciled, one of them being the notion of universal salvation, the other christological exclusivism. See, for example, his short chapter "Paul," in *Early Christian Thought in Its Jewish Context* (ed. John Barclay and John Sweet; Cambridge: Cambridge University Press, 1996), 112–29. For a fuller exploration of exactly this idea and its implications for theology today, see Sven Hillert, *Limited and Universal Salvation: A Text-Oriented and Hermeneutical Study of Two Perspectives in Paul* (ConBNT 31; Stockholm: Almqvist & Wiksell, 1999). Nevertheless, when one sets Paul's thought into its religio-cultural milieu, it is difficult to see how one can maintain that he ultimately advocated universal salvation. Thus, Stendahl brilliantly shows how even passages that have been read as holding out hope for the repentance of one's enemies are really about leaving retaliation to God. Krister Stendahl, "Hate, Non-Retaliation, and Love: 1QS x, 17–20 and Rom 12:19-21," *HTR* 55 (1962): 343–55.

10. Scot McKnight, *A Light Among the Gentiles: Jewish Missionary Activity in the Second Temple Period* (Minneapolis: Fortress Press, 1991), 48. For a much more skeptical view toward the whole notion of Jewish proselytization, see Martin Goodman, *Mission and Conversion: Proselytizing in the Religious History of the Roman Empire* (Oxford: Clarendon Press, 1994).

11. Goldenberg, *The Nations that Know Thee Not*, 94. Marc Hirshman ("Rabbinic Universalism in the Second and Third Centuries," *HTR* 93.2 [April 2000]: 101–15) has argued that texts associated with the school of Rabbi Ishmael were much more open to proselytizing, although these traditions eventually fell out of favor. While the texts that Hirshman discusses deserve much greater attention than they have received previously, Hirshman overstates his case when he argues that this school of ancient Jewish thought had a missionary orientation. The texts he discusses are proof that the ancient rabbis saw Torah as universally available to all, not that they believed Jews should actively seek to convert all Gentiles to Judaism.

12. "Evil upon evil will befall those who receive proselytes" and "proselytes are as annoying to Israel as scabs" from *b. Yebamot* 109b (cf. 48b). Also see *b. Niddah* 13b. See Goldenberg, *Nations that Know Thee Not*, 93–94 for a balanced assessment of the diverse opinions on converts in rabbinic literature.

13. Another possible factor for rabbinic reserve concerning missionizing may be that Judaism preserves certain tribal/familial aspects of ancient Israelite identity.

14. Rowley, *Election*, 164.

15. Ibid., 165.

16. N. T. Wright, *What Saint Paul Really Said* (Grand Rapids: Eerdmans, 1997), 84 (emphasis his). For a critique of Wright's position, see Douglas Harink, *Paul Among the Postliberals: Pauline Theology Beyond Christendom and Modernity* (Grand Rapids: Brazos Press, 2003), 153–68. Such views are widespread among more evangelical Christians as evidenced by articles such as Gerald Bray's "The Promises Made to Abraham and the Destiny of Israel," *Scottish Bulletin of Evangelical Theology* 7 (Autumn 1989): 69–87, esp. 77.

17. Rabbi Joshua understands this verse to mean only those of the nations who forget God will end up in Sheol. This translation is taken from *The Tosefta, Neziqin* (trans. Jacob Neusner; New York: KTAV, 1981), 238. See the similar statement attributed to Rabbi Joshua in Midrash Prov 19:1: "Anyone who lives blamelessly before his Creator in this world will be saved from the torment of Gehenna in the coming future." This translation is from *The Midrash on Proverbs* (trans. Burton Visotzky; Yale Judaica Series; New Haven: Yale University Press, 1992), 87. For a deeper introduction to this subject see the following works: Benjamin Helfgott, *The Doctrine of Election in Tannaitic Literature* (New York: King's Crown Press, 1954); Novak, *The Image of the Non-Jew*; and Gary Porton, *Goyim: Gentiles and Israelites in Mishnah-Tosefta* (BJS 155; Atlanta: Scholars Press, 1988).

18. In fairness the rabbis were often pessimistic about the ability of non-Jews to observe even the seven Noahide commandments and thus at times were pessimistic about their ultimate salvation (e.g., *b. 'Avod. Zar.* 2b–3a). Similar negative treatments of the Gentiles' inability to act righteously that imply or assert their ultimate destruction could be multiplied many times over, as demonstrated by even a quick perusal through Sacha Stern's *Jewish Identity in Early Rabbinic Writings* (Leiden: Brill, 1994).

19. Marc Hirshman, *Torah for the Entire World* (Tel Aviv: Hakkibbutz Hameuchad, 1999) [Hebrew], has cogently argued that there is an alternative rabbinic position on Gentile salvation, which did not survive the talmudic period, in which Gentiles can keep the Torah (or at least parts of it) without converting to Judaism rather than observing only the seven Noahide commandments.

20. Henry Chadwick, "Christian and Roman Universalism in the Fourth Century," in *Christian Faith and Greek Philosophy in Late Antiquity* (ed. L. Wickham and C. Bammel; FS C. G. Stead; Leiden: Brill, 1993), 26–42.

21. See chapter 9 for detailed argumentation.

22. This is not to imply that Paul had no interest in works or that James was directly attacking Paul's theology. Paul clearly thought one could not be a member of the Christian community and engage in immoral behavior (1 Cor 5). Scholars debate whether James is an early or late composition and thus who his opponents were. Even if it is a late letter, it may be directed less against Paul's theology per se than against a group who may have distorted Paul's theology. The fact remains that the theologies put forward by James and Paul stand in tension, as recognized by Luther's highly negative assessment of James.

23. *The Mekilta de Rabbi Ishmael* (trans. J. Z. Lauterbach; Philadelphia: Jewish Publication Society, 1976 [1933]), 1.253 (בשלח ז). In general, I have opted to use the standard English translations of the midrashic texts under discussion so as to allow the reader to access the complete text with ease. The reader should be aware that many of the collections of midrashim have not yet been published in critical editions. For more background on these texts and translations, see Hermann L. Strack and Günter Stemberger,

Introduction to the Talmud and Midrash (Minneapolis: Fortress, 1992). I have left all translations of biblical verses that occur within midrashic translations as is; however, I have opted to standardize how they are marked off from the surrounding midrashic expansions by italicizing all such quotations.

24. I am aware that a number of scholars associated with the "New Perspective" see Paul's approach to the law as much less derogatory than the more standard Lutheran reading imagines. But aside from scholars on the far end of the debate, like Gager, who argue that Paul preserves the full law for Jewish-Christians, most others end up affirming that the law is derogated to some extent. Thus, even a scholar like Dunn recognizes that for Paul, the law cannot function salvifically. Furthermore, according to Dunn, while Paul preserves certain functions of the law and argues that people will be judged on the basis of their works, Paul dissolves the law's specificity by reducing it down to the notion of loving one's neighbor. From a Jewish perspective, this remains a highly derogatory view of the law and its salvific ability as it is described in the Torah. See James Dunn, "Was Paul Against the Law?" in idem, *The New Perspective on Paul* (WUNT 185; Tübingen: Mohr Siebeck, 2005), 259–77.

25. This problem is one that came to the fore long before the rabbinic period. For some of the various exegetical solutions proposed by differing groups in the Second Temple period, see Gary Anderson, "The Status of the Torah Before Sinai: The Retelling of the Bible in the Damascus Covenant and the Book of Jubilees," *DSD* 1.1 (April 1994): 1–29. In fact, there was even an ancient Jewish propensity to import the revelation at Sinai back into Eden as indicated by texts like Sir 17:11-13. For a more in-depth discussion of this issue, see John J. Collins, "Wisdom, Apocalypticism and the Dead Sea Scrolls," in *Jedes Ding Hat seine Zeit . . .* (ed. Anja Diesel et al.; Berlin: Walter de Gruyter, 1996), 19–32, esp. 21–26.

26. *m. Qiddušin.* 4:14, translation from Jon D. Levenson, "The Conversion of Abraham to Judaism, Christianity, and Islam," in *The Idea of Biblical Interpretation: Essays in Honor of James L. Kugel* (ed. Hindy Najman and Judith Newman; Leiden: Brill, 2004), 3–40, at 22. This essay contains many thoughtful reflections on the variant portrayals of Abraham's observance of the law in ancient Jewish and Christian sources.

27. *ER* 5, *Tanna Debe Eliyyahu* (trans. W. G. Braude and I. J. Kapstein; Philadelphia: JPS, 1981), 67. The rabbis are here building upon the notion that Jacob studied in the academy of Shem and Eber, an idea facilitated by the word "tents" used in Gen 9:27 and 25:27.

28. The Christian Old Testament and the Jewish Tanakh are ordered differently, and this has significant theological implications. Judaism puts the strongest emphasis on the Torah, the first five books, and the canon closes with 2 Chronicles pointing toward the rebuilding of the temple in Jerusalem. Christianity ends the Old Testament with Malachi pointing ahead to the return of Elijah and the coming eschatological judgment, a prophecy Christians see fulfilled in John the Baptist and Jesus. Additionally, the church drew on the Greek Septuagint that at times contains a substantially different text than the Hebrew Masoretic Tanakh.

29. For full argumentation to support this contention, see Michael David Goldberg, *Jews and Christians: Getting Our Stories Straight* (Philadelphia: Trinity Press International, 1991 [1985 1st ed.]), 135–210.

30. *Gen. Rab.* 38:13. *Midrash Rabbah, Genesis,* vol. 1 (trans. H. Freedman; 3rd ed.; London: Soncino, 1983), 310–11.

31. Clearly, there are rabbinic texts that enhance God's arbitrariness while diminishing Israel's role in God's plan. Note the following text from *b. Shabb* 88a, which comments on the fact that Israel stood "at the foot of" or literally "under" Mount Sinai immediately before receiving God's commandments: "*And they stood under the mount* [Exod 19:17]. R. Abdimi b. Ḥama b. Ḥasa said: This teaches us that the Holy One, blessed be He, overturned the mountain upon them like an (inverted) cask, and said to them, 'If ye accept the Torah, 'tis well: if not, there shall be your burial.'" This is not a portrait of a willing and deserving Israel or of a non-arbitrary God. This translation is from *The Babylonian Talmud, Seder Moed,* vol. 1 (trans. Rabbi I. Epstein; London: Soncino, 1938), 417.

32. *The Mekilta de Rabbi Ishmael*, 2.234–35 (דבחודש ה").

33. Moberly, "Earliest Commentary."

34. Thus, Irving Mandelbaum, "Tannaitic Exegesis of the Golden Calf Episode," in *A Tribute to Geza Vermes* (ed. Philip Davies and Richard White; JSOTSup 100; Sheffield: JSOT, 1990), 207–23, finds substantial differences between the Tannaitic discussions of the golden calf episode and those attributed to later Amoraic sources. In particular, he sees the Tannaitic material as much more critical of Israel's idolatrous behavior while the Amoraic midrashim introduce a variety of mitigating explanations that function in an apologetic manner. This may indicate that the rabbis softened their approach to this material in reaction to early Christian claims that the golden calf story demonstrated that the relationship between God and Israel had been totally abrogated.

35. Examples of those who see many midrashim as direct responses to Christian charges include L. Smolar and M. Aberbach, "The Golden Calf Episode in Postbiblical Jewish Literature," *HUCA* 39 (1968): 91–116, and A. Marmorstein, "Judaism and Christianity in the Middle of the Third Century," in *Studies in Jewish Theology* (ed. J. Rabbinowitz and M. S. Lew; London: Oxford University Press, 1950), 179–224.

36. One scholar who deserves praise for her careful analysis is Judith Baskin, *Pharaoh's Counsellors: Job, Jethro and Balaam in Rabbinic and Patristric Tradition* (BJS 47; Chico: Scholars Press, 1983). Note her clear statement "that in certain times and places, most especially Palestine of the third, fourth and fifth centuries of our era, some rabbis were aware of and combatted through their exegeses various claims of the Christian Church which were seen as threatening to Judaism. Ultimately, however, the differences between rabbinic and patristic biblical interpretations are far greater than their points of contact. The contrasting principles and aims that inform these two bodies of commentary account for the vast differences in the interpretations of Job, Jethro and Balaam" (p. 120). For a careful comparison of Jewish and Christian interpretive techniques and an investigation into the question of the ways in which interreligious polemics might have shaped certain interpretations, see Marc Hirshman, *A Rivalry of Genius: Jewish and Christian Biblical Interpretation in Late Antiquity* (trans. Batya Stein; Albany: SUNY Press, 1996).

37. Levenson, *Death and Resurrection*, 200–232.

38. Heard, *Dynamics of Diselection*.

39. Here I disagree with the argument of J. Louis Martyn, "The Covenants of Hagar and Sarah," in *Faith and History: Essays in Honor of Paul W. Meyer* (ed. John Carroll and Charles Cosgrove; Atlanta: Scholars Press, 1990), 160–92, who argues that Hagar here is not a reference to Judaism but to a law-observant mission to the Gentiles. In any case, even if Martyn were correct about his point, within a century of Paul's time the church understood this passage as an endorsement of the idea that the church superseded the old

Israel as argued at length in Jeffrey S. Siker, *Disinheriting the Jews: Abraham in Early Christian Controversy* (Louisville: Westminster/John Knox, 1991).

40. See chapter 2, note 20 for an explanation of the pun at the end of this Hebrew verse.

41. Coats, "Strife Without Reconciliation," 97.

42. "Behaving wantonly with someone," as suggested in von Rad, *Genesis*, 232. The rabbis (*Gen. Rab.* 53:11) also think that Ishmael may have committed some type of sexual immorality by linking the use of the root צחק in this verse to Gen 39:17 in which Potiphar's wife uses the same root to suggest Joseph tried to seduce her. However, they imagine that Sarah saw Ishmael acting improperly toward other women rather than toward Isaac.

43. One finds a similar idea expressed in *Gen. Rab.* 53:11 in which Rabbi Simeon Bar Yochai, commenting on the word מצחק in Gen 21:9, says the following: "But I say: This term sport [mockery] refers to inheritance. For when our father Isaac was born all rejoiced, whereupon Ishmael said to them, 'You are fools, for I am the firstborn and I receive a double portion.'" Cited from *Midrash Rabbah, Genesis*, vol. 1 (trans. H. Freedman; 3rd ed.; London: Soncino, 1983), 470; compare *t. Sotah* 6:6. For a fuller analysis of the character of Ishmael in various rabbinic sources, see Carol Bakhos, *Ishmael on the Border: Rabbinic Portrayals of the First Arab* (Albany: SUNY Press, 2006).

44. *Sifre, Piska* 312, p. 318.

45. Eugene Mihaly, "A Rabbinic Defense of the Election of Israel," *HUCA* 35 (1964): 103–43.

46. Alan Segal, *Rebecca's Children* (Cambridge: Harvard University Press, 1986), 1.

47. For a fuller treatment of the rabbinic sources demonstrating the existence of God-fearers and the closely related category of the *ger toshav* (resident alien), see Louis Feldman, *Jew and Gentile in the Ancient World* (Princeton: Princeton University Press, 1993), 353–56. Feldman also treats pagan and Christian sources that mention Gentiles partially allied with Judaism on pp. 344–48 and 356–58, respectively.

48. Thus, even when a thinker like Maimonides views Christianity and Islam as mistaken, he believes that they are serving a divine purpose by preparing the larger world to accept Jewish teachings once the messianic king appears. See Baruch Frydman-Kohl, "Covenant, Conversion and Chosenness: Maimonides and Halevi on 'Who Is a Jew,'" *Judaism* 41.1 (January 1992): 64–79.

49. Karl Rahner, "Christianity and the Non-Christian Religions," *Theological Investigations*, vol. 5 (London: Darton, Longman, and Todd; New York: Seabury Press, 1966), 115–34.

50. Krister Stendahl, *Paul Among Jews and Gentiles* (Philadelphia: Fortress Press, 1976). This book includes his famous essay "Paul and the Introspective Conscience of the West" first published in English in *HTR* 56 in 1963. A good exemplar of a more recent scholar fully embracing the two covenant theory in its most radical form would be John Gager, *Reinventing Paul* (New York: Oxford University Press, 2000).

51. For a thoughtful argument in support of this idea, see Robert W. Jenson, "Toward a Christian Theology of Judaism," in *Jews and Christians: People of God* (ed. Carl Braaten and Robert Jenson; Grand Rapids: Eerdmans, 2003), 1–13.

52. Leora Batnitzky, "Dialogue as Judgment, not Mutual Affirmation: A New Look at Franz Rosenzweig's Dialogical Philosophy," *JR* 79.4 (October 1999): 523–44 and Jon D. Levenson, "Must We Accept the Other's Self-Understanding?" *JR* 71.4 (October 1991): 558–67.

Concluding Reflections

1. Herberg, "The 'Chosenness' of Israel and the Jew of Today," 281 (emphasis his).

2. Levenson, "Universal Horizon," 167.

3. Ibid., 166.

4. Thus, Walter Moberly has noted the close linkage in Deuteronomy between texts such as the *Shema* in Deut 6:4ff. and some of Israel's most articulate meditations on election found in Deut 7:7ff. W. Moberly, "Are Election and Monotheism Bad for You?" (paper presented at SBL, Philadelphia, Pa., 2005). For the fuller implications of this paper, see R. W. L. Moberly, "How Appropriate Is 'Monotheism' as a Category for Biblical Interpretation?" in *Early Jewish and Christian Monotheism* (ed. Loren Stuckenbruck and Wendy North; JSNTSup 263; London: T&T Clark, 2004), 216–34. Similarly, in 2nd Isaiah one finds a very tight interlinking between claims about Israel's God as the only true God and those concerning Israel as God's chosen people. This is explored at length in Kaminsky and Stewart, "God of All the World."

5. See Joel Kaminsky, "Attempting the Impossible: Eliminating Election from the Jewish Liturgy," *Midstream* (January/February 2005): 23–27.

Index of Ancient Sources

Hebrew Bible

Church Fathers

INDEX OF MODERN AUTHORS